Philosophical Logic

Also available from Continuum:

Phenomenology, Michael Lewis and Tanja Staehler
The Philosophy of History, Mark Day
The Philosophy of Mind, Dale Jacquette
The Philosophy of the Social Sciences, Robert C. Bishop

Forthcoming:

Classical Chinese Philosophy, Im Manyul
Critical Thinking, Robert Arp and Jamie Carlin Watson
Ethics, Robin Attfield
Introduction to Indian Philosophy, Christopher Bartley
Metaphysics, Jonathan Tallant
Philosophy of Language, Chris Daly
Philosophy of Law, Jeffrey Brand-Ballard
Philosophy of Science, Emma Tobin
Pragmatism, John Capps

Philosophical Logic
An Introduction to
Advanced Topics

George Englebretsen and
Charles Sayward

continuum

Continuum International Publishing Group
The Tower Building   80 Maiden Lane
11 York Road   Suite 704
London SE1 7NX   New York, NY 10038

www.continuumbooks.com

British Library Cataloguing-in-Publication Data
A catalogue record for this book is available from the British Library.

ISBN: HB: 978-1-4411-7385-0
       PB: 978-1-4411-1911-7

Library of Congress Cataloging-in-Publication Data
Englebretsen, George.
Philosophical logic: an introduction to advanced topics / George Englebretsen
and Charles Sayward.
    p. cm.
Includes bibliographical references and index.
ISBN 978-1-4411-1911-7 – ISBN 978-1-4411-7385-0
1. Logic–Textbooks. I. Sayward, Charles. II. Title.

BC71.E55 2011
160–dc22   2010023063

Typeset by Newgen Imaging Systems Pvt Ltd, Chennai, India
Printed and bound in India by Replika Press Pvt Ltd

from Charlie
to Lela

from George
to Libbey

Contents

List of Symbols

$\wedge$	sign for conjunction
$\neg$	sign for negation
$\supset$	sign for conditional
$\equiv$	sign for biconditional
$\vee$	sign for disjunction
$\exists$	sign for existential quantification (there is at least one)
$\forall$	sign for universal quantification
$\vdash$	sign for derivability
$\exists!$	sign for uniqueness quantification (there is exactly one)
$\vDash$	sign for semantic consequence
$+$	sign for unsplit positive logical copula
$-$	sign for unsplit negative logical copula
$\Diamond$	sign for possibility
$\square$	sign for necessity
P	sign for permissibility
O	sign for obligation
$\in$	sign for set membership
$\subseteq$	sign for set inclusion
$\subset$	sign for proper inclusion
$\cup$	sign for set union
$\cap$	sign for set intersection
$\varnothing$	sign for the null set

Introduction

1

Chapter Outline

Post-Fregean mathematical logic began with a concern for foundational issues in mathematics. However, by the 1930s philosophers had not only contributed to the building and refinement of various formal systems, but they had also begun an exploitation of them for primarily philosophical ends. While many schools of philosophy today eschew any kind of technical, logical work, an ability to use (or at least a familiarity with) the tools provided by formal logic systems is still taken as essential by most of those who consider themselves analytic philosophers. Moreover, recent years have witnessed a growing interest in formal logic among philosophers who stand on friendly terms with computer theory, cognitive psychology, game theory, linguistics, economics, law, and so on. At the same time, techniques developed in formal logic continue to shed light on both traditional and contemporary issues in epistemology, metaphysics, philosophy of mind, philosophy of science, philosophy of language, and so forth.

In what follows, students who have already learned something of classical mathematical logic are introduced to some other ways of doing formal logic: classical logic rests on the concepts of truth and falsity, whereas *constructivists* logic accounts for inference in terms of defense and refutation; classical logic usually makes use of a semantic theory based on models, whereas the alternative introduced here is based on the idea of truth sets; classical logic tends to interpret quantification objectually, whereas this alternative allows for a substitutional interpretation of quantifiers. As well, a radically different approach, fundamentally different from *any* version of mathematical logic, is also introduced. It is one that harkens back to the earliest stages in the history of formal logic but is equipped with the resources demanded of any formal logic today.

Sentences

In the expository sections of this text the word "sentence" primarily signifies declarative sentences, construed to include, for example, arithmetical equations and statements of science, as well as many sentences from common speech and writing.

Truth and Falsity

If, in response to the question of who won the 1996 presidential election, I say "Clinton defeated Dole" then I get things right, and what I have said with that sentence is something *true*. But had I instead answered "Dole defeated Clinton" I would have gotten things wrong, and what I would have said with that sentence would have been something *false*. This illustrates one way in which the terms "true" and "false" are used in relation to many everyday sentences. We do not ordinarily say of the *sentences* that they are true or are false, but rather apply those terms via such phrases as "what is said with the sentence." So, here the terms "true" and "false" are applied *in relation to* sentences though not directly applied to sentences themselves. We also apply these terms in relation to such quite different sentences as arithmetical equations. The multiplication of 25 with itself equals 625. So if I report "25 squared equals 625" I get things right and can be said to have said something true. But if I mistakenly multiply and report "25 squared equals 725" then I get things wrong, and so may be said to have said something false.

In some cases what we say with a sentence in no way varies from one to another of its standard utterances. This is how things are with, for example, the sentence "Gold is an element." And since gold *is* an element, what is said with this sentence is invariably true. For this kind of case we can apply the word "true" to the sentence itself. Another example of a sentence in the standard utterances of which we always say the same thing is "Gold is a chemical compound." But in this case what we say is false. So, what is said by "Gold is a chemical compound" is invariably false, and we thus can apply that term to the sentence itself.

Classical logic—the type of account of inference that will be primarily used in this text—makes free use of the notions of truth and falsity.

Truth-Values

The *truth-value* of something said is *truth*, if what is said is true, or is *falsity*, if what is said is false. For the cases in which we can speak of a *sentence* as true, or as false, we can also speak of *its* truth-value, saying that the truth-value of the true sentence is truth, and that the truth-value of the false sentence is falsity.

Defense and Refutation

For great many sentences there are associated activities of defense and refutation, where one may not *successfully* defend what one seeks to defend, and may not *successfully* refute what one seeks to refute. For example, if asked to defend the statement that there is a red vase in the living room we might go to the living room, spot the vases in that room, and look to see whether any is red. In other cases defending a statement is very difficult and complex. Think in this connection of what might be involved in defending the statement that there are electrons. There is a connection between defending a statement and truth, and refuting a statement and falsity. For we say that our statement is true if we have done what we regard as successfully defending it. And if we have done what we regard as successfully refuting some statement, then we will say that it is false.

The reason why we write these brief observations about defending and refuting statements is that there is a type of account of inference—constructivist logic—that employs these notions, rather than the notions of truth and falsity, in its discussion of inference, the main features of which will be sketched later in this text.

Inference, Form and Implication

Logic is a study of formally valid (correct) inference. Here is an example of such an inference:

> All whales are mammals.
> All mammals are animals.
> *Thus*, all whales are animals.

The *form* of this inference can be seen from the following schema:

> All A are B
> All B are C
> All A are C

where the letters stand in for plural nouns and noun phrases. An inference is said to be of this form if it is an *instance* of this form, that is, if it results from a uniform replacement of letters in the schema by plural nouns or noun phrases. No inference of this form is incorrect. And so we speak of each such inference as *formally valid*. Coordinate with this we also say that for each such inference, its initial sentences *formally imply* its final sentence.

By a *uniform* replacement is meant (for this case) a replacement of both occurrences of "A" by the same word or phrase, and a replacement of both occurrences of "B" by the same word or phrase (possibly different from the word or phrase replacing the occurrences of "A"), and similarly for the occurrences of "C." The general notion of a uniform replacement is the obvious generalization of this case.

Formally Valid Inference

We noted that all instances of the above schema are valid. But what does it mean to say of any *one* of those instances that *it* is valid? Classical logic suggests that the instance is valid because, for every instance of the schema, if its beginning sentences are true, so is its final sentence. On the constructivist view, the instance is valid because, for every instance of the schema, if its initial sentences are defensible, so is its final sentence.

On the classical view, an inference is formally valid because it is "truth-preserving." On the constructivist view, an inference is formally valid because it is "defense preserving."

Conjunctions

The word "and" is used in various constructions, for example, to form conjunctive subject terms as in:

> *Plato and Socrates* are among the best-known classical philosophers.

Or to form conjunctive predicates, as in:

> Apples are tasty and healthful.

There is also the use of "and" to form conjunctive sentences, as in:

> Apples are tasty *and* apples are healthful.

Contemporary logical discussion of conjunction focuses on *this* use of the word "and," the one in which it links two occurrences of sentences to form therefrom yet another sentence. The construction here noted is one that forms *complete* sentences from *complete* sentences. Within that discussion, a sentence thus formed is called a *conjunction* and the sentences from which it is formed are called its *conjuncts*.

Both "Snow is white and grass is green" and "Snow is white and snow is white" are conjunctions. In the first there occur two sentences, in the second just one sentence. But in both conjunctions there are two *occurrences* of sentences.

In its use to form conjunctions, the word "and" is called a sentential operator. Because it links *two* occurrences of sentences, it is said to be a *binary* or *two-place* sentential operator. There are many such words and phrases in our language, for example, "or," "if," "unless," "because," "only if."

Inference with Conjunctions

From a constructivist point of view an inference is valid if it is of some form such that for every inference of its form if its premises are defensible, so is its conclusion. For example, to defend the conjunctive claim that apples are tasty and apples are healthful we must defend both the claim that apples are tasty and the claim that apples are healthful. Thus, if we can defend the claim that apples are tasty and also defend the claim that apples are healthful, we can defend the conjunction claim that apples are tasty and apples are healthful. Here, what suffices to defend the premises of the inference suffices as well for defending its conclusion. Similar considerations show that what suffices to defend the premise of an inference from a conjunction to either of its conjuncts also is valid, suffices as well for defending its conclusion.

From a classical point of view an inference is valid if it is of some form no instance of which proceeds from truth to falsity. And nothing seems plainer than that we count a conjunction true just in case we take both its conjuncts to be true, and false just in case we take either or both of its conjuncts to be false.

From both points of view, formally valid inferences involving just conjunctions can be summed up by two "rules of inference," commonly labeled *the rule of conjunction* and *the rule of simplification*. They can be put as follows:

> Conj: To infer a conjunction from its conjuncts.
> Simp: To infer its conjuncts from a conjunction.

Truth-Functionality and Conjunctions

Consider the case of any conjunction both conjuncts of which are truth-valued. In that case the conjunction also is truth-valued, and precisely as follows: it is true if and only if both conjuncts are true and otherwise is false, that is, it is false if and only if either or both of its conjuncts are false. The truth-value of a conjunction (both conjuncts of which are truth-valued) is thus entirely fixed by the truth-values of those conjuncts. We express this point by saying that in its use as a sentential operator, the word "and" is *truth-functional*.

Negation

A variety of linguistic devices fall under the rubric "negation." Some examples are:

The engine is running.
The engine is *not* running.
Some of the engines are running.
None of the engines are running.
All of the engines are running.
Not all of the engines are running.

In the first case the word "not" is *added* to the sentence's predicate to form its negation. In the second case the word "none" *replaces* the word "some" in the sentence "Some of the engines are running" to form its negation. In the third, the word "not" is *prefixed* to a sentence to form its negation. Contemporary logical discussion takes the third manner of forming negations as its paradigm for negation. A phrase of English that (unlike "not") can always prefix a sentence to form its negation is "it is not the case that." Taken as a whole, this phrase functions as a sentential operator. Since it applies to a single occurrence of a sentence, it is said to be a *unary* or *one-place* sentential operator.

Inference with Negation

There are two forms of inference for negation that are accepted as valid by both classical and constructivist logicians. The first is the inference from a sentence to its double negation. From the classical point of view negation is like the operation of flipping a coin. From truth to falsity, and then back to truth. So, if a sentence is true its negation is false, and so the negation of that negation—the double negation of the original sentence—is again true. The constructivist reasons instead as follows: To defend the negation of some sentence it is enough to refute that sentence. To refute the negation of some sentence it is enough to defend the sentence of which it is a negation. So suppose that there is a defense of sentence S. Then that is enough to refute its negation. And that is enough to defend the negation of that negation. Otherwise put, what defends S refutes the negation of S and thus defends the double negation of S.

The second generally accepted negation inference is the method of argument that affirms the negation of any sentence that validly implies a contradiction. From the classical point of view, since a contradiction is false, whatever validly implies a contradiction also is false, in which case its negation is true. From the constructivist point of view, that a sentence validly implies a contradiction suffices to refute that sentence and thus to defend its negation.

The first of the inferences just considered might be called the rule of *inference to a double negation*, and the second is often called the rule of *negation introduction*, or, more traditionally, the rule of *reductio ad absurdum*.

The converse of the first form of inference just noted might be called *inference from a double negation*. Classical logic accepts this inference as formally valid. Its idea might be put as follows: If the double negation of sentence S is true, then its single negation will have been false, in which case S will have been true. Constructivist logic does not accept inference from a double negation. Here the reasoning runs roughly as follows: There are two ways of refuting the negation of sentence S. One is to directly defend S. The other is to infer a contradiction from the negation of S. Thus it is possible to refute the negation of S, and thereby defend the *double negation* of S, without therein defending S itself. Defending a double negation can occur without defending the sentence of which it is a double negation, and thus the inference is not formally valid.

In this connection, consider the claim

> It is not the case that not all of Nebraska's US senators in the 1990s were Caucasian.

To defend this claim we need to refute the claim

> Not all of Nebraska's US senators in the 1990s were Caucasian.

This can be done by examining the public record and taking a look at the persons therein identified as US senators from Nebraska in the 1990s. Doing this *also* defends the claim

> All of Nebraska's US senators in the 1990s were Caucasian.

So it is clear that, in some cases at any rate, defending a double negation is one with defending the sentence of which it is a double negation.

But now consider the case of the claim that there is no odd prime number. This could be refuted by noting that the number 11 is odd and then carrying out the calculations that show that the only numbers of which it is a product are itself and 1. This way of *refuting* the claim there is *no* odd prime number is one with *defending* the claim of which it is the negation, namely the claim that there *is* an odd prime. But one might also refute the claim that there is no odd prime number by the following argument:

Suppose there is no odd prime number. Then, since 2 is the only even prime, and every number is either odd or even, 2 is the only prime. Thus, every number but 2 is composite. So, since every number is a product of primes, every number is a product of 2. Thus every number is even. But since there are odd numbers, not every number is even. So, if there is no odd prime number then every number is even and not every number is even, which is a contradiction.

This refutes the claim

> There is no odd prime number

without defending the claim

> There is an odd prime number

or, at any rate, without defending it *in the usual way*, that is, by citing an odd number and carrying out the appropriate calculations.

In this text we primarily present logic from the classical point of view, but will frequently draw comparisons with the constructivist conception of inference.

Exercise 1.1 The following derivations are correct according to classical logic and incorrect according to constructivist logic. Locate the line in each derivation with which the constructivist would object. (Numerals within "{" and "}" indicate the premises upon which the line depends. Numerals within parentheses indicate line numbers. "¬" is the operator for negation; "∧" is the operator for conjunction.)

1. {1}   (1)   p   premise
    {2}   (2)   ¬ (p ∧ ¬ q)   premise
    {3}   (3)   ¬ q   premise
    {1, 3}   (4)   p ∧ ¬ q   from lines 1 and 3 by Conj
    {1, 2, 3} (5)   (p ∧ ¬ q) ∧ ¬ (p ∧ ¬ q)   from lines 2 and 4 by Conj
    {1, 2}   (6)   ¬ ¬ q   from lines 3–5 by negation introduction
    {1, 2}   (7)   q   from line 6 by inference from a double negation
2. {1}   (1)   ¬ p ∧ ¬ q   premise
    {2}   (2)   q   premise
    {3}   (3)   ¬ p   premise

{1}	(4)	¬ q	from line 1 by Simp
{1, 2}	(5)	q ∧ ¬ q	from lines 2 and 4 by Conj
{1, 2, 3}	(6)	¬ ¬ p	from lines 3–5 by negation introduction
{1, 2}	(7)	p	from line 6 by inference from a double negation

Exercise 1.2 Give a constructivist rationale for the inference from ¬ ¬ p to p.

Truth-Functionality and Negation

Let S be a truth-valued sentence. Then, if S is true, its negation is false, and if S is false, its negation is true. But might not the negation of S be false and S *not* be true? Not if S is truth-valued. It thus appears that the phrase "it is not the case that" is, like the word "and," a *truth-functional* sentential operator.

Grouping

The sentence

It is not the case that Tom went to the store and Bill went to the store

has two readings. On one, this sentence is the negation of a conjunction. On the other, it is a conjunction the left conjunct of which is a negation. If we wanted to rule out the second reading we might write:

It is not the case *both* that Tom went to the store and Bill went to the store.

Here the word "both" groups the two sentences as a conjunction to which the negation operator "it is not the case that" attaches as a whole. To rule out the first reading we might write:

It is not the case that Tom went to the store and, *furthermore*, Bill went to the store.

Here the word "furthermore" serves to indicate that the negation is limited to the left conjunction. The elimination of multiple readings could also be achieved through the use of parentheses. So we might write:

It is not the case that (Tom went to the store and Bill went to the store) to secure the first reading, and use the convention that the negation operator is to apply to the *shortest* sentence to which it is prefixed, as in

> It is not the case that Tom went to the store and Bill went to the store

to secure just the second reading.

In most logic texts definiteness of grouping is achieved by stipulating that binary operators are to occur *between* occurrences of the sentences they join, the whole being enclosed in parentheses, and that unary operators modify the shortest sentence to which they are prefixed. The outermost parentheses are, as it were, the limiting case of grouping. For this case the leftmost parenthesis is like a capital letter beginning a sentence, and the rightmost parenthesis is like the period ending a sentence. In practice, if a sentence begins with "(" and thus also ends with ")," these outermost parentheses can be omitted.

There is also a method of avoiding the kind of ambiguity here under discussion that dispenses with parentheses altogether, utilizing in its place *order*. For example, instead of writing "¬ (p ∧ q)" we would write "¬ ∧ p q," and instead of writing "(¬ p ∧ q)" we would write "∧ ¬ p q." This is called the method of *Polish* notation, a name drawn from the nationality of the logicians by whom this form of notation was first developed.

Exercise 1.3 The following are in Polish notation. Rewrite them using parentheses.

1. ¬ ∧ ∧ ¬ p ¬ q ∧ q ¬ p
2. ¬ ∧ ∧ p ¬ ∧ p ¬ q ¬ q
3. ∧ ¬ ∧ p ¬ q ¬ q
4. ¬ ∧ ¬ p ¬ q
5. ¬ ∧ p ¬ q
6. ¬ ∧ ¬ ∧ p q ¬ ∧ ¬ p ¬ q
7. ∧ ∧ p q ∧ ¬ p ¬ q
8. ¬ ∧ ∧ ¬ p q ∧ p ¬ q
9. ∧ ∧ ¬ ¬ p ¬ q ∧ p ¬ q
10. ∧ ¬ ∧ ¬ p q ¬ ∧ q ¬ p

Exercise 1.4 The following are in standard notation, using parentheses. Rewrite them using Polish notation.

1. ¬ (¬ p ∧ ¬ q)
2. p ∧ ¬ (¬ q ∧ ¬ r)

3. ¬ (p ∧ ¬ q)
4. ¬ p ∧ ¬ q
5. ¬ (¬ (p ∧ q) ∧ ¬ r)
6. (p ∧ q) ∧ r
7. (p ∧ ¬ q) ∧ (¬ p ∧ q)
8. ¬ ¬ (p ∧ q) ∧ ¬ r
9. p ∧ ¬ (¬ p ∧ ¬ r)
10. ¬ (p ∧ ¬ ¬ (q ∧ ¬ r))

Sentential Logic

Chapter Outline

We begin with a system of logic based on conjunction and negation. It is a system of *sentential logic*, so called because every sentence in the system is either a simple sentence or a compound of simple sentences.

The general procedure will be to first define what in logic is called a *language*, and then define the notion of a *derivation* (argument) in that language. The aim is to thereby codify all the formally valid inferences that turn on the notions of conjunction and negation.

Simple Sentences

The part of logic that deals with the sentential operators has no interest in the particular words that make up simple (non-compound) sentences. So, various marks are used in place of such sentences. The marks we shall employ to that end are (i) the lowercase letters of the alphabet, and (ii) the mark "'". We specify the *simple sentences* of language *SL* as follows:

Definition 2.1   (i) each lowercase letter of the alphabet is a simple sentence of *SL*, and (ii) for any simple sentence ϕ of *SL*, ϕ followed by "'" is also a simple sentence of *SL*.

The Greek letters as "ϕ" and "ψ" are not themselves simple sentences of the language *SL*, but rather stand for such sentences. In the next passage they will stand for sentences of the language *SL*. They, and other Greek letters, are used when we want to write about the various terms of the language in a general way. Just which terms they are to be understood as standing for in this or that context will either be explicitly noted, or clear from that context.

So, the following are all simple sentences of *SL*:

> p
>
> q
>
> p'
>
> q''

Sentences

Definition 2.2   (i) each simple sentence of *SL* is a sentence of *SL*, (ii) for any sentence ϕ of *SL*, the sign consisting of "¬" followed by ϕ is a sentence of *SL*, (iii) for any sentences ϕ and ψ of *SL*, the sign consisting of "(" followed by ϕ followed by "∧" followed by ψ followed by ")" is a sentence of *SL*.

The clauses using "followed by" are clumsy. Fortunately, there is a convention whereby we can drop quotation marks and signify a sequence of marks by the *left to right ordering* of symbols (usually Greek letters) standing for certain marks together with certain of those marks themselves (in what follows, the "'"and the two parentheses). So, instead of writing

> ϕ followed by "'"

we will write

φ′

a sign in which the mark "′" follows the Greek letter "φ". And for

"("followed by φ followed by "∧" followed by ψ followed by")"

we will write

(φ ∧ ψ)

and similarly for other cases. Rewriting our definitions using this convention we have:

Definition 2.3   (i) each lowercase letter of the alphabet is a simple sentence of *SL*, and
(ii) for any simple sentence φ of *SL*, φ′ is also a simple sentence of *SL*.

Definition 2.4   (i) each simple sentence of *SL* is a sentence of *SL*, (ii) for any sentence φ
of *SL*, ¬ φ is a sentence of *SL*, and (iii) for any sentences φ and ψ of *SL*,
(φ ∧ ψ) is a sentence of *SL*.

For any sentences φ and ψ, (φ ∧ ψ) is a *conjunction* with sentences φ and ψ as its *conjuncts*. For any sentence φ, the sentence ¬φ is the *negation* of φ.

In writing out sentences the outermost parentheses may be dropped. For example, instead of writing

((p ∧ ¬ q) ∧ ¬ (p ∧ ¬ q))

the sentence will instead be written

(p ∧ ¬ q) ∧ ¬ (p ∧ ¬ q)

Derivations: A First Look

Consider the following derivations:

(1)   ¬ (p ∧ ¬ q)   P
(2)   p   P
(3)   ¬ q   P

(4)	$p \wedge \neg q$	2, 3 Conj
(5)	$(p \wedge \neg q) \wedge \neg (p \wedge \neg q)$	1, 4 Conj
(6)	$\neg\neg q$	5 RAA
(7)	q	6 DN

The capital letter "P," written to the far right of the first three lines, indicates that the sentences at those lines occur as *premises* in this derivation. The indent, beginning with line 3 and ending with line 5, marks a sub-derivation, and thereby indicates that the third premise is, as it were, "temporary"—made in anticipation of a later application of the *reductio* rule. The notation "2, 3 Conj" at the right on the fourth line indicates that the conjunction at that line has been inferred from the sentences at lines 2 and 3 by the rule of conjunction formation. The notation "1, 4 Conj" at line 5 indicates that the conjunction at this line has been formed by the same rule from the sentences at lines 1 and 4. The sub-derivation is now completed. What has been shown in the sub-derivation is that adding the assumption "$\neg q$" to the derivation yields a contradiction. The *reductio* rule (RAA) is then applied to obtain at line 6 the negation of the assumption introduced at the start of the sub-derivation at line 3. The out dent indicates that this conclusion depends only on the first two premises. Finally, the rule of double negation (DN) is applied to obtain the sentence with which the derivation ends.

The type of derivation just given is perspicuous with respect to sub-derivations and overall premise dependency. But it does not make it explicit on *which* premises the sentence on this or that line depends. This lack can be remedied by adding a bit of set notation to the far left, using line numbers to stand for sentences on lines. Following these conventions our derivation could take the following form:

{1}	(1)	$\neg (p \wedge \neg q)$
{2}	(2)	p
{3}	(3)	$\neg q$
{2, 3}	(4)	$p \wedge \neg q$
{1, 2, 3}	(5)	$(p \wedge \neg q) \wedge \neg (p \wedge \neg q)$
{1, 2}	(6)	$\neg\neg q$
{1, 2}	(7)	q

That the premise set at a line has the sentence at that line as its sole member indicates that the line is a premise line. For every other case, the sentences at the lines whose numbers are in the premise set are the premises on which the sentence at that line depends in the derivation. Beyond that, for the derivation to be correct is for each of its lines to satisfy an inference condition.

The derivation just displayed is not annotated. Annotating a derivation involves saying what justifies each line of the derivation. Annotated, the last displayed derivation would have been written as follows:

{1}	(1)	$\neg (p \wedge \neg q)$	P
{2}	(2)	p	P
{3}	(3)	$\neg q$	P
{2, 3}	(4)	$p \wedge \neg q$	2, 3 Conj
{1, 2, 3}	(5)	$(p \wedge \neg q) \wedge \neg (p \wedge \neg q)$	1, 4 Conj
{1, 2}	(6)	$\neg \neg q$	5 RAA
{1, 2}	(7)	q	6 DN

Exercise 2.1 Following are derivations. Say what premise or premises each line depends on.

1.	{1}	(1)	$\neg (\neg p \wedge \neg q)$
	{2}	(2)	$\neg q$
	{3}	(3)	$\neg p$
	{2, 3}	(4)	$\neg p \wedge \neg q$
	{1, 2, 3}	(5)	$(\neg p \wedge \neg q) \wedge \neg (\neg p \wedge \neg q)$
	{1, 2}	(6)	$\neg \neg p$
	{1, 2}	(7)	p
2.	{1}	(1)	$\neg (p \wedge \neg q)$
	{2}	(2)	$\neg q$
	{3}	(3)	p
	{2, 3}	(4)	$p \wedge \neg q$
	{1, 2, 3}	(5)	$(p \wedge \neg q) \wedge \neg (p \wedge \neg q)$
	{1, 2}	(6)	$\neg p$
3.	{1}	(1)	p
	{2}	(2)	$\neg p \wedge \neg q$
	{2}	(3)	$\neg p$
	{1, 2}	(4)	$p \wedge \neg p$
	{1}	(5)	$\neg (\neg p \wedge \neg q)$
4.	{1}	(1)	p
	{2}	(2)	q
	{3}	(3)	$\neg (p \wedge q) \wedge \neg (\neg p \wedge q)$
	{1, 2}	(4)	$p \wedge q$
	{3}	(5)	$\neg (p \wedge q)$
	{1, 2, 3}	(6)	$(p \wedge q) \wedge \neg (p \wedge q)$
	{1, 2}	(7)	$\neg (\neg (p \wedge q) \wedge \neg (\neg p \wedge \neg q))$

5.

{1}	(1)	$\neg\,(\neg\,(p \wedge q) \wedge \neg\,(\neg\, p \wedge \neg\, q))$
{2}	(2)	p
{3}	(3)	$\neg\, q$
{4}	(4)	$p \wedge q$
{4}	(5)	q
{3, 4}	(6)	$q \wedge \neg\, q$
{3}	(7)	$\neg\,(p \wedge q)$
{8}	(8)	$\neg\, p \wedge \neg\, q$
{8}	(9)	$\neg\, p$
{2, 8}	(10)	$p \wedge \neg\, p$
{2}	(11)	$\neg\,(\neg\, p \wedge \neg\, q)$
{2, 3}	(12)	$\neg\,(p \wedge q) \wedge \neg\,(\neg\, p \wedge \neg\, q)$
{1, 2, 3}	(13)	$(\neg\,(p \wedge q) \wedge \neg\,(\neg\, p \wedge \neg\, q)) \wedge \neg\,(\neg\,(p \wedge q) \wedge \neg\,(\neg\, p \wedge \neg\, q))$
{1, 2}	(14)	$\neg\,\neg\, q$
{1, 2}	(15)	q

Exercise 2.2 Each of the deductions (or derivations) in exercise 2.1 are correct in classical logic. Does the same hold for constructivist logic? Identify any to which the constructivist would object.

Exercise 2.3 Annotate each of the derivations in exercise 2.1.

A Note on Sets

In this text the words "set" and "class" are used interchangeably. All sets but one have members. The one set lacking members is called the *empty set*. Our symbol for this set is "∅." To indicate membership in a set we use the symbol "∈." So we might write: 7 ∈ the set of primes.

Some sets have just one member. These are called *unit sets*. We indicate a unit set by placing a sign for its single member between brackets. Thus, "{7}" signifies the unit set whose only member is 7.

If a set has just a few members, we can write it out by placing terms for those members within brackets. So we might write "{2, 3, 5, 7}" for the set whose members are exactly 2, 3, 5, and 7—the set of prime numbers less than 10. When this method of indicating a set is unavailable or too lengthy, we can use brackets together with a phrase for exactly the members of the set we wish to designate. So we might write "{x: x is a natural number}" for the set of natural numbers, reading the sign using brackets as follows: the set of all x such that x is a natural number. Finally, in some cases it will be enough to write terms for three or four set elements to indicate the remaining members, as when we write {1, 2, 3, . . .} for the set of natural numbers, or {2, 4, 6, . . .} for the set of even natural numbers.

For any sets A and B, the *union* of those sets is the set whose members are exactly the members of A and the members of B. So, for example, if A is the set of even prime numbers and B is the set of odd prime numbers, then the union of A and B is the set of all prime numbers. We write the union of sets A and B with the sign "∪." Thus, A ∪ B is the union of sets A and B.

For any sets A and B, the intersection of those sets is the set whose members are common to both A and B. So, for example, if A is the set of male humans and B is the set of humans that wear glasses, the intersection of A and B is the set of male humans that wear glasses. We write the intersection of sets A and B with the sign "∩." Thus, A ∩ B is the intersection of sets A and B.

Sets A and B are said to be *disjoint* just in case nothing is a member of both. For sets A and B, A *less* B (written "A ~ B") is the set of all members of A that are not members of B. So, for example, the set of natural numbers less the set of even natural numbers is the set of odd natural numbers.

For any sets A and B, if every member of B is also a member of A, then B is said to be a *subset* of A. Since every member of a set is a member of that set, every set is a subset of itself. To indicate that B is a subset of A we write: B ⊆ A. To indicate that B is a *proper* subset of A, that is, a subset of A other than A itself, we write: B ⊂ A. Finally, a set A is identical with a set B (written "A = B") just in case A and B have the same members. For example, the set of humans and the set of primates whose nasal cavities are lined with hair are identical.

A relation is a special kind of set. A set of ordered pairs is a binary relation; a set of ordered triples is ternary relation; and so on. To indicate an ordered pair of objects a and b, we write <a, b>, where a is the first element of the pair and b is the second element of the pair. To indicate an ordered triple of objects a, b, and c, we write <a, b, c>, and so on for ordered n-tuples. While {a, b} = {b, a}, <a, b> ≠ <b, a> unless a = b. With ordered n-tuples order matters.

Exercise 2.4

Let A = {4, 6}
   B = {1, 3, 5, 7, 9}
   C = {x: x is a positive integer less than 9}
   D = {x: x is a positive integer that is prime}
   E = {1, 4, 3, 4 + 3}
   F = {2, 2^3, 2}
   G = {2^2}

$$H = \{1\}$$
$$K = \{8\}$$

Which of the following are true?

1. $G \in A$
2. $G \subseteq A$
3. $G \cap H \subseteq D$
4. $(A \cap B) \cup E \subset F$
5. $(F \cap C) \cap K = B$
6. $B \subset C$
7. $A \cup D \subset G \cup H$
8. $B \subset F$
9. $A \cap B = \emptyset$
10. $E \cup K = K$

Exercise 2.5   Answer the following:

1. Give an example of sets A, B, and C such that $A \in B$, $B \in C$, and $A \notin C$ (it is not the case that $A \in C$).
2. Explain why $\emptyset \subseteq A$, for any set A. Explain why it is not the case that, for any set A, $\emptyset \in A$. (That is, explain why it is false that the null set is a member of every set).
3. Is $\{1, 2\} \subset \{\{1, 2, 3\}, \{1, 3\}, 1, 2\}$? Explain why or why not.
4. Is $\{1, 2\} \in \{\{1, 2, 3\}, \{1, 3\}, 1, 2\}$? Explain why or why not.
5. Which of the following is true for all sets A, B, and C?

   (a) $A \sim B = B \sim A$
   (b) $(A \sim B) \sim C = A \sim (B \sim C)$
   (c) $A \sim \emptyset = A$
   (d) $A \sim (B \cup C) = (A \sim B) \cup C$
   (e) $A \sim (B \sim C) = (A \sim B) \sim C$
   (f) $B \sim (B \sim A) = A$

Lines

Definition 2.5   We will call a pair the first element of which is a finite set A of *SL* sentences and the second element of which is some *SL* sentence ϕ, a *line*.

Note that the set of *SL* sentences referred to may be empty. We will write

<A, ϕ>

for a line consisting of finite set A of *SL* sentences and *SL* sentence ϕ.

Derivations Again

We will define a derivation as a finite sequence of lines, each of which satisfies a rule of inference. Those rules will take the form of *conditions* that a sequence of lines must satisfy in order to constitute a derivation. Our official definition is:

Definition 2.6   An *SL derivation* is any finite sequence S of lines each satisfying one of the following conditions, for sets of sentences A and B and sentences ϕ and ψ:

P   For every ϕ, <{ϕ}, ϕ> is a derivation.

Simp   If S is a derivation and <A, ($\phi \wedge \psi$)> occurs in S, then S, <A, ϕ> and S, <A, ψ> also are derivations.

Conj   If S is a derivation and both <A, ϕ> and <B, ψ> occur in S, then S, <A ∪ B, ($\phi \wedge \psi$)> also is a derivation.

DN   If S is a derivation and <A, $\neg \neg \phi$> occurs in S, then S, <A, ϕ> also is a derivation, and conversely.

RAA   If S is a derivation and <A ∪ {ϕ}, ($\psi \wedge \neg \psi$)> occurs in S, then S, <A, $\neg \phi$> also is a derivation.

The first condition corresponds to a rule of *premise introduction*. That ϕ is the only member of its set of premises in one of its occurrences in a derivation indicates that in that occurrence in the derivation it is not derived from other sentences in that derivation, and thus occurs as a premise of that derivation. The second condition corresponds to a rule of *simplification*. It says that either conjunct of a conjunction may be derived from that conjunction, taking as its premises in the derivation all those of that conjunction. The third condition corresponds to a rule of *conjunction*. It says that a conjunction may be derived from its two conjuncts, taking as its premises in the derivation all those of the conjuncts. The fourth condition corresponds to a rule of *double negation*. The idea is that if two sentences are different and only just by the interchange of some sentence with its double negation, then each may be derived from the other, retaining the same premises.

The fifth condition corresponds to a rule of *negation introduction*, known also as a rule of *reductio ad absurdum*. It says that from a contradiction any sentence $\neg \phi$ can be derived taking as its premises all those of the contradiction less ϕ itself.

Expressed as *rules of inferences*, these conditions are:

P   To introduce a sentence ϕ at a new line with the set {ϕ} as the premise set of that new line.

Conj   To introduce a sentence φ ∧ ψ at a new line if the sentences φ and ψ are at earlier lines, with the union of the sets of premises at those earlier lines as the premise set of the new line.

Simp   To introduce a sentence φ at a new line if either φ ∧ ψ or ψ ∧ φ is the sentence at an earlier line, with the premise set of that earlier line as the premise set of the new line.

DN   To introduce a sentence ¬ ¬ φ at a new line if φ is the sentence at an earlier line, or conversely, with the premise set of the earlier line as the premise set of the new line.

RAA   To introduce a sentence ¬ φ at a new line if ψ ∧ ¬ ψ is the sentence at an earlier line, with the premise set of that earlier line less the sentence φ as the premise set of the new line.

As expressed, the rules Conj, Simp, and DN lack specificity with respect to premises for the cases in which there are several earlier lines, or several pairs of earlier lines, which are all of the right form for drawing the inference. This is not a problem in practice.

Definition 2.7   There is a *derivation of* φ *from* A if and only if there is a derivation with line <A, φ>.

Definition 2.8   φ *is derivable from* A if and only if, for some set B, B ⊆ A and there is a derivation of φ from B. We write: A ⊢ φ.

Note that it is possible for sentence to be derivable from an infinite set of sentences. But if sentence φ is derivable from some set of *SL* sentences A, then, for some finite subset B of A, B ⊢ φ. For if A ⊢ φ, then, for some subset B of A, there is a derivation with line <B, φ>, in which case (by definition 2.5) B is a finite set. So, for any set A of *SL* sentences and any *SL* sentence φ, if A ⊢ φ, then, for some finite subset B of A, B ⊢ φ.

Theorems

Definition 2.9   φ is an *SL theorem* if and only if there is a derivation of φ from ∅, the empty set of *SL* sentences. We write: ∅ ⊢ φ or ⊢ φ.

To establish that a sentence is a theorem we construct a derivation the last line of which consists of the sentence and the empty set of premises. To construct such a derivation, take as its initial premise the negation of the sentence you want to establish as a theorem. Then apply the various rules until a contradiction is derived with just the negation of that theorem as premise. Then apply rule RAA. This yields the double negation of the theorem from the empty set of premises. Then apply the rule of double negation to obtain the theorem, still from the empty set of premises. Here is an example.

(1)	¬ ¬ (p ∧ ¬ ¬ (¬ q ∧ ¬ p))		P
(2)	(p ∧ ¬ ¬ (¬ q ∧ ¬ p))		1 DN
(3)	p		2 Simp
(4)	¬ ¬ (¬ q ∧ ¬ p)		2 Simp
(5)	¬ q ∧ ¬ p		4 DN
(6)	¬ p		5 Simp
(7)	p ∧ ¬ p		3, 6 Conj
(8)	¬ ¬ ¬ (p ∧ ¬ ¬ (¬ q ∧ ¬ p))		7 RAA
(9)	¬ (p ∧ ¬ ¬ (¬ q ∧ ¬ p))		8 DN

Here is the same derivation with the premises upon which each line depends made explicit.

{1}	(1)	¬ ¬ (p ∧ ¬ ¬ (¬ q ∧ ¬ p))	P
{1}	(2)	(p ∧ ¬ ¬ (¬ q ∧ ¬ p))	1 DN
{1}	(3)	p	2 Simp
{1}	(4)	¬ ¬ (¬ q ∧ ¬ p)	2 Simp
{1}	(5)	¬ q ∧ ¬ p	4 DN
{1}	(6)	¬ p	5 Simp
{1}	(7)	p ∧ ¬ p	3, 6 Conj
∅	(8)	¬ ¬ ¬ (p ∧ ¬ ¬ (¬ q ∧ ¬ p))	7 RAA
∅	(9)	¬ (p ∧ ¬ ¬ (¬ q ∧ ¬ p))	8 DN

Exercise 2.6 Prove each of the following:

1. ∅ ⊢ ¬ (p ∧ ¬ p)
2. ∅ ⊢ ¬ (p ∧ ¬ ¬ ¬ p)
3. ∅ ⊢ ¬ ((p ∧ q) ∧ ¬ p)
4. ∅ ⊢ ¬ (¬ (p ∧ ¬ q) ∧ (¬ q ∧ ¬ ¬ p))
5. ∅ ⊢ ¬ ((¬ q ∧ ¬ ¬ p) ∧ ¬ (p ∧ ¬ q))
6. ∅ ⊢ ¬ (¬ (p ∧ ¬ q) ∧ (¬ ¬ p ∧ ¬ q))

Truth Sets

The semantics of *SL* is usually done in terms of truth tables and truth-value assignments. We shall instead employ truth sets. Truth sets are introduced by Hugues Leblanc in chapter 3 of his *Truth-Value Semantics* (Leblanc 1976) For reasons of economy in the development of truth sets we will, for now, keep the language *SL* to just the two operators "¬" and "∧." Later we will use further operators.

Let T be a set (possibly empty) of simple *SL* sentences. We can then think of expanding this set in accord with the following rules (where, as usual, "ϕ" and "ψ" are variables for *SL* sentences):

    1. ¬ ϕ ∈ T if and only if ϕ ∉ T, and

    2. ϕ ∧ ψ ∈ T if and only if ϕ ∈ T and ψ ∈ T.

Every set of the sentences of *SL* satisfying the characterization just given is called a *truth set* of *SL*. (We will use the letter "F" to designate the class of *SL* sentences that are not members of truth set T.)

For any simple sentence ϕ there will be unlimitedly many truth sets of which ϕ is a member. Equally, there will be unlimitedly many truth sets of which ϕ is not a member. (There is no limit to simple *SL* sentences. So, there is no limit to the ways in which these sentences can form sets.) That there will be unlimitedly many truth sets of which ϕ is not a member corresponds to the idea that for a simple sentence there is both the possibility of being true and the possibility of being not true—which, if all the simple sentences are truth-valued, comes to the possibility of being false. The same holds for many compound sentences. For example, there will be truth sets to which both "p" and "q" belong. So, the conjunction "p ∧ q" will also belong to those truth sets. On the other hand, there are truth sets to which "p" does not belong, which then will be truth sets to which the conjunction "p ∧ q" also will not belong. This corresponds to the idea that a conjunction of simple sentences also has *two* truth-value possibilities.

There also are *SL* sentences that belong to all truth sets. A simple example is "¬ (p ∧ ¬ p)." To see this just note that if "p" belongs to a truth set, then "¬ p" does not, in which case "p ∧ ¬ p" also does not. But then "¬ (p ∧ ¬ p)" does. So, if "p" belongs to a truth set, so does "¬ (p ∧ ¬ p)." Now suppose that "p" does not belong to some truth set. Then "p ∧ ¬ p" also does not belong to that truth set, in which case "¬ (p ∧ ¬ p)" does. So, if "p" does not belong to some truth set, "¬ (p ∧ ¬ p)" does. So, "¬ (p ∧ ¬ p)" is a member of every truth set. And, of course, there are *SL* sentences which belong to no truth sets, one being "p ∧ ¬ p."

We now define an *SL truth set* (or truth set, for short) as follows:

Definition 2.10 Set T is an *SL* truth set if and only if T is a set of *SL* sentences such that (i) for any *SL* sentence ϕ ∧ ψ, ϕ ∧ ψ ∈ T if and only if ϕ ∈ T and ψ ∈ T, and (ii) for any *SL* sentence ¬ ϕ, ¬ ϕ ∈ T if and only if ϕ ∉ T.

Further terminology is as follows:

Definition 2.11 An *SL* sentence φ is a *semantical truth* if and only if φ is a member of every truth set. We write: ⊨ φ.

Definition 2.12 An *SL* sentence φ is a *semantically inconsistent* sentence if and only if φ is a member of no truth set.

Definition 2.13 A set A of *SL* sentences is *semantically inconsistent* if and only if there is no truth set of which each sentence in A is a member.

Definition 2.14 An *SL* sentence φ is *semantically consistent* if and only if φ is a member of some truth set.

Definition 2.15 A set A of *SL* sentences is *semantically consistent* if and only if there is some truth set of which each sentence in A is a member.

Definition 2.16 An *SL* sentence φ is *semantically contingent* if and only if there is some truth set of which φ is a member, and also some truth set of which φ is not a member.

Definition 2.17 An *SL* sentence φ is a *semantical consequence* of a set A of *SL* sentences if and only if there is no truth set to which every sentence in A belongs but φ does not belong. We also say that A *semantically implies* φ and write: A ⊨ φ. If A is the unit set {ψ} we say that φ is a semantical consequence of ψ (that ψ semantically implies φ) and write ψ ⊨ φ. Where A = {ψ$_1$, ψ$_2$, . . . , ψ$_n$} and φ is any *SL* sentence, ψ$_1$, ψ$_2$, . . . , ψ$_n$ ∴ φ will be said to be an argument. Such an argument is valid if and only if A ⊨ φ.

Truth sets are prompted by the thought that our letters are intended to represent truth-valued sentences for which both truth and falsity are in some sense possible, and that our operation symbols function, relative to truth and falsity, as do "and" and "it is not the case that."

If, for each simple sentence, both truth and falsity are possible, and if all compatibilities and incompatibilities of truth and falsity are due to circumstances external to the simple sentences, then one possibility is that all such sentences are true. Another will be that all such sentences are false. And, since we suppose no upper limit on the number of simple sentences, there will be unlimitedly many combinations of truth and falsity between these two extremes. Each truth set represents, relative to the simple sentence, one way in which they might be true and false.

Then the thought is that "and" and "it is not the case that" are truth-functional operators. If so, then once it is determined which simple sentences are true and which are false—once the basis of a truth set is fixed—then all the remaining sentences fall into line, picking up their truth-values from the truth-values of their component sentences, in accord with the modes of truth-functionality associated with the two operators.

It is sometimes thought that by means of these truth sets it will be possible to test the system of inference laid down for *SL*, to determine whether they *really* are good rules—ones which never lead sentences all of which are true to a sentence that is not true—ones which are, to use the standard term, *sound*. But it would perhaps be better to say that we test the adequacy of our formulation of truth sets. For there is no serious question about whether a conjunction follows from its conjuncts taken together, or implies each of them, or about whether a sentence implies its double negation.

And, as to the disputed principle of inferring a sentence from its double negation, truth sets leave that matter unsettled.

It might be best to say that what is done in a proof of soundness is to show that the kind of coordination between inference and the calculus of "true" and "false" that we sought to secure in constructing truth sets was thereby secured.

In this connection we should note that when, for example, we stipulate that a conjunction belongs to any T set to which both its conjuncts belong we thereby stipulate that the rule of conjunction (to infer a conjunction from its conjuncts) will never lead from sentences belonging to some truth set to a sentence not belonging to that truth set. A proof of soundness is, it thus seems, a way of showing that these stipulations work as anticipated.

An argument formulated in *SL* may be one in which its conclusion belongs to a truth set if its premises do. We want a guarantee that our rules provide for a corresponding derivation. If so, these rules are said to be *complete*. So we want our rules to be complete.

Soundness

Definition 2.18   The *SL* derivation system is *sound* if and only if for any *SL* sentence ϕ and set A of *SL* sentences, if ϕ is derivable from A, then ϕ is a semantical consequence of A, that is, if A $\vdash \phi$ then A $\models \phi$.

That is, if there is a derivation with a line $<A', \phi>$, where A' is a finite subset of a set A of *SL* sentences (i.e., if A $\vdash \phi$), then A semantically implies ϕ (i.e., then A $\models \phi$).

We shall prove something slightly stronger: for every finite set of *SL* sentences B and *SL* sentence ψ, every line $<B, \psi>$ of a derivation is such that ψ is a semantical consequence of B; that is, every line of a derivation is valid.

This follows from the following two points: (1) the first line of a derivation is valid; (2) a given line is valid if all the earlier lines are valid.

The first line of a derivation is justified by rule P; thus, it is of the form <{ψ}, ψ>, for some sentence ψ of SL, and, trivially, {ψ} ⊨ ψ (for any truth set T, if {ψ} ⊆ T then ψ ∈ T). Thus the first line of every derivation is valid. So point (1) is proven.

Proof of (2). Now we shall show that a given line of a derivation is valid if all earlier lines of that derivation are valid. We shall proceed by cases.

Case 1. The given line is justified by rule P. Then, by virtue of the argument for point (1), the given line is obviously valid.

Case 2. Simp justifies the given line. Then, for some SL sentence φ and set of SL sentences A, the given line is

<A, φ>.

With regard to earlier lines there are two subcases.

Subcase 1. There is an earlier line

<A, φ ∧ ψ>.

By hypothesis

A ⊨ φ ∧ ψ.

Thus,

A ⊨ φ.

For suppose A ⊆ T, for some truth set T. Then, by the hypothesis, φ ∧ ψ ∈ T. Thus, φ ∈ T by the definition of a truth set.

Subcase 2. There is an earlier line

<A, ψ ∧ φ>.

Then, by the same reasoning as just given, A ⊨ φ.

Case 3. Conj justifies the given line. Then, for some SL sentences φ and ψ and set of SL sentences A, the given line is the pair

<A ∪ B, φ ∧ ψ>

with there being earlier lines

$<A, \phi>$

and

$<B, \psi>$.

By hypothesis

$A \models \phi$

and

$B \models \psi$.

Thus,

$A \cup B \models \phi \wedge \psi$.

For suppose $A \cup B \subseteq T$, for some truth set T. Then $A \subseteq T$ and $B \subseteq T$. Thus $\phi \in T$ and $\psi \in T$ by the hypothesis. Thus $\phi \wedge \psi \in T$ by the definition of a truth set (definition 2.10).

Case 4. DN justifies the given line.

Subcase 1. For some *SL* sentence ϕ and set of *SL* sentences A, the given line is

$<A, \phi>$

and there is an earlier line

$<A, \neg \neg \phi>$.

By hypothesis

$A \models \neg \neg \phi$.

Thus

$A \models \phi$.

For suppose $A \subseteq T$, for some truth set T. Then, by the hypothesis, $\neg \neg \phi \in T$. Then, by the definition of a truth set, $\neg \phi \notin T$. Thus, by the same definition, $\phi \in T$.

Subcase 2. For some *SL* sentence ϕ and set of *SL* sentences A, the given line is

<A, ¬¬ϕ>

and there is an earlier line

<A, ϕ>.

By hypothesis

A $\models \phi$.

Thus

A $\models \neg\neg\phi$.

For suppose A ⊆ T, for some truth set T. Then, by the hypothesis, ϕ ∈ T. Then, by the definition of a truth set, ¬ϕ ∉ T. Thus, by the same definition, ¬¬ϕ ∈ T.

Case 5. The given line is justified by RAA. Then, for some *SL* sentence ϕ and set of *SL* sentences A, the given line is

<A ~ {ϕ}, ¬ϕ>

and the earlier line is

<A ∪ {ϕ}, ψ ∧ ¬ψ>

for some *SL* sentence ψ. By hypothesis

A ∪ {ϕ} $\models$ ψ ∧ ¬ψ.

Thus

A ~ {ϕ} $\models \neg\phi$.

For suppose A ~ {ϕ} ⊆ T, for some truth set T. By the hypothesis, if ϕ ∈ T then ψ ∧ ¬ψ ∈ T. But, by the definition of a truth set, ψ ∧ ¬ψ ∉ T. Thus ϕ ∉ T. Thus, again by the definition of a truth set, ¬ϕ ∈ T. So, if A ~ {ϕ} ⊆ T then ¬ϕ ∈T.

This completes the proof of soundness of the derivational system defined by definition 2.6.

Exercise 2.7 An *SL* rule of inference is *valid* if and only if the sentence whose derivation it allows is a semantical consequence of its premises if the sentence or sentences from which it is inferred are semantical consequences of their premises. Prove the following rules valid:

1. For *SL* sentences φ and ψ and set of *SL* sentences A: the given line is <A, ¬ (φ ∧ ψ)>, and there is an earlier line <A, ¬ φ> or there is an earlier line <A, ¬ ψ>.
2. For *SL* sentences φ and ψ and set of *SL* sentences A: the given line is <A, ¬ (¬ φ ∧ ¬ ψ)>, and there is an earlier line <A, φ> or there is an earlier line <A, ψ>.
3. For *SL* sentences φ and ψ and sets of *SL* sentences A and B: the given line is <A ∪ B, ψ>, and there is an earlier line <A, φ > and there is an earlier line <B, ¬ (φ ∧ ¬ ψ)>.
4. For *SL* sentences φ and ψ and sets of *SL* sentences A and B: the given line is <A ∪ B, ¬ φ>, and there is an earlier line <A, ¬ ψ> and there is an earlier line <B, ¬ (φ ∧ ¬ ψ)>.
5. For *SL* sentences φ, ψ, and γ, and sets of *SL* sentences A and B: the given line is <A ∪ B, ¬ (φ ∧ ¬ γ)>, and there is an earlier line <A, ¬ (φ ∧ ¬ ψ)> and there is an earlier line <B, ¬ (ψ ∧ ¬ γ)>.
6. For *SL* sentences φ and ψ and set of *SL* sentences A: the given line is <A, ¬ (φ ∧ ¬ ψ)>, and there is an earlier line <A, ψ>.

Exercise 2.8 Use the general soundness result to prove that all theorems are tautologies (or semantical truths).

Completeness

Definition 2.19 The *SL* derivation system is *complete* if and only if for any *SL* sentence φ and set A of *SL* sentences, if φ is a semantical consequence of A, then φ is derivable from A, that is, if A ⊨ φ then A ⊢ φ.

To say that if A ⊨ φ then A ⊢ φ is to say that *if*, for all truth sets T, φ ∈ T if A ⊆ T *then*, for some finite subset A* of A, there is a derivation with a line <A*, φ>.

We start with a definition of consistency with respect to derivability ("d-consistency," for short):

Definition 2.20 A set of *SL* sentences B is d-consistent if and only if for no *SL* sentence ψ is it the case that B ⊢ ψ ∧ ¬ ψ.

Now we shall prove completeness by means of a series of propositions. The first of our propositions is:

Proposition 1   For any set A of *SL* sentences and *SL* sentence ϕ: A $\vdash \phi$ if and only if it is not the case that A $\cup \{\neg \phi\}$ is d-consistent.

We shall write "A $\cup \{\neg \phi\}$ is d-inconsistent" as short for "it is not the case that A $\cup \{\neg \phi\}$ is d-consistent."

Proof of proposition 1. Suppose A $\vdash \phi$. Then by definitions 2.5–2.8, for some finite subset A* of A, there is a derivation of the following form:

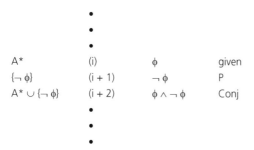

A*	(i)	ϕ	given
$\{\neg \phi\}$	(i + 1)	$\neg \phi$	P
A* $\cup \{\neg \phi\}$	(i + 2)	$\phi \wedge \neg \phi$	Conj

So if A $\vdash \phi$ then $<A^* \cup \{\neg \phi\}, \phi \wedge \neg \phi>$ is a line of a derivation. Since A* $\cup \{\neg \phi\}$ is a finite subset of A $\cup \{\neg \phi\}$, it follows by definitions 2.5–2.8 that A $\cup \{\neg \phi\} \vdash \phi \wedge \neg \phi$. So if A $\vdash \phi$ then A $\cup \{\neg \phi\}$ is d-inconsistent.

Now suppose A $\cup \{\neg \phi\}$ is d-inconsistent. Then, for some finite subset A* of A and some *SL* sentence ψ, there is a derivation of the form:

A* $\cup \{\neg \phi\}$	(i)	$\psi \wedge \neg \psi$	given
A*	(i + 1)	$\neg \neg \phi$	i RAA
A*	(i + 2)	ϕ	i + 1DN

Thus, $<A^*, \phi>$ is a line of a derivation. Since A* is a finite subset of A, it follows by definitions 2.5–2.8 that A $\vdash \phi$. So if A $\cup \{\neg \phi\}$ is d-inconsistent then A $\vdash \phi$.

A second proposition is:

> Proposition 2　For any set of *SL* sentences A and *SL* sentence ϕ, A $\models \phi$ if and only if A $\cup$ {$\neg \phi$} is semantically inconsistent.

Proof of proposition 2. Suppose

$$A \models \phi.$$

This means that, for any truth set T, if A $\subseteq$ T then $\phi \in$ T. Now suppose that there is a truth set T* such that

$$A \cup \{\neg \phi\} \subseteq T^*.$$

Then

$$\phi \in T^*$$

and

$$\neg \phi \in T^*$$

which, by definition 2.10 (the definition of a truth set), is impossible. So if A $\models \phi$ then A $\cup$ {$\neg \phi$} is a subset of no truth set, that is, A $\cup$ {$\neg \phi$} is semantically inconsistent.

Suppose A $\cup$ {$\neg \phi$} is semantically inconsistent. That is,

$$(A \cup \{\neg \phi\}) \cap T = \varnothing$$

for all truth sets T. So, for any truth set T, if

$$A \subseteq T$$

then

$$\neg \phi \notin T$$

in which case

$$\phi \in T$$

by definition 2.10. So if $A \cup \{\neg \phi\}$ is semantically inconsistent, $A \models \phi$.
From propositions 1 and 2 it follows that

> Proposition 3 $A \not\models \phi$ only if $A \vdash \phi$ if, and only if, $A \cup \{\neg \phi\}$ is semantically inconsistent only if $A \cup \{\neg \phi\}$ is d-inconsistent

holds for every set A of *SL* sentences and every *SL* sentence ϕ. Thus to prove completeness it suffices to prove:

> Proposition 4   Every set of *SL* sentences that is d-consistent is semantically consistent.

To prove proposition 4 we start by letting A be any d-consistent set of *SL* sentences. Then we consider an enumeration of all the sentences of *SL*:

$$\phi_1, \phi_2, \ldots, \phi_n, \ldots$$

Then we consider a series of sets of *SL* sentences

$$A_0, A_1, \ldots, A_n, \ldots$$

defined as follows:

$$A_0 = A$$

and

$$A_n = \begin{cases} A_{n-1} \cup \{\phi_n\} \text{ if } A_{n-1} \cup \{\phi_n\} \text{ is d-consistent,} \\ A_{n-1} \text{ otherwise.} \end{cases}$$

Finally we let

$$T = A_0 \cup A_1 \cup \ldots \cup A_n \cup \ldots$$

Thus T is a union of nested subsets.
To prove proposition 4 it suffices to prove:

> Proposition 5   T is a truth set.

And to prove proposition 5 it suffices to prove

> Proposition 6 T is d-consistent,
> Proposition 7 For any *SL* sentence ϕ, $\phi \in$ T if and only if T $\cup$ {ϕ} is d-consistent,
> Proposition 8 For any *SL* sentence ϕ, $\phi \in$ T if and only if T $\vdash \phi$,
> Proposition 9 For any *SL* sentences ϕ and ψ, $\phi \wedge \psi \in$ T if and only if $\phi \in$ T and $\psi \in$ T,

and

> Proposition 10 For any *SL* sentence ϕ, $\neg \phi \in$ T if and only if $\phi \notin$ T.

Propositions 6–8 are used to prove propositions 9 and 10; and propositions 9 and 10 directly entail proposition 5. Proposition 5 enables a proof of proposition 4. Proposition 4, in conjunction with propositions 1–3 enable a proof of completeness.

Proof of proposition 6. $T = A_0 \cup A_1 \cup \ldots \cup A_n \cup \ldots$ The first set, A_0, is A, which is d-consistent by hypothesis. And a given set, A_i, is d-consistent if all earlier sets in the union are d-consistent. For $A_i = A_{i-1} \cup \{\phi_i\}$ if that set is d-consistent; otherwise $A_i = A_{i-1}$. So if A_{i-1} is d-consistent so also is A_i. Thus, for any i, A_i is d-consistent.

Now suppose T is d-inconsistent. Then T $\vdash \psi \wedge \neg \psi$, for some *SL* sentence ψ. By definitions 2.5–2.8, there is some finite subset T* of T such that T* $\vdash \psi \wedge \neg \psi$. Since T* is finite, some sentence in T* comes after all the other sentences in T* in the enumeration

$$\phi_1, \phi_2, \ldots, \phi_n, \ldots$$

of the sentences of *SL*. Let that sentence be ϕ_j. Then T* $\subseteq A_j$. Then A_j is d-inconsistent, which by the previous paragraph, is impossible.

Proof of proposition 7. This proposition is: for any *SL* sentence ϕ, $\phi \in$ T if and only if T $\cup$ {ϕ} is d-consistent. The left to right implication follows from proposition 6, which says that T is d-consistent. For, if $\phi \in$ T, T $\cup$ {ϕ} = T. Let us then focus on the right to left implication. Assume T $\cup$ {ϕ} is d-consistent. For some k, $\phi = \phi_k$ in the enumeration

$$\phi_1, \phi_2, \ldots, \phi_n, \ldots$$

of the sentences of *SL*. Thus T $\cup$ {ϕ} = T $\cup$ {ϕ_k}. From definition 2.8 and definition 2.20 it follows that if a set is d-consistent so is every subset of that set.

Since $A_{k-1} \cup \{\phi_k\} \subseteq T \cup \{\phi_k\}$, $A_{k-1} \cup \{\phi_k\}$ is d-consistent. Thus $A_k = A_{k-1} \cup \{\phi_k\}$. Thus $\phi_k \in A_k$. Thus $\phi \in T$.

Proof of proposition 8. This proposition is: for any *SL* sentence ϕ, $\phi \in T$ if and only if $T \vdash \phi$. The left to right implication follows from the fact that $\{\phi\} \vdash \phi$. Let us then focus on the right to left implication. Assume $T \vdash \phi$. Assume $\phi \notin T$. Then, by proposition 7, $T \cup \{\phi\}$ is d-inconsistent. Thus $T \vdash \neg \phi$ by proposition 1. Thus T is d-inconsistent, which contradicts proposition 6.

Proof of proposition 9. This proposition is: for any *SL* sentences ϕ and ψ, $\phi \wedge \psi \in T$ if and only if $\phi \in T$ and $\psi \in T$. Assume $\phi \wedge \psi \in T$. By proposition 8 $T \vdash \phi \wedge \psi$. By Simp, it follows that $T \vdash \phi$ and $T \vdash \psi$. Let us now focus on the right to left implication. Assume $\phi \in T$ and $\psi \in T$. By proposition 8, $T \vdash \phi$ and $T \vdash \psi$. By Conj, $T \vdash \phi \wedge \psi$.

Proof of proposition 10. This proposition is: for any *SL* sentence ϕ, $\neg \phi \in T$ if and only if $\phi \notin T$. Assume $\neg \phi \in T$. By proposition 8, $T \vdash \neg \phi$. Now assume $\phi \in T$. By proposition 8, $T \vdash \phi$. By Conj, $T \vdash \phi \wedge \neg \phi$. Thus T is d-inconsistent. This contradicts proposition 6. Let us now focus on the right to left implication. Assume $\phi \notin T$. By proposition 7, it follows that $T \cup \{\neg \phi\}$ is d-inconsistent. By proposition 1, $T \vdash \neg \phi$. By proposition 8, $\neg \phi \in T$.

From propositions 9 and 10 it follows that T is a truth set. Thus every d-consistent set is a subset of a truth set. By definition 2.15, every d-consistent set is semantically consistent (proposition 4). By propositions 1–3, it follows that, for any set of *SL* sentences A and *SL* sentence ϕ, if $A \vDash \phi$ then $A \vdash \phi$.

Exercise 2.9   Show that, for any set of *SL* sentences A and for any *SL* sentence ϕ, $A \cup \{\phi\}$ is d-inconsistent only if $A \vdash \neg \phi$.

Exercise 2.10   Show, for any set of *SL* sentences A, A is d-consistent only if every subset of A is d-consistent.

Exercise 2.11   Call a set M maximal d-consistent if and only if (i) M is d-consistent and (ii) for any sentence ϕ, $\phi \in M$ if and only if $M \cup \{\phi\}$ is d-consistent. Show every maximal consistent set is a truth set. Show every truth set is maximal consistent.

Exercise 2.12   Use these definitions

Definition	$\phi \vee \psi = \neg(\neg \phi \wedge \neg \psi)$
Definition	$\phi \supset \psi = \neg(\phi \wedge \neg \psi)$
Definition	$\phi \equiv \psi = \neg(\phi \wedge \neg \psi) \wedge \neg(\psi \wedge \neg \phi)$

to prove the following, for any *SL* sentences ϕ and ψ, and for any set truth set T:

1. $\phi \vee \psi \in$ T if and only if $\phi \in$ T or $\psi \in$ T
2. $\phi \supset \psi \in$ T if and only if $\phi \notin$ T or $\psi \in$ T
3. $\phi \equiv \psi \in$ T if, and only if, $\phi \in$ T if and only if $\psi \in$ T.

Exercise 2.13 Use propositions 1–4 to derive: for any set of *SL* sentences A and *SL* sentence ϕ, if A $\models \phi$ then A $\vdash \phi$ (completeness).

Exercise 2.14 Prove: for any set of *SL* sentences A, A is semantically consistent if and only if every finite subset of A is semantically consistent. (Hint: use proposition 4 plus soundness to get the right to left implication.)

Exercise 2.15 Show that proposition 3 is superfluous in the proof of completeness. That is, show propositions 1, 2, and 4 entail if A $\models \phi$ then A $\vdash \phi$ (completeness).

Extensions of SL

SL uses just two sentential operators, "$\neg$" and "$\wedge$." Other operators can be introduced by definition, as in exercise 2.12:

Definition 2.21 $(\phi \vee \psi) = \neg(\neg \phi \wedge \neg \psi)$

Definition 2.22 $\phi \supset \psi = \neg(\phi \wedge \neg \psi)$

Definition 2.23 $\phi \equiv \psi = \neg(\phi \wedge \neg \psi) \wedge \neg(\psi \wedge \neg \phi)$

"$\vee$," "$\supset$," and "$\equiv$" are standard symbols for respectively forming disjunctions, conditionals and biconditionals. A sentence $\varphi \vee \psi$ is a *disjunction*, with ϕ and ψ as its *disjuncts*. A sentence $\phi \supset \psi$ is a *conditional* with ϕ as *antecedent* and ψ as *consequent*. A sentence $\phi \equiv \psi$ is a *biconditional*.

That we are justified in using these signs (as defined) as operators for forming disjunctions, conditionals, and biconditionals is something that needs to be established by showing that the basic inference rules for conditionals, disjunction, and biconditionals hold for these symbols as just defined. So, for example, it would have to be shown that under the above definition for "$\supset$" (together with the basic rules for negations and conjunctions) the rule *modus ponens* holds for sentences formed with that symbol. This can be done, for example, by construction of the following derivation schema:

	•		
	•		
	•		
A	(i)	$\neg\,(\phi \wedge \neg\,\psi)$	given
	•		
	•		
	•		
B	(j)	ϕ	given
	•		
	•		
	•		
{k}	(k)	$\neg\,\psi$	P
B ∪ {k}	(k + 1)	$\phi \wedge \neg\,\psi$	j, k Conj
A ∪ B ∪{k}	(k + 2)	$(\phi \wedge \neg\,\psi) \wedge \neg\,(\phi \wedge \neg\,\psi)$	i, k + 1 Conj
A ∪ B	(k + 3)	$\neg\,\neg\,\psi$	k, k + 2 RAA
A ∪ B	(k + 4)	ψ	k + 3 DN
	•		
	•		
	•		

Note that the final inference from $\neg\,\neg\,\psi$ to ψ is not available in a constructivist system. This precludes a constructivist definition of the conditional in terms of conjunction and negation. Note also we continue the convention of dropping outermost parentheses.

The negation at line (i) definitionally corresponds to the conditional $\phi \supset \psi$. The entire derivation schema shows that from earlier lines on which there occur the sentence ϕ and the sentence to which $\phi \supset \psi$ is definitionally equivalent, the sentence ψ may be derived at some later line using just the basic inference rules.

By means of such derivation schemas as the one just constructed it can be shown that whatever derivations would hold using these new operators in accord with their usual rules of inference are available in *SL*. This availability claim can be put as follows. Let A′ be a set of sentences, including ones that use the newly defined symbols, and let ϕ′ be a sentence, possibly one using one or more of the newly defined symbols. Let A be the set of sentences which results from A′ by replacing each occurrence of each newly defined symbol in the sentences in A by the symbols which define it, and let ϕ be obtained from ϕ′ in the same fashion. Then it can be shown that if ϕ′ is derivable from A′ using our rules of inference plus the usual rules of inference for the newly defined operators, then ϕ is derivable from A using just our rules of inference.

For example, the following is a standard derivation of the theorem "p ⊃ (q ∨ p)":

{1}	(1)	p	P
{1}	(2)	q ∨ p	1 Addition
∅	(3)	p ⊃ (q ∨ p)	2 Conditionalization

using the addition rule for introducing disjunctions and the conditionalization rule for introducing conditionals. This theorem is obtained from the sentence "¬ (p ∧ ¬ ¬ (¬ q ∧ ¬ p))," by applying the definition for "∨" to "¬ (¬ q ∧ ¬ p)" and the definition for "⊃" to "¬ (p ∧ ¬ (q ∨ p))." The derivation establishing this sentence as a theorem of *SL* was given earlier. Here it is again:

{1}	(1)	¬ ¬ (p ∧ ¬ ¬ (¬ q ∧ ¬ p))	P
{1}	(2)	p ∧ ¬ ¬ (¬ q ∧ ¬ p)	1 DN
{1}	(3)	p	2 Simp
{1}	(4)	¬ ¬ (¬ q ∧ ¬ p)	2 Simp
{1}	(5)	¬ q ∧ ¬ p	4 DN
{1}	(6)	¬ p	5 Simp
{1}	(7)	p ∧ ¬ p	3, 6 Conj
∅	(8)	¬ ¬ ¬ (p ∧ ¬ ¬ (¬ q ∧ ¬ p))	7 RAA
∅	(9)	¬ (p ∧ ¬ ¬ (¬ q ∧ ¬ p))	8 DN

Consider the following schema:

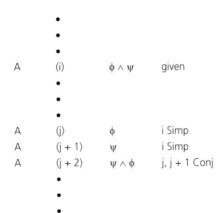

A	(i)	ϕ ∧ ψ	given
A	(j)	ϕ	i Simp
A	(j + 1)	ψ	i Simp
A	(j + 2)	ψ ∧ ϕ	j, j + 1 Conj

No rule for reversing conjuncts (a rule "Com" for the "commutation" of conjuncts) is among our *basic* rules of inference. But the above schema shows that any derivation using a reversal of conjuncts rule (retaining premises) could be replaced by another derivation using only the basic rules Simp and Conj, deriving the new sentence with the same set of premises as was associated with that sentence in the derivation using the rule for reversing conjuncts. This justifies accepting the rule:

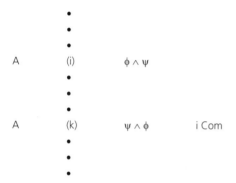

as a *derived* rule of inference. In practice, we will justify new rules of inference by exhibiting a sample derivation using (i) the usual lowercase letters, (ii) the basic rules of inference, and (iii) antecedently justified derived rules of inference. For example:

{1}	(1)	p ∧ q	P
{1}	(2)	p	1 Simp
{1}	(3)	q	1 Simp
{1}	(4)	q ∧ p	2, 3 Conj

To construct a derivation to justify the following rule:

	•		
	•		
	•		
A	(i)	¬ φ	given
	•		
	•		
	•		

B	(j)	$\neg(\neg\phi \wedge \neg\psi)$	given
		•	
		•	
		•	
A ∪ B	(k)	ψ	i, j Com
		•	
		•	
		•	

we write:

{1}	(1)	$\neg p$	P
{2}	(2)	$\neg(\neg p \wedge \neg q)$	P
{3}	(3)	$\neg q$	P
{1, 3}	(4)	$\neg p \wedge \neg q$	1, 3 Conj
{2, 3}	(5)	$(\neg p \wedge \neg q) \wedge \neg(\neg p \wedge \neg q)$	2, 4 Conj
{1, 2, 3}	(6)	$\neg\neg q$	5 RAA
{1, 2}	(7)	q	6 DN

(Note that this derivation is not available within a constructivist system since that system has no rule permitting the inference from "$\neg\neg q$" to "q.")

We will often write rules using an arrow (assuming that the premises of the sentence to the right are all those of the sentences to the left), for example,

$$\neg\phi, \neg(\neg\phi \wedge \neg\psi) \rightarrow \psi$$

Conditionalization

A very convenient rule is a rule for conditionalization. The schema for that rule is as follows:

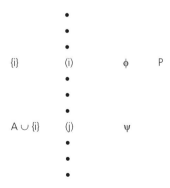

A   (k) $\phi \supset \psi$ i, j C
·
·
·

Now consider the following derivation schema:

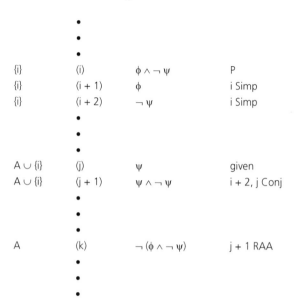

By the above definition for "⊃," the sentence at line k of the above schema can be replaced by "$\phi \supset \psi$." Thus, rule C is also an acceptable derived rule of inference.

A convenient set of inference rules for the new operators runs as follows:

Disjunctive Addition (Add)

$\phi \rightarrow \phi \lor \psi$
$\psi \rightarrow \phi \lor \psi$

Disjunctive Syllogism (DS)

$\neg \phi, \phi \lor \psi \rightarrow \psi$
$\neg \psi, \phi \lor \psi \rightarrow \phi$

Modus Ponens (MP)

$\phi, \phi \supset \psi \rightarrow \psi$

Modus Tollens (MT)

$$\neg \psi, \phi \supset \psi \rightarrow \neg \phi$$

Conditionalization (C)

$$\psi \rightarrow \phi \supset \psi$$
where ϕ is among the premises of ψ. As premises of the new line take all those of the earlier line less ϕ

Biconditional Elimination (BE)

$$\phi \equiv \psi \rightarrow \phi \supset \psi$$
$$\phi \equiv \psi \rightarrow \psi \supset \phi$$

Biconditional Introduction (BI)

$$(\phi \supset \psi) \wedge (\psi \supset \phi) \rightarrow \phi \equiv \psi$$

Dilemma (DI)

$$\phi \vee \psi, \phi \supset \chi, \psi \supset \chi \rightarrow \chi$$

As stated above, we use the arrow to informally indicate rules of inference. Except for rule C, it is always to be understood that the premises of the sentence derived by the rule are to be those of the sentences from which it is derived by the rule.

Exercise 2.16   Construct derivations justifying the following rules:

1. $\neg \phi, \neg (\neg \phi \wedge \neg \psi) \rightarrow \psi$
2. $\neg \psi, \neg (\neg \phi \wedge \neg \psi) \rightarrow \phi$
3. $\phi \rightarrow \neg (\neg \phi \wedge \neg \psi)$
4. $\psi \rightarrow \neg (\neg \phi \wedge \neg \psi)$
5. $\phi, \neg (\phi \wedge \neg \psi) \rightarrow \psi$
6. $\neg \psi, \neg (\phi \wedge \neg \psi) \rightarrow \neg \phi$
7. $\psi \rightarrow \neg (\phi \wedge \neg \psi)$
8. $\neg (\neg \phi \wedge \neg \psi), \neg (\phi \wedge \neg \chi), \neg (\psi \wedge \neg \chi) \rightarrow \chi$

Note that if we define "∨" and "⊃" by means of definitions 2.21 and 2.22, the first two derived rules are rules for disjunctive syllogism (DS), the next two are for disjunctive addition (Add), and the next two are, respectively, rules for *modus ponens* (MP), *modus tollens* (MT). The seventh derived rule corresponds to a rule that permits the derivation, for any sentence φ, of the sentence φ ⊃ ψ given a derivation of ψ (C).

Exercise 2.17   Use rules P, Conj, Simp, DN, RAA plus rules Add, DS, MP, MT, C, BI, BE, and DI to prove the following:

1. p ∨ q ⊢ q ∨ p (Note that this is a shorthand way of writing "{'p ∨ q'} ⊢ 'q ∨ p.'")
2. p ∧ (q ∨ r) ⊢ (p ∧ q) ∨ (p ∧ r)
3. p ∨ (q ∧ r) ⊢ (p ∨ q) ∧ (p ∨ r)
4. ¬(p ∧ q) ⊢ ¬p ∨ ¬q
5. ¬(p ∨ q) ⊢ ¬p ∧ ¬q
6. ¬p ∧ ¬q ⊢ ¬(p ∨ q)
7. ¬(p ⊃ ¬q) ⊢ p ∨ q
8. ¬p ∨ ¬q ⊢ ¬(p ∧ q)
9. ¬(¬p ∨ ¬q) ⊢ p ∧ q
10. p ⊃ q, q ⊃ r ⊢ p ⊃ r
11. ¬p ⊃ ¬q ⊢ q ⊃ p
12. p ⊢ p ∧ (p ∨ q)
13. p ⊃ q ⊢ ¬p ∨ q
14. ¬p ∨ q ⊢ p ⊃ q
15. ¬p ⊃ q ⊢ p ∨ q
16. ⊢ p ∨ (p ⊃ q) (Note that this is a short way of writing "'p ∨ (p ⊃ q)' is derivable from the null class" or "Ø ⊢ 'p ∨ (p ⊃ q).'")
17. ⊢ (p ⊃ q) ∨ (q ⊃ p)
18. p, ¬p ⊢ q
19. p ∨ q ⊢ ¬p ⊃ q
20. ¬p ⊃ q ⊢ p ∨ q
21. ⊢ (¬p ⊃ p) ⊃ p
22. ¬(p ⊃ q) ⊢ p ∧ ¬q
23. p ∧ ¬q ⊢ ¬(p ⊃ q)
24. (p ⊃ q) ⊃ q ⊢ p ∨ q
25. p ∨ q ⊢ (p ⊃ q) ⊃ q
26. (p ⊃ q) ∨ (p ⊃ r) ⊢ p ⊃ (q ∨ r)
27. p ⊃ (q ∨ r) ⊢ (p ⊃ q) ∨ (p ⊃ r)
28. p ⊃ q ⊢ (p ≡ q) ∨ q
29. (p ≡ q) ∨ q ⊢ p ⊃ q

30. $q \vdash (p \land q) \equiv p$
31. $\neg q \vdash (p \lor q) \equiv p$

Model Sets

In "Modality and Quantification" Jaakko Hintikka introduces the notion of a model set (Hintikka 1969b, pp. 57–59). Model sets give a method for testing sets of sentences for consistency and hence, indirectly, a method for testing arguments for validity. A model set is a set of sentences meeting certain conditions that insure that the set is consistent.

Normal form. We say a sentence is in Hintikka normal form (hnf, after Hintikka) if and only if the only truth-functional connectives it contains are "$\neg$," "$\land$," and "$\lor$," and "$\neg$" is applied only to atomic sentences (simple sentences).

Every sentence of *SL* is equivalent to a sentence in hnf. For any given sentence ϕ, an equivalent sentence in hnf can be found by repeatedly replacing one well-formed part by its equivalent in the following list of equivalences ("$\Leftrightarrow$" stands for "is equivalent to").

a. $\neg (\phi \supset \psi) \Leftrightarrow (\phi \land \neg \psi)$
b. $(\phi \supset \psi) \Leftrightarrow (\neg \phi \lor \psi)$
c. $\neg (\phi \equiv \psi) \Leftrightarrow (\phi \land \neg \psi) \lor (\neg \phi \land \psi)$
d. $(\phi \equiv \psi) \Leftrightarrow (\phi \land \psi) \lor (\neg \phi \land \neg \psi)$
e. $\neg (\phi \land \psi) \Leftrightarrow \neg \phi \lor \neg \psi$
f. $\neg (\phi \lor \psi) \Leftrightarrow \neg \phi \land \neg \psi$

Conditions (a) through (d) eliminate $\supset$ and $\equiv$. The other conditions allow us to move $\neg$ inside until it has smallest scope. Double negations are eliminated as they occur.

A model set is a set of sentences in hnf that satisfies all of the following conditions:

1. If $\phi \in m$, then it is not the case that $\neg \phi \in m$. (C $\neg$)
2. If $(\phi \land \psi) \in m$, then $\phi \in m$ and $\psi \in m$. (C $\land$)
3. If $(\phi \lor \psi) \in m$, then $\phi \in m$ or $\psi \in m$. (C $\lor$)

Consistency and validity. We can now redefine the following notions. The subscripts are to indicate that we are defining consistency and validity in the model set sense, or the Hintikka sense. These subscripted notions are equivalent to the standard notions defined in terms of truth sets. For every truth set is a model set. And any set is included in a truth set if and only if the set consisting of the hnf of each of its members is included in a model set.

1. A sentence ϕ in hnf is consistent$_h$ if and only if there is a model set m such that $\phi \in$ m.
2. A sentence that is not in hnf is consistent$_h$ if and only if its hnf is consistent$_h$.
3. A sentence is valid$_h$ ϕ if and only if $\neg \phi$ is not consistent$_h$.
4. A finite set is consistent$_h$ if and only if the set consisting of the hnf of each of its members is included in a model set.
5. An argument, $\phi_1, \ldots, \phi_n$ ∴ ψ, is valid$_h$ if and only if $\{\phi_1, \ldots, \phi_n, \neg \psi\}$ is not consistent$_h$. (That is, there is no model set that contains all of the premises and the negation of the conclusion.)

Model sets are a semantical test of consistency. A set is semantically consistent if and only if the set consisting of the hnf of each of its members is embeddable in a model set. The conditions on model sets can be viewed as directions for constructing model sets. Each of the conditions other than (C $\neg$) tells us what must be added to a set to make it a model set. C $\neg$ is a negative condition that tells us what a model set cannot have.

To test a finite set to see if it is semantically consistent, list the hnf of the members of the set, and then attempt to add sentences to the list to satisfy the conditions on model sets. If you can do this, so that every condition is satisfied for every sentence we list, and there are no violations of C $\neg$, then we have a model set, and the original set of sentences is semantically consistent. If every attempt to add sentences to satisfy the other conditions is blocked by (C $\neg$), then the set is semantically inconsistent.

Here is an example. Is

$$\{p \wedge q, \neg (p \supset q)\}$$

semantically consistent? First, put each sentence in the set in hnf. The first sentence

$$p \wedge q$$

is already in hnf. The second sentence can be put in hnf thus:

$\neg (p \supset q),$
$\neg (\neg p \vee q),$

$\neg\neg p \wedge \neg q,$
$p \wedge \neg q.$

We end up with a pair of sentences

$p \wedge q,$
$p \wedge \neg q,$

that cannot be embedded in a model set. Thus the original set of sentences is semantically inconsistent.

Let us now consider this set:

$\{p \supset q, p \vee q\}.$

Is it semantically consistent? Consider:

1. $\neg p \vee q$ $\in m$
2. $p \vee q$ $\in m$
3. q $\in m$, from 1 using $(C \vee)$

The set

$m = \{q, \neg p \vee q, p \vee q\}$

is a model set. Thus, the set

$\{p \supset q, p \vee q\}$

can be embedded in a model set; thus it is semantically consistent.

To test an argument for validity, take the hnf of the premises and the negation of the conclusion and attempt to construct a model set. If you succeed, it is not valid. If you must fail, then the argument is valid. Exhibiting a model set that contains the premises and the negation of the conclusion shows that the argument is not valid. Thus, we have a method of disproof.

For example, consider the argument

$p, p \supset q \therefore q \vee r$

Putting the premises in hnf, we get

    1. p
    2. ¬p ∨ q

Putting the negation of the conclusion in hnf, we get

    3. ¬q ∧ ¬r

If we suppose 1–3 can be embedded in a model set, we violate (C ¬). For suppose

    1. p   ∈ m
    2. ¬p ∨ q   ∈ m
    3. ¬q ∧ ¬r ∈ m

for some model set m. Then

    4. ¬q   ∈ m   from 3 by (C ∧)

And either

    5. ¬p   ∈ m   from 2 by (C ∨)

which violates (C ¬), or

    6. q   ∈ m   from 2 by (C ∨)

which also violates (C ¬). Thus the original argument is valid.
    For a final example, consider

    p, p ⊃ q ∴ q ∧ r

Putting the premises in hnf, we get

    1. p
    2. ¬p ∨ q

Putting the negation of the conclusion in hnf, we get

    3. $\neg q \vee \neg r$

If we suppose 1–3 can be embedded in a model set, we do **not** violate (C $\neg$). For suppose

    1. p $\in m$
    2. $\neg p \vee q$ $\in m$
    3. $\neg q \vee \neg r$ $\in m$

for some model set m. Then

    4. $\neg r$ $\in m$ from 3 by (C $\vee$)
    5. q $\in m$ from 2 by (C $\vee$)

Thus

    $m = \{ q, \neg p \vee q, \neg r, \neg q \vee \neg r, p \}$

is a model set into which the premises and negation of the conclusion of our original argument can be embedded. Thus the original argument is invalid.

    The sentences required by (C $\wedge$) and (C $\vee$) are always shorter than the sentence referred to in the antecedent of these conditions. Thus, starting with a finite set of sentences and repeatedly adding what is needed to satisfy (C $\wedge$) and (C $\vee$), we must eventually get down to atomic sentences. Either there is a contradiction among these sentences—a violation of (C $\neg$)—and the original set is semantically inconsistent, or there is no contradiction and the original set is semantically consistent. Thus we have a decision procedure for the propositional calculus, and one which in general involves fewer calculations than the use of truth tables.

Exercise 2.18   Test the following arguments for validity by the model set method:

    1. $p \vee q, p \therefore p \supset q$
    2. $p \vee q, \neg p \therefore q$
    3. $p \supset q \therefore \neg q \equiv \neg p$
    4. $\neg q \equiv \neg p \therefore p \supset q$
    5. $\neg p, p \supset q \therefore \neg q$
    6. $p \therefore q \supset p$
    7. $\neg q \therefore q \supset p$

8. $p \wedge \neg p \therefore q$
9. $q \therefore p \vee \neg p$
10. $p \vee q \therefore p \equiv q$
11. $p \supset r, r \supset \neg p \therefore p$
12. $p \vee q, p \supset r, q \supset r \therefore r$
13. $p \vee q, q \vee r \therefore p \vee r$
14. $p \supset q, q \vee p \therefore p \equiv q$
15. $p \equiv q, q \supset r \therefore p \equiv r$

Syntax and Semantics

Let's review the overall situation regarding syntax and semantics. On the one hand we specify languages together with inferential systems. On the other we specify truth sets and model sets.

The distinction between inferential systems, on the one hand, and truth sets and model sets, on the other hand, is often characterized in terms of a distinction between the syntax and the semantics of a language.

Syntax concerns those features of language that can be specified in terms of the perceptible features of signs together with rules (for forming complex signs and structures of complex signs from simpler signs) that also refer only to the perceptible features of signs.

Semantics concerns those features of language that make for meaning.

Think of what you might learn about a written language without coming to understand the language. You might learn that such and such marks are its letters, that such and such sequences of letters are its words, that there are such and such categories of words that combine in such and such ways to form the sentences of the language. What you here learn is all part of what is called the syntax of the language.

Inference (reasoning in words, written proofs, etc.), at the strictly syntactic level, is a sequencing of sentences that makes it recognizable what's inferred from what. We can call any such sequence an inference sequence, or, for short, an inference.

Prior to the development of any kind of theory, we draw, for example, a distinction between what does and doesn't follow from something said or written. An inference to what follows is called valid and an inference to what doesn't follow is called invalid. Theory begins when we reckon certain accepted inferences to have something in common, and come to hold that any inferences with that in common also are to be accepted. These are the inferences we call formally valid, using the word "form" to signify what it is that is common to the inferences we group together.

In some cases it is possible to characterize the "form" of a group of inferences all of which we regard as valid in terms of the word "sentence." So we might write:

> For any declarative sentences φ and ψ, the sentence sequence consisting of (i) φ and (ii) the sentence consisting of ψ followed by "if" followed by φ, and (iii) ending with the sentence consisting of the word "thus" followed by ψ is an inference.

Now, if, as is usually assumed, the notion declarative sentence is itself strictly syntactic, or can be rendered strictly syntactic by one or another device of grammar, then what we have just displayed is a strictly syntactic specification of a class of inferences.

One of the key ideas of modern formal logic is that all formally valid inferences can be specified in strictly syntactic terms, as was just done for the formally valid inference typically known by the name *modus ponens*.

It is not known how to characterize a natural language in strictly syntactic terms (nor, is it known that it could be thus characterized). On the other hand, it is known, since Frege, how to stipulate sign systems in strictly syntactic terms, and how to do so in a way that makes it possible to decide, for any given sign, whether or not it is a sign of that system, and to which subclasses of signs within that system it belongs. Sign systems thus stipulated are the so-called languages of logical theory. We shall stipulate a number of such languages in our text.

Given a language (of the kind just described) it is possible to stipulate rules of inference for that language, guided by our feel for what is common to various inferences, for example, those involving terms like "and" and "not." In this text we have stipulated rules of inference by laying down definitions for derivations.

The language in which we write when we do the work of logic is one or another natural language. In our case, English. Since it is a language in the use of which we stipulate certain systems of signs and call them "languages," it is often useful and sometimes important to keep it in mind that the language in the use of which we make these stipulations is distinct from the languages we thereby stipulate and of which we write. Granting the nomenclature of "language" to such stipulated systems, it is common to speak of them as object languages, meaning by the word "object" something like "object of study."

By contrast with this, it is common to refer to the language in the use of which we stipulate systems of signs, and their associated inferential and semantical systems, as a metalanguage. Our metalanguage is English.

In some logical studies a metalanguage is itself a stipulated system of signs. In those cases it is common to speak of a formalized metalanguage.

But some natural language will still be the language in the use of which further languages, including, formalized metalanguages, are stipulated.

It often happens that one or another symbol or device or notation "created" by one or another stipulation, or by some combination of stipulations, "returns" to the natural language. (The natural language is, after all, the language we speak and write and what we find useful for speaking and writing we use, and it thereby becomes part of our language. And this is why natural language is not colloquial language. English contains all sorts of technical terms, special symbols, etc.) This means we must sometimes exercise considerable care to be clear about whether this or that bit of writing occurs as a part of our natural language or as a bit of one or another stipulated system of signs.

Once these stipulations are in place (the one that specifies a language together with the one that specifies the derivations for that language) it is possible to establish all sorts of sentences pertaining to the overall stipulated system (consisting of the language and its derivations) and to do so from those stipulations. These sentences are often called syntactic theorems. They are sentences of the metalanguage. In our case, English.

Once a semantical system is in place it is possible to establish various things about the language relative to a semantical system. For example, it might be established that every truth set members a certain sentence.

Sentences like

> For any truth set T, "p ∨ ¬ p" ∈ T.
> For every T, if ("¬ (p ∨ q)") ∈ T and "q" ∈ T, then "¬ p" ∈ T.

are often called semantic theorems. In our case, they are sentences of English.

It is common to compare inferential systems with semantical systems. Two key points (put in terms of truth sets) are as follows: First, to show that if some sentence ϕ is derivable from a set of sentences A, then for every truth set T, if ψ ∈ T for each sentence ψ ∈ A, then ϕ ∈ T; second, to show that if, for every truth set T, if ψ ∈ T for each sentence ψ ∈ A, then ϕ ∈ T, then ϕ is derivable from A. The first point is called soundness and the second is called completeness.

3 Quantificational Logic

Singular Terms

Language contains many terms that are both *singular* and *particular*. Any ordinary proper name is a term of this type. So are many descriptive phrases formed with the definite article, phrases like "the man who climbed Everest with Sir Edmund Hillary." But not all "definite descriptions" are terms of this type, for some, like "the men who first climbed Everest" are plural, not singular. Nor are singular terms like "someone" terms of this type, since they are general, not particular.

Further examples of terms of the type here under consideration are place names like "Nebraska" and "New York City," arabic numerals, terms for events like "World War II," and so on.

Following the custom in much of the literature influenced by modern logic, we shall call words and phrases of the type we are now considering "singular terms," recalling always that a term of this type is not a general term.

Predicates

The general notion of a *predicate* seems to be this: a declarative sentence less one or more occurrences of one or more of its singular terms. So, for example, "Socrates was a philosopher" less "Socrates" is the predicate "ζ was a philosopher." (The "ζ" serves to indicate a place for a singular term. It is not a part of the predicate.) Or, "Plato knew Socrates" less "Plato" and "Socrates" yield the predicate "ζ knew ξ." Since the first of these predicates results from the deletion of just *one* occurrence of a singular term, it is called a *unary* or *one-place* predicate. And since the second of these predicates results from the deletion of exactly *two* occurrences of terms, it is called a *binary* or *two-place* predicate. There also are higher-place predicates. For example, three deletions from "Socrates was standing between Plato and Crito" results in the three-place predicate "ζ is standing between κ and γ."

Some Symbolic Conventions

We shall use uppercase letters to represent predicates, affixing a superscript to indicate the "place" of the predicate. So, we might use "P^1" for the one-place predicate "ζ was a philosopher," "K^2" for the two-place predicate "ζ knew κ," and "S^3" for the three-place predicate "ζ was standing between κ and γ."

We will use lowercase letters from the beginning of the alphabet to represent singular terms, and will adopt the convention of placing those letters to the *right* of the letter representing a predicate. So, using the letters "a," "b," and "c" for "Socrates," "Plato," and "Crito" we can pair up sentences as follows:

Socrates was a philosopher.
P^1a
Plato knew Socrates.
K^2ba
Socrates was standing between Plato and Crito.
S^3abc

Once the predicate letter is associated with letters for singular terms we can allow the number of occurrences of those terms to tell us the place of the predicate, and thereby, in practice, omit the superscripts. So we can write:

Socrates was a philosopher.
Pa
Plato knew Socrates.
Kba
Socrates was standing between Plato and Crito.
Sabc

Some

Consider the following inference:

Socrates was a philosopher.
Thus, someone was a philosopher.

The second sentence results from the first by replacing its subject term, "Socrates," by the general term "someone." Another inference to the same effect is:

Socrates was a philosopher.
Thus, someone is such that he or she was a philosopher.

The complication concerning gender can be avoided by using a non-gendered pronoun, yielding yet another inference to the same effect as the first:

Socrates was a philosopher.
Thus, some thing is such that it was a philosopher.

Following the mathematical practice of using letters from the end of the alphabet as pronouns, we can express this inference as follows:

Socrates was a philosopher.
Thus, some x is such that x was a philosopher.

Following yet another convention, we can replace the words "some . . . is such that" by the symbol "∃," and write the above inference as follows:

Socrates was a philosopher.
Thus, ∃ x x was a philosopher.

Then, using the symbols and conventions discussed in the preceding section, we can write our inference as follows:

Pa
Thus, "∃x Px"

In similar fashion we can express the inference:

Plato knew Socrates.
Thus, someone knew someone.

by

Plato knew Socrates.
Thus, some x is such that some y is such that x knew y,

using different letters to indicate that it is not ruled out that the two "some-ones" might be different.

Using our new symbol for "some . . . . is such that" we obtain:

Plato knew Socrates.
Thus, ∃x ∃y x knew y.

Then, again using the symbols discussed in the preceding section, we obtain:

Kba
Thus, ∃x ∃y Kxy

Adding phrases for negation and conjunction we can further obtain symbolic forms of inference such as

Kab
¬ (Kab ∧ Kad)
Thus, ∃x ∃y ¬ Kxy

Representing, for example, the inference

Plato knew Socrates.
It is not the case both that Plato knew Socrates and Plato knew Parmenides.
Thus, someone did not know someone.

Letters that go in for pronouns are called *variables*. Letters that go in for singular (non-general) terms are called *constants*. Letters that go in for predicates are called *predicate letters*. The symbol "∃" followed by a variable is called a *quantifier*.

The Language QL

Predicate letters are uppercase letters with arabic numeral superscripts and with or without arabic numeral subscripts. The arabic numeral subscripts serve only to provide additional orthographically distinct predicate letters. These subscripts can be regarded as part of how the letter is written. By way of contrast, the superscripted numeral indicates the place of the predicate letter.

Constants are lowercase letters "a" through "e" with or without arabic numeral subscripts.

Variables are lowercase letters "s" through "z" with or without arabic numeral subscripts.

Quantifiers are, for any variable α, $\exists\alpha$.
Operators are "∧" and "¬."
Parentheses are ")" and "(."

Simple formulas are any n-place predicate letter followed by n occurrences of individual symbols (= constants or variables).

Formulas are as follows: Every simple formula is a formula. If ϕ is a formula, $\neg\phi$ also is a formula. If ϕ and ψ are formulas, $(\phi \wedge \psi)$ also is a formula. If ϕ is a formula and α is a variable, $\exists\alpha\,\phi$ also is a formula.

Sentences are as follows: ϕ is a sentence if and only if ϕ is a formula and, for every variable α, each occurrence of α in ϕ is in a part of ϕ that, for some formula ψ, is a formula $\exists\alpha\,\psi$. A sentence of *QL*, ψ, is a *simple sentence* if and only if ψ is a simple formula of *QL* free of individual variables. We write: $\Phi\beta_1 \ldots \beta_n$ for n-ary predicate Φ and constants $\beta_1, \ldots, \beta_n$. A sentence of *QL* is a *compound* sentence if and only if it is either a negation or a conjunction. A sentence of *QL* is a some-quantification if and only if it is a formula of *QL* beginning with an occurrence of "∃."

Free and bound occurrences of individual symbols are as follows: An occurrence of an individual symbol α in a formula ϕ is *bound in* ϕ if and only if it is a variable and is in a part of ϕ which, for some formula ψ, is a formula $\exists\alpha\,\psi$; otherwise, that occurrence of individual symbol α is *free in* ϕ. (Note that by this definition all constants have only free occurrences and any occurrence of a variable in a quantifier is bound.)

Substitution instances are as follows: A sentence is a substitution instance of sentence $\exists\alpha\ \phi$ if and only if constant β replaces exactly the free occurrences of variable α in ϕ. Such a substitution instance will be written $\phi\ \beta/\alpha$. So, for example, "Fx" "a" / "x" (= "Fa") is a substitution instance of "$\exists$x Fx." Generalizing, we use the notation "$\phi\ \beta/\alpha$" to signify the formula like ϕ except for replacing zero or more occurrences of individual symbol α by individual symbol β.

Derivations

A derivation in language *QL* is like a derivation in language *SL* except for two additional conditions for quantificational sentences. These conditions are as follows:

EG Where α is a variable and β is a constant, if S is a derivation and <A, ϕ> occurs in S, then, S, <A, $\exists\alpha\psi$> is also a derivation if ψ results from replacing one or more occurrences of constant β in ϕ by variable α not in ϕ.

ES Where α is a variable and β is a constant, if S is a derivation and <B, ψ>, <A, $\exists\alpha\phi$>, and <{$\phi\ \beta/\alpha$}, $\phi\ \beta/\alpha$ > occur in S, then S, <(A $\cup$ B) ~ {$\phi\ \beta/\alpha$}, ψ> is also a derivation if the constant β occurs neither in ϕ nor in ψ nor in any sentence in A or B.

The first of these conditions formulates the usual rule of generalization for some-quantifications. The second condition formulates a rule for specifying some-quantifications. The basic idea behind this rule is as follows: At some point in a derivation there occurs a some-quantification with a set A of premises. To use that sentence we introduce a *new premise* that is an instantiation of that sentence to a constant that is *new to the derivation*. Further inferences are drawn until a desired sentence ϕ *free of that new constant* occurs in the derivation with a set B of premises. At any point thereafter ϕ may be *reintroduced* with a *change of premises* as follows: All the sentences in B are retained except for the sentence which instantiated $\exists\alpha\ \psi$, together with all the sentences in A. At this point the *new premise has been dropped*. The idea is this: To reason with an *instance* of the some-quantification making *no further assumptions* with respect to the new constant β. That instantiation serves only for *further inferences*—not to introduce any new assumptions. Conclusions that can thus be arrived at depend only on the premises of that some-quantification.

{1}	(1)	$\exists x (Fx \wedge Gx)$	P
{2}	(2)	$Fa \wedge Ga$	P
{2}	(3)	Ga	2 Simp
{2}	(4)	$\exists x\, Gx$	3 EG
{2}	(5)	Fa	2 Simp
{2}	(6)	$Fa \wedge \exists x\, Gx$	5 Conj
{2}	(7)	$\exists x (Fx \wedge \exists y\, Gy)$	6 EG
{1}	(8)	$\exists x (Fx \wedge \exists y\, Gy)$	1, 2, 7 ES

Here the second premise begins the ES portion of the derivation. This takes the form of a sub-derivation (lines 2–7). Note that the sub-derivation ends with a sentence that is repeated on the next line (line 8) by a sentence justified by ES. The last line indicates that the additional premise at line (2) has been dropped, leaving only the premise at line (1).

Definition 3.1 We will call a pair the first element of which is a finite set A of QL sentences and the second element of which is some QL sentence ϕ, a *line*.

Definition 3.2 A QL *derivation* is any finite sequence S of lines each satisfying one of the following conditions, for sets of QL sentences A and B, QL sentences ϕ and ψ, variable α, and constant β:

P   For every ϕ, $<\{\phi\}, \phi>$ is a derivation.

Simp   If S is a derivation and $<A, (\phi \wedge \psi)>$ occurs in S, then S, $<A, \phi>$ and S, $<A, \psi>$ also are derivations.

Conj   If S is a derivation and both $<A, \phi>$ and $<B, \psi>$ occur in S, then S, $<A \cup B, (\phi \wedge \psi)>$ also is a derivation.

DN   If S is a derivation and $<A, \neg\neg\phi>$ occurs in S, then S, $<A, \phi>$ also is a derivation, and conversely.

RAA   If S is a derivation and $<A \cup \{\phi\}, (\psi \wedge \neg\psi)>$ occurs in S, then S, $<A, \neg\phi>$ also is a derivation.

EG   If S is a derivation and $<A, \phi>$ occurs in S, then, S, $<A, \exists\alpha\psi>$ is also a derivation if ψ results from replacing one or more occurrences of constant β in ϕ by variable α not in ϕ.

ES   If S is a derivation and $<B, \psi>$, $<A, \exists\alpha\phi>$, and $<\{\phi\ \beta/\alpha\}, \phi\ \beta/\alpha>$ occur in S, then S, $<(A \cup B) \sim \{\phi\ \beta/\alpha\}, \psi>$ is also a derivation if the constant β occurs neither in ϕ nor in ψ nor in any sentence in A or B.

The following definitions, 3.3–3.4, hold for sets of QL sentences A and B and QL sentences ϕ and ψ:

Definition 3.3 There is a *derivation of φ from* A if and only if there is a derivation with line <A, φ>.

Definition 3.4 φ *is derivable from* A if and only if for some set B, B ⊆ A and there is a derivation of φ from B. We write: A ⊢ φ.

Note that, as in the case of *SL*, it is possible for sentence to be derivable from an infinite set of sentences. But if sentence φ is derivable from some set of *QL* sentences A, then, for some finite subset B of A, B ⊢ φ. For if A ⊢ φ, then, for some subset B of A, there is a derivation with line <B, φ>, in which case (by definition 3.1) B is a finite set. So, for any set A of *QL* sentences and any *QL* sentence φ, if A ⊢ φ, then, for some finite subset B of A, B ⊢ φ.

Definition 3.5 φ is a *QL theorem* if and only if there is a derivation of φ from ∅, the empty set of *QL* sentences. We write: ∅ ⊢ φ or ⊢ φ.

Truth Sets

In the beginning of his article published in *The Journal of Symbolic Logic*, Hugues Leblanc writes: "As those of us who instruct him are well aware, customary accounts of validity and implication often bewilder the novice. For his benefit I present here [accounts] ... which add up to what the better textbooks say, but, in making no mention whatever of domains, say it far more simply" (Leblanc 1968, p. 231). We invoke those simpler accounts here.

We begin with truth sets.

Definition 3.6 T is a truth set of *QL* if and only if T is a set of *QL* sentences such that (i) ¬ φ ∈ T if and only if φ ∉ T, (ii) (φ ∧ ψ) ∈ T if and only if φ ∈ T and ψ ∈ T, and (iii) ∃α φ ∈ T if and only if there is a constant β such that φ β/α ∈ T.

As before, we will use "F" to designate the compliment of T in the set of *QL* sentences. A semantics for *QL* based on truth sets is called *substitutional* (since it assigns T or F to quantifications in a way fixed by the truth sets of their substitution instances). For many purposes of logic truth sets suffice. But it is common to replace truth sets by what are usually called *models*.

The main motivation for moving to models is the desire to allow for the consistency of sets of sentences that include the negation of a universal quantification together with each of its instances, and the consistency of sets of sentences that include an existential quantification together with the negations of each of its instances. Such sets are said to be ω-inconsistent. The aim, then, is to allow for ω-inconsistent sets of sentences that are nonetheless consistent.

The notion of *inconsistency* is semantical, defined in terms of truth sets. The notion of *ω-inconsistency* is defined syntactically. So there is no contradiction in saying that some set of formulas is ω-inconsistent but nonetheless consistent.

We shall first define the semantical notion of consistency for finite sets of sentences and then generalize that concept to cover all sets of sentences.

Definition 3.7   For any finite set of *QL* sentences A, A is semantically consistent if and only if A is a subset of a truth set.

Definition 3.8   For any set of *QL* sentences A, A is semantically consistent if and only if every finite subset of A is consistent.

Definition 3.9   For any set of *QL* sentences A, A is semantically inconsistent if and only if it is not the case that A is semantically consistent.

Exercise 3.1   Show that for any set of *QL* sentences A, A is semantically inconsistent if and only if some finite subset of A is a subset of no truth set.

On the notion of a truth set defined above, the truth set of *every* sentence is fixed by the truth sets of the atomic sentences. That is, truth sets, as just defined, differ on non-atomic sentences only if they differ on atomic sentences. So, in particular, the truth sets of the quantifications are fixed by the truth sets of the atomic sentences. There is, for example, no truth set on which each sentence in the ω-inconsistent set $\{$"$\exists x\ F^1x$," "$\neg\ F^1a$," "$\neg\ F^1b$," ...$\}$ is a member. The reason is that for every truth set T, formula ϕ, and variable α of *QL*, $\exists \alpha\ \phi \in T$ if and only if for some constant β of *QL*, $\phi\ \alpha/\beta \in T$. Thus the ω-inconsistent set $\{$"$\exists x\ F^1x$," "$\neg\ F^1a$," "$\neg\ F^1b$," ...$\}$ is a subset of no truth set. It is nonetheless semantically consistent, since each of its finite subsets is a subset of some truth set. And, intuitively, the ω-inconsistent set $\{$"$\exists x\ F^1x$," "$\neg\ F^1a$," "$\neg\ F^1b$," ...$\}$ *is* semantically consistent, since it is clearly possible for something to F even though everything for which there is a singular term is not F.

Exercise 3.2   Show that truth set T_1 contains the same atomic sentences as truth set T_2 only if $T_1 = T_2$; that is, show that, for any atomic sentence ϕ of *QL*, *if* $\phi \in T_1$ if and only if $\phi \in T_2$, *then*, for any sentence ψ of *QL*, $\psi \in T_1$ if and only if T_2.

Given the semantical notion of a consistent set of sentences, various other semantical notions can be defined:

Definition 3.10 A QL sentence ϕ is a *semantical consequence* of an infinite set A of QL sentences if and only if there is no truth set to which every sentence in A* belongs but ϕ does not belong, for some finite subset A* of A. If A is a finite set of QL sentences, then QL sentence ϕ is a *semantical consequence* of set A if and only if there is no truth set to which every sentence in A belongs and to which ϕ does not belong. We also say that A *semantically implies* ϕ and write: A ⊧ ϕ. If A is the unit set {ψ} we say that ϕ is a semantical consequence of ψ (that ψ semantically implies ϕ) and write ψ ⊧ ϕ. Where A = {ψ$_1$, ψ$_2$, . . . , ψ$_n$} and ϕ is any SL sentence, ψ$_1$, ψ$_2$, . . . , ψ$_n$ ∴ ϕ will be said to be an argument. Such an argument is valid if and only if A ⊧ ϕ.

Exercise 3.3 Show that for any set of QL sentences A and QL sentence ϕ: A ⊧ ϕ if and only if A ∪ {¬ ϕ} is semantically inconsistent.

Definition 3.11 A QL sentence ϕ is a semantical truth if and only if {¬ ϕ} is semantically inconsistent.

Exercise 3.4 Show that for any truth set of QL sentences T and QL sentence ϕ: ϕ is a semantical truth if and only if ϕ ∈ T.

Definition 3.12 A QL sentence ϕ is a semantical falsehood if and only if ¬ ϕ is a semantical truth.

Definition 3.13 The QL derivation system is sound if and only if for any QL sentence ϕ and set A of QL sentences, if ϕ is derivable from A, then ϕ is a semantical consequence of A, that is, if A ⊢ ϕ then A ⊧ ϕ.

Exercise 3.5 Show that for any finite set of QL sentences A, QL sentence ϕ, variable α, constant β: A ⊧ ϕ β/α only if A ⊧ ∃α ϕ.

Definition 3.14 The QL derivation system is complete if and only if for any QL sentence ϕ and set A of QL sentences, if ϕ is a semantical consequence of A, then ϕ is derivable from A, that is, if A ⊧ ϕ then A ⊢ ϕ.

The proofs of soundness and completeness of QL are not included in this text. They proceed along the same lines as the proofs of soundness completeness of SL.

All

Just as the usual sentential operators for forming disjunctions, conditionals, and biconditionals can, within a classical system, be introduced by definition, the usual quantifiers for forming "all" sentences may be added by the following definition

Definition 3.15 $\forall\alpha\ \phi = \neg\ \exists\alpha\ \neg\ \phi$

along with the inference conditions:

UG   If S is a derivation and <A, φ β/α> occurs in S and constant β occurs in no sentence in A, then S, <A, ∀α φ> is also a derivation.

US   If S is a derivation and <A, ∀α φ> occurs in S, then S, <A, φ β/α> is also a derivation.

Exercise 3.6 Show for any variable α, QL sentence ∀α φ, and truth set T: ∀α φ ∈ T if and only if φ β/α ∈ T, for all constants β. (Hint: use definition 3.15.)

Exercise 3.7 Mistakes are made in applying the quantificational rules of inference in each of the following putative derivations. In each case locate the line at which the mistake is made and explain the nature of the mistake.

1.	{1}	(1)	∀x Fxx	P
	{1}	(2)	Faa	1 US
	{1}	(3)	∀x Fxa	2 UG
2.	{1}	(1)	Fa	P
	{2}	(2)	∃x Gx	P
	{3}	(3)	Ga	P
	{1, 3}	(4)	Fa ∧ Ga	1, 3 Conj
	{1, 3}	(5)	∃x (Fx ∧ Gx)	4 EG
	{1, 2}	(6)	∃x (Fx ∧ Gx)	2, 3, 5 ES
3.	{1}	(1)	∀x ∃y Fyx	P
	{1}	(2)	∃y Fya	US
	{3}	(3)	Faa	P
	{3}	(4)	∃x Fxx	3 EG
	{1}	(5)	∃x Fxx	2, 3, 4 ES
4.	{1}	(1)	∃x Fx	P
	{2}	(2)	Fa	P
	{1}	(1)	Fa	ES

Definition 3.16 For any sentences φ and ψ of *QL*, φ is semantically equivalent to ψ if and only if φ and ψ belong to the same truth sets. We write φ ⇔ ψ.

Exercise 3.8 From definition 3.15 it is trivial that ∀α φ is semantically equivalent to ¬ ∃α ¬ φ. Using definitions 3.6, 3.15, 3.16, and exercise 3.6, prove the following:

1. ¬ ∀α φ ⇔ ∃α ¬ φ
2. ∀α ¬ φ ⇔ ¬ ∃α φ
3. ¬ ∀α ¬ φ ⇔ ∃α φ

Exercise 3.9 Construct derivational schemas to show UG and US are dispensable rules of inference. You may use any other rule of inference that has been introduced previously: P, Simp, Conj, DN, RAA, ES, EG.

Further Extension of QL

The set of inference rules for our three primitive logical constants—¬, ∧, ∃—are rules P, Simp, Conj, DN, RAA, EG, and ES. In addition, these operators have been introduced by definition: ∨, ⊃, ≡, ∀.

A convenient set of inference rules for the new operators runs as follows:

Disjunctive Addition (Add)

φ → φ ∨ ψ
ψ → φ ∨ ψ

Disjunctive Syllogism (DS)

¬ φ, φ ∨ ψ → ψ
¬ ψ, φ ∨ ψ → φ

Modus Ponens (MP)

φ, φ ⊃ ψ → ψ

Modus Tollens (MT)

¬ ψ, φ ⊃ ψ → ¬ φ

Conditionalization (C)

$$\psi \rightarrow \phi \supset \psi$$

where ϕ is among the premises of ψ. As premises of the new line take all those of the earlier line less ϕ

Biconditional Elimination (BE)

$$\phi \equiv \psi \rightarrow \phi \supset \psi$$
$$\phi \equiv \psi \rightarrow \psi \supset \phi$$

Biconditional Introduction (BI)

$$(\phi \supset \psi) \wedge (\psi \supset \phi) \rightarrow \phi \equiv \psi$$

Dilemma (DI)

$$\phi \vee \psi, \phi \supset \chi, \psi \supset \chi \rightarrow \chi$$

Universal Specification (US)

$$\forall \alpha \ \phi \rightarrow \phi \ \beta/\alpha \text{ where } \beta \text{ is any constant}$$

Universal Generalization (UG)

$$\phi \ \beta/\alpha \rightarrow \forall \alpha \ \phi \text{ where } \beta \text{ is not in } \phi \text{ nor in any premise of } \phi \ \beta/\alpha$$

Quantifier Negation (QN)

$$\neg \exists \alpha \ \phi \rightarrow \forall \alpha \ \neg \phi$$
$$\neg \forall \alpha \ \phi \rightarrow \exists \alpha \ \neg \phi$$
$$\exists \alpha \ \neg \phi \rightarrow \neg \forall \alpha \ \phi$$
$$\forall \alpha \ \neg \phi \rightarrow \neg \exists \alpha \ \phi$$

As stated before, we use the arrow to informally indicate rules of inference. Except for rule C, it is always to be understood that the premises of the sentence derived by the rule are to be those of the sentences from which it is derived by the rule.

Exercise 3.10 Use rules P, sentential logic, plus rules US, UG, ES, EG, and QN to prove the following (if a line follows from one or more preceding lines by sentential logic then to the right of that line write the line number[s] of the preceding line[s] plus "SL"):

¬ ∃x (Fx ∧ Gx) ⊢ ∀x (Fx ⊃ ¬ Gx) (Note that this is a shorthand way of writing "{¬ ∃x (F¹x ∧ G¹x)'} ⊢ '∀x (F¹x ⊃ ¬ G¹x).'" Note also we are retaining the convention of dropping the outmost parentheses.)

1. ∀x (Fx ∧ Gx) ⊢ ∀x Fx ∧ ∀x Gx
2. ∀x Fx ∧ ∀x Gx ⊢ ∀x (Fx ∧ Gx)
3. ∃x (Fx ∨ Gx) ⊢ ∃x Fx ∨ ∃x Gx
4. ∃x Fx ∨ ∃x Gx ⊢ ∃x (Fx ∨ Gx)
5. ∀x (Fx ∧ Gx) ⊢ ∀x Fx ∧ ∀x Gx
6. ∀x Fx ∨ ∀x Gx ⊢ ∀x (Fx ∨ Gx)
7. ∀x (Fx ⊃ Gx) ⊢ ¬ ∃x (Fx ∧ ¬ Gx)
8. ¬ ∃x (Fx ∧ ¬ Gx) ⊢ ∀x (Fx ⊃ Gx)
9. ∀x (Fx ⊃ Gx) ⊢ ∀x Fx ⊃ Ga
10. ∀x Fx ⊃ Ga ⊢ ∃x (Fx ⊃ Ga)
11. ∃x (Fx ⊃ Ga) ⊢ ∀x Fx ⊃ Ga
12. ∃x Fx ⊃ Ga ⊢ ∀x (Fx ⊃ Ga)
13. ∀x ∀y Fxy ⊢ ∀y ∀x Fxy
14. ∃x ∃y Fxy ⊢ ∃y ∃x Fxy
15. ∃x ∀y Fxy ⊢ ∀y ∃x Fxy
16. ∀x (Fx ⊃ Gx) ⊢ ∀x (∃y (Fy ∧ Hxy) ⊃ ∃z (Gz ∧ Hxz))
17. ∃x (Fx ∧ ∀y (Gy ⊃ Hxy)), ∀x (Fx ⊃ ∀y (By ⊃ ¬ Hxy)) ⊢ ∀x (Gx ⊃ ¬ Bx)
18. ∃x (Fx ∧ Gx), ∃x (Fx ∧ ∀y (Gy ⊃ ¬ Hxy)) ⊢ ∃x (Fx ∧ ¬ ∀y (Fy ⊃ Hxy))
19. ∀x ∀y (Fxy ⊃ ∃z Izxy), ∀x ∀y ∀z (Izxy ⊃ (Gzx ∧ Gzy)), ∀x Fxm ⊢ ∀x ∃y (Iyxm ∧ Gym)
20. ∃x ∃y ∀z Fxyz ⊢ ∀z ∃y ∃x Fxyz

Exercise 3.11 Use rules P, sentential logic, plus rules US, UG, ES, and EG to prove the following (you may not use QN on these):

1. ∀x Fx ⊢ ¬ ∃x ¬ Fx
2. ¬ ∃x ¬ Fx ⊢ ∀x Fx
3. ¬ ∀x Fx ⊢ ∃x ¬ Fx
4. ∃x ¬ Fx ⊢ ¬ ∀x Fx
5. ¬ ∃x Fx ⊢ ∀x ¬ Fx
6. ∀x ¬ Fx ⊢ ¬ ∃x Fx
7. ¬ ∀x ¬ φ ⊢ ∃x φ
8. ∃x Fx ⊢ ¬ ∀x ¬ Fx

Model Sets

Model set construction for *QL* proceeds along the same lines that it did for *SL*. We again follow Hintikka in his paper "Modality and Quantification" (Hintikka 1969b, pp. 57–59).

First, to the conditions defining Hintikka normal form (hnf) we add:

$$\neg \exists\alpha\,\phi \Leftrightarrow \forall\alpha\,\neg\,\phi$$
$$\neg \forall\alpha\,\phi \Leftrightarrow \exists\alpha\,\neg\,\phi$$

Second, to conditions (C ¬), (C ∨), (C ∧), we add (where "m" stands for a model set):

> If $\exists\alpha\,\phi \in m$, then $\phi\,\beta/\alpha \in m$, for at least one constant β. (C ∃)
>
> If $\forall\alpha\,\phi \in m$, then $\phi\,\beta/\alpha \in m$, for any constant β that occurs in any formula in m. (C ∀)
>
> If $\forall\alpha\,\phi \in m$, then $\phi\,\beta/\alpha \in m$, for at least one constant β. (C u)

Without condition (C u) we could not prove that $\exists\alpha\,(\Phi\alpha \vee \neg\,\Phi\alpha)$ is a truth of logic where $\Phi\alpha$ is any degree-1 formula, that is, any formula Φ in which α is the only free variable.

A finite set is consistent if and only if the set consisting of the hnf of each of its members is embeddable in a model set. The conditions on model sets can be viewed as directions for constructing model sets as before. Each of the conditions other than (C ¬) tells us what must be added to a set to make it a model set. (C ¬) is a negative condition that tells us what a model set cannot have.

To test a finite set to see if it is consistent, list the hnf of the members of the set, and then attempt to add sentences to the list to satisfy the conditions on model sets. If you can do this, so that every condition is satisfied for every sentence we list, and there are no violations of (C ¬), then we have a model set, and the original set of sentences is consistent. If every attempt to add sentences to satisfy the other conditions is blocked by (C ¬), then the set is inconsistent.

To test an argument for validity, take the hnf of the premises and the negation of the conclusion and attempt to construct a model set. If you succeed, it is not valid. If you must fail, then the argument is valid. Exhibiting a model set that contains the premises and the negation of the conclusion shows that the argument is not valid. Thus, we have a method of disproof.

We do not have a decision procedure. The reason is that we may neither succeed nor fail in a finite number of steps.

The conditions pertaining to the propositional calculus are (C ¬), (C ∧), and (C ∨). The sentences required by (C ∧) and (C ∨) are always shorter than the sentence referred to in the antecedent of these conditions. Thus, starting with a finite set of sentences and repeatedly adding what is needed to satisfy (C ∧) and (C ∨), we must eventually get down to atomic sentences. Either there is a contradiction among these sentences—a violation of (C ¬)—and the original set is inconsistent, or there is no contradiction and the original set is consistent. Thus we have a decision procedure for the propositional calculus, and one which in general involves fewer calculations than the use of truth tables.

But when we add quantifiers, the situation changes. It may happen that no matter how many sentences we have added, it is still necessary to add more sentences to satisfy all the conditions. This is due, in particular, to the interplay of (C ∃) and (C ∀). (C ∃) may force us to add new constants to the model set. This will then require new instances of universal quantifications to satisfy (C ∀). When there are existential quantifiers inside the scope of universal quantifiers, these new instances will be existential quantifications, which force new applications of (C ∃), adding new constants to the model set, and so forth. Thus, the test will never come to an end. In some such cases, it is possible to see that no contradiction will turn up no matter how far we go. But this is not always the case. Thus, some consistent sets of sentences can be contained in infinite model sets, but do not have finite model sets. No matter how far you have gone in adding sentences in an attempt to construct a model set, there is no general procedure for determining whether we are dealing with such a set or whether a contradiction will turn up later.

Here are some examples. First, is ¬ ∀x (Fx ⊃ Gx), ∃x (¬ Gx ∧ Hx) ∴ ∃x (Fx ∧ Hx) valid?

i.   ∃x ¬ (Fx ⊃ Gx)
ii.   ∃x (Fx ∧ ¬ Gx)

In i and ii we put the first premise in hnf. The second premise is already in hnf.

iii.   ¬ ∃x (Fx ∧ Hx)
iv.   ∀x ¬ (Fx ∧ Hx)
v.   ∀x (¬ Fx ∨ ¬ Hx)

In iii–v we put the negation of the conclusion in hnf.

In the following 1–3 assume there is a model set containing the hnfs of the premises and the negation of the conclusion. In lines 4–13 we attempt to satisfy each of the conditions. We indicate on the right which condition is being satisfied with respect to which line.

1.	∃x (Fx ∧ ¬ Gx)	∈ m	assumption	
2.	∃x (¬ Gx ∧ Hx)	∈ m	assumption	
3.	∀x (¬ Fx ∨ ¬ Hx)	∈ m	assumption	
4.	Fa ∧ Ga	∈ m	1	(C ∃)
5.	Fa	∈ m	4	(C ∧)
6.	¬ Ga	∈ m	4	(C ∧)
7.	¬ Gb ∧ Hb	∈ m	2	(C ∃)
8.	¬ Gb	∈ m	7	(C ∧)
9.	Hb	∈ m	7	(C ∧)
10.	¬ Ga ∨ ¬ Ha	∈ m	3	(C ∀)
11.	¬ Ha	∈ m	10	(C ∨)
12.	¬ Fb ∨ ¬ Hb	∈ m	3	(C ∀)
13.	¬ Fb	∈ m	12	(C ∨)

Since 1–13 make m a model set, the original argument is not valid.

For another example, let us consider

∀x (∃y Fxy ∨ ∃y ¬ Fxy).

Is it a logical truth? (As in *SL*, a *QL* sentence is a logical truth just in case its negation in hnf is a member of no model set). Let us negate it:

¬ ∀x (∃y Fxy ∨ ∃y ¬ Fxy).

And let us put that negation into hnf:

∃x (∀y ¬ Fxy ∧ ∀y Fxy).

It turns out that this is not a member of a model set. For example, consider the following:

1.	∃x (∀y ¬ Fxy ∧ ∀y Fxy)	∈ m	assumption
2.	∀y ¬ Fay ∧ ∀y Fay	∈ m	1 (C ∃)
3.	∀y ¬ Fay	∈ m	2 (C ∧)
4.	∀y Fay	∈ m	2 (C ∧)

5.	¬ Faa	∈ m	3 (C ∀)
6.	Faa	∈ m	4 (C ∀)

Since the hnf of the negation of "∀x (∃y Fxy ∨ ∃y ¬ Fxy)" is a member of no model set, "∀x (∃y Fxy ∨ ∃y ¬ Fxy)" is a valid sentence.
For a final example, consider

Fa ∧ ∀x (Fx ⊃ Gax) ∴ Gaa.

Is this argument valid? Consider:

1.	Fa ∧ ∀x (¬ Fx ∨ Gax)	∈ m	hnf of premise
2.	¬ Gaa	∈ m	hnf of the negation of the conclusion
3.	Fa	∈ m	1, (C ∧)
4.	∀x (¬ Fx ∨ Gax)	∈ m	1, (C ∧)
5.	¬ Fa ∨ Gaa	∈ m	4, (C ∀)

We cannot add either disjunct of line 5 to m without violating (C ¬), since "¬ Fa" contradicts line 3 and "Gaa" contradicts line 2. Thus it is impossible to construct a model set containing lines 1 and 2. Thus the argument is valid.

Exercise 3.12 For each of the following arguments, show the argument is invalid by means of a model set:

1. ∀x (Hx ⊃ Gx), ∀x (Fx ⊃ Gx) ∴ ∃x (Fx ∧ Hx)
2. ∃x Fx, ∃xGx ∴ ∃x (Fx ∧ Gx)
3. ∀x ∃y Fxy ∴ ∃y ∀x Fxy
4. ∀x (Fx ∨ Gx) ∴ ∀x Fx ∨ ∀x Gx
5. ∀x Fx ⊃ Ga ∴ ∀x (Fx ⊃ Ga)

Exercise 3.13 For each of the following sets of sentences, show it is consistent by embedding it in a model set:

1. {∀x ∃y Fxy, ∀x (Gx ⊃ ∃y Fyx), ∃x Gx, ∀x ¬ Fxx}
2. {∀x (Px ∨ Qx), ∀x (Rx ⊃ Qx), ∃x (Px ∧ ¬ Qx)}
3. {∃x Fx, ∃x ¬ Fx}
4. {¬ ∀x ¬ Fx, ∀x (Fx ⊃ Gx), ∃x (Gx ∧ ¬ Fx)}
5. {∀x (¬ Gx ⊃ Fx), ∃x (Gx ∧ Fx), Fa ⊃ ¬ Ga}

Exercise 3.14 Use the model set technique to determine the validity of the following arguments:

1. $\exists x \neg Fx \therefore \neg \exists x \neg Fx$
2. $\forall x\, Fx \therefore \neg \forall x \neg Fx$
3. $\forall x\, Fx \vee \forall x \neg Gx \therefore \forall x\, (\neg Fx \supset \neg Gx)$
4. $\forall x\, Fx \vee \forall x\, Gx \therefore \forall x\, (Fx \vee Gx)$
5. $\forall x\, (Fx \wedge Gx) \therefore \forall x\, Fx \wedge \forall x\, Gx$
6. $\forall x\, Fx \wedge \forall x\, Gx \therefore \forall x\, (Fx \wedge Gx)$
7. $\forall x\, (Fx \vee Gx) \therefore \forall x\, Fx \vee \forall x\, Gx$
8. $\exists x\, Fx \vee \exists x\, Gx \therefore \exists x\, (Fx \vee Gx)$
9. $\exists x\, (Fx \vee Gx) \therefore \exists x\, Fx \vee \exists x\, Gx$
10. $\exists x\, Fx \wedge \exists x\, Gx \therefore \exists x\, (Fx \wedge Gx)$
11. $\exists x\, (Fx \vee Gx) \therefore \exists x\, Fx \vee \exists x\, Gx$
12. $\forall x\, \exists y\, Fxy \therefore \exists y\, \forall x\, Fxy$
13. $\exists y\, \forall x\, Fxy \therefore \forall x\, \exists y\, Fxy$
14. $\forall x\, (Fx \supset Ga) \therefore \exists x\, Fx \supset Ga$
15. $\forall x\, (Fx \supset Ga) \therefore \forall x\, Fx \supset Ga$
16. $\exists x\, (Fx \supset Ga) \therefore \forall x\, Fx \supset Ga$
17. $\exists x\, (Fx \supset Ga) \therefore \exists x\, Fx \supset Ga$
18. $\exists x\, Fx \supset Ga \therefore \exists x\, (Fx \supset Ga)$

Identity

In addition to $\neg$, $\wedge$, and $\exists$, there is a further logical primitive $=$, the sign of identity. We shall call the language formed by adding $=$ to QL, QLI. Unlike $\vee, \supset$, $\equiv$, and $\forall$, the sign $=$ is not eliminable.

Simple formulas of QLI consist of any n-place predicate letter followed by n occurrences of individual symbols (constants or variables) or else the identity sign flanked by individual symbols.

As in QL, every simple formula is a formula. If ϕ is a formula, $\neg \phi$ also is a formula. If ϕ and ψ are formulas, $(\phi \wedge \psi)$ also is a formula. If ϕ is a formula and α is a variable, $\exists \alpha \square \phi$ also is a formula. Also, as in QL, ϕ is a sentence if and only if ϕ is a formula and, for every variable α, each occurrence of α in ϕ is in a part of ϕ that, for some formula ψ, is a formula $\exists \alpha\, \psi$.

Definition 3.17   A *QLI derivation* is any finite sequence of lines each satisfying one of the conditions for a derivation for *QL* and for following two conditions:

II   For every constant β, the line $<\varnothing, \beta = \beta>$ is a derivation;

IE   if S is a derivation and $<A, \phi>$ occurs in S and $<B, \beta = \gamma>$ occurs in S, where ϕ is like ψ except that constants β and γ have been exchanged at one or more places, then S, $<A \cup B, \psi>$ is a derivation.

The derivative operators $\lor, \supset, \equiv, \forall$ may be introduced in the usual way along with the usual rules of inference, yielding P, Conj, Simp, DN, RAA, Add, DS, MP, MT, C, BI, BE, US, UG, ES, EG, QN, plus rules II and IE.

Here is an example of a derivation:

{1}	1.	a = b	P
∅	2.	a = a	II
{1}	3.	b = a	1, 2 IE
∅	4.	a = b ⊃ b = a	1–2, C
∅	5.	∀y (a = y ⊃ y = a)	3, UG
∅	6.	∀x ∀y (x = y ⊃ y = x)	4, UG

Exercise 3.15 For each of the following sentences of QLI, prove the sentence is a theorem of QLI. Use rule P, sentential logic, plus quantificational logic, plus II and IE to prove items 1–6. If a line follows from one or more preceding lines by sentential logic, write the line numbers and "SL" to the right of that line. If a line follows from one or more preceding lines by quantificational logic, write the line numbers and "QL" to the right of that line.

1. $\forall x \, (x = x)$
2. $\forall x \, \forall y \, \forall z \, ((x = y \land y = z) \supset x = z)$
3. $\forall x \, (Fx \equiv \exists y \, (x = y \land Fy))$
4. $\forall x \, (Fx \equiv \forall y \, (x = y \supset Fy))$
5. $\forall x \, \forall y \, (x = y \supset (Fx \equiv Fy))$
6. $\forall x \, \forall y \, ((Fx \land x = y) \equiv (Fy \land x = y))$
7. $\exists x \, \forall y \, (Fy \equiv x = y) \supset (\exists x \, Fx \land \forall x \, \forall y \, ((Fx \land Fy) \supset x = y))$

Model Sets for QLI

To get model sets suitable for *QLI*, we add two conditions to (C ¬), (C ∨), (C ∧), (C ∃), (C ∀), and (C u):

> For any names β_1 and β_2, if $\beta_1 = \beta_2 \in m$, then if $\phi \in m$, then $\psi \in m$ where ψ differs at most from ϕ in the exchange of β_1 and β_2 in one or more places. (C =)
> For every constant β that occurs in a member of m, $\beta = \beta \in m$. (C self =)

Here are some examples. Is

$Fa, \neg Fb \therefore \neg a = b$

valid? Let us see if the premises and the negation of the conclusion belong to a model set, m.

1.	Fa	∈ m	assumption about the first premise
2.	¬ Fb	∈ m	assumption about the second premise
3.	a = b	∈ m	assumption about the negation of the conclusion

From steps 1 and 3 we get

4.	Fb	∈ m	1, 3 (C =)

Lines 2 and 4 violate (C ¬). Thus the argument is valid.
    For another example, consider

∃x (x = a ∧ Fa) ∴ Fb

The premise and negation of the conclusion are already in hnf:

1.	∃x (x = a ∧ Fa)	∈ m
2.	¬ Fb	∈ m

Using the methods of model set construction, we get the following:

3.	b = a ∧ Fa	∈ m	1 (C ∃)
4.	Fa	∈ m	3 (C ∧)
5.	b = a	∈ m	3 (C ∧)
6.	Fc	∈ m	4, 5 (C =)
7.	a = a	∈ m	1–6 (C self =)
8.	b = b	∈ m	1–6 (C self =)

Since (C ¬) or (C self =) are not violated, the argument is invalid. In practice, steps such as 7 and 8, which are justified by (C self =), may be omitted in model set construction.

Exercise 3.16   Use the model set technique to determine the validity of the following arguments:

1. a = b ∴ ∃x (Fbx ∨ ¬ Fax)
2. a = b, ∀x (Fxa ⊃ ¬ Gxb) ∴ ∃x ¬ Gxa

3. a ≠ b, b ≠ c ∴ a ≠ c
4. Fab, ¬ Fba ∴ a ≠ b
5. ∀x Fxx, ∀x x = a ∴ ∀x ∀y Fxy
6. ∃x (Fax ∧ ¬ Fbx) ∴ a ≠ b
7. ∀x ∀y x = y ∴ ∀x ∀y ∀z (z = y ∨ z = x)

4

Sentential Modal Logic

Non-Truth-Functional Sentential Operators

For any truth-valued sentence ϕ, the sentence that results from prefixing it with the phrase "it is not the case that" has the opposite truth-value. This marks the unary sentential operator "it is not the case that" as truth-functional.

But not all unary sentential operators are like "it is not the case that" in this respect. For example, though the sentences

Some odd numbers are prime
Some old men are republicans

are both true, the sentences that result from prefixing them with the unary sentential operator "it is necessary that" are respectively true and false. So, that operator is not truth-functional. And though the sentences

Some even number in addition to 2 is prime
Some classical philosopher in addition to Socrates was executed in Athens

are both false, the sentences that result from prefixing them with "it is possible that" are respectively false and true. So this operator also is not truth-functional.

Sentential operators that involve the notions of necessity and possibility are customarily called *modal* operators. The idea behind this usage seems to be this, that we use such phrases as "it is necessary that" and "it is possible that" to assert something *in a certain way*—as necessary, or as possible. The phrases do not add to the *content* of what is said, but express its *mode* of its assertion. However this may be, the terminology is pretty well fixed, and we will not deviate from it, and call sentential operators involving terms kindred to "necessarily" and "possibly" *modal* operators.

We noted the feature of *non*-truth-functionality in introducing modal operators. But they are not the only type of non-truth-functional operator. The phrases "it ought to be that" and "it is permissible that" also are non-truth-functional. Prefix the first phrase to the false sentence "No innocent children are tortured" and you get something true, but if you prefix the same phrase to the equally false sentence "Bananas are not eaten" and you get something false, not something true. And if you prefix the second phrase to the true sentence "Some innocent children are tortured" you get something false, though if you prefix it to the equally true sentence "Bananas are eaten" you get something true.

There also are non-truth-functional unary sentential operators of other types. For example, the phrase "Harry Truman hoped that" attaches to some true sentences to form a true sentence, but to other true sentences to form a false sentence. (Some but not all of his hopes were realized.)

Exercise 4.1   Give five examples of non-truth-functional unary sentential operators other than those mentioned in this section. Give one example of a truth-functional unary sentential operator other than the one mentioned for negation.

Sentential Modal Operators

We begin with a language *SML*—a language for *sentential modal logic*. Syntactically, this is the language that results from the language *SL* for sentential logic by adding the two unary connectives "□" and "◊" (for necessities and possibilities) and the three binary operators "∨," "≡," and "⊃" (for disjunctions, biconditionals, and conditionals).

Definition 4.1   Every *SL* sentence is an *SML* sentence.

If φ *is an SML* sentence, so are ¬ φ, □ φ, and ◊ φ.

If φ and ψ are *SML* sentences, so are (φ ∧ ψ) (φ ∨ ψ), (φ ⊃ ψ), and (φ ≡ ψ).

It is plain that the rules of conjunction and simplification hold for conjunctions, and there is no dispute about whether adding negation signs two at a time is a correct inference. The same general agreement holds for the *reductio*, and for the rules for reasoning with disjunctions. Of the rules for conditionals, *modus ponens* and *conditionalization* also are not in dispute. Disagreements arise only—or mostly—about the acceptability of deleting negation signs two at a time and certain aspects of inference with conditionals (e.g., the inference to φ from "It is not the case that if φ, then ψ").

But in the case of "it is possible that" and "it is necessary that" disagreements abound. Having noted this, we will begin with a set of rules for modal inference on the basis that it is a well-known set of rules for which it is quite simple to provide a semantics based on model sets.

Derivations

We first stipulate that if S is a derivation and φ is a theorem of *SL* <∅, φ> is also a derivation of *SML*.

We now add conditions for the two new unary operators.

D   If S is a derivation and <A, □ φ> occurs in S, S, <A, ¬ ◊ ¬ φ> is also a derivation.
If S is a derivation and <A, ¬ ◊ ¬ φ> occurs in S, S, <A, □ φ> is also a derivation.
If S is a derivation and <A, ◊ φ> occurs in S, S, <A, ¬ □¬ φ> is also a derivation.
If S is a derivation and <A, ¬ □ ¬ φ> occurs in S, S, <A, ◊ φ> is also a derivation.

ND   If S is a derivation and <A, □ (φ ⊃ ψ)> occurs in S, then S, <A, (□ φ ⊃ □ ψ)> is also a derivation.

◊I   If S is a derivation and <A, φ> occurs in S, then S, <A, ◊ φ> is also a derivation.

□I   If S is a derivation and <∅, φ> occurs in S, then S, <∅, □ φ> is also a derivation.

□E   If S is a derivation and <A, □ φ> occurs in S, then S, <A, φ> is also a derivation.

□□ If S is a derivation and <A, □ φ> occurs in S, then S, <A, □ □ φ> is also a derivation.

□◊ If S is a derivation and <A, ◊ φ> occurs in S, then S, <A, □ ◊ φ> is also a derivation.

The D rules ("duality" rules) are rules of equivalence for the diamond and square. Rule ND serves for "necessity distribution" for conditionals.

We can informally express these rules as follows:

D	□ φ → ¬ ◊ ¬ φ	¬ □ ¬ φ → ◊ φ
	◊ φ → ¬ □ ¬ φ	¬ ◊ ¬ φ → □ φ
ND	□ (φ ⊃ ψ) → (□ φ ⊃ □ ψ)	
◊I	φ → ◊ φ	
□I	⊢ φ → □ φ	
□E	□ φ → φ	
□□	□ φ → □ □ φ	
□◊	◊ φ → □ ◊ φ	

To introduce □ φ into a derivation by rule □I, some earlier segment of the derivation must itself be a derivation of φ from the empty set of premises. In practice we omit that earlier segment if we could construct an empty set derivation for φ in *SL*. So, for example, if we could construct an empty set derivation of "(p ⊃ (p v q))" in *SL*, we can appeal to rule □I in introducing "□ (p ⊃ (p v q))" into a later derivation without needing to reproduce that derivation in that later derivation.

Note that our rules all are *implication* rules, not *equivalence* rules. So, for example, the rules do not provide for a *one step* derivation of "□ ¬ p" from "¬ ◊ p," or of "□ ◊ p" from "□ ¬ □ ¬ p," just as our rules for sentential logic do not provide for a *one step* derivation of "(p ⊃ q)" from "(p ⊃ ¬ ¬ q)."

We will now establish some basic derivability theorems of sentential modal logic. In doing so we will justify lines by reference to previously established theorems *and their substitution instances*. Note also that to each derivability theorem φ ⊢ ψ there corresponds the derivability theorem ⊢ (φ ⊃ ψ).

T1   ¬ ◊ p ⊢ □ ¬ p

Proof

{1}	(1)	¬ ◊ p	P
{2}	(2)	¬ □ ¬ p	P

{2}	(3)	◊ p	2 D
{1, 2}	(4)	◊ p ∧ ¬ ◊ p	1, 3 Conj
{1}	(5)	¬ ¬ □ ¬ p	4 RAA
{1}	(6)	□ ¬ p	5 DN

T2   ◊ ¬ p ├ ¬ □ p

Proof

{1}	(1)	◊ ¬ p	P
{2}	(2)	¬ ¬□ p	P
{2}	(3)	□ p	2 DN
{2}	(4)	¬ ◊ ¬ p	3 D
{1, 2}	(5)	(◊ ¬ p ∧ ¬ ◊ ¬ p)	1, 4 Conj
{1}	(6)	¬ ¬ ¬ □ p	5 RAA
{1}	(7)	¬ □ p	6 DN

T3   ¬ □ p ├ ◊ ¬ p

Proof

{1}	(1)	¬ □ p	P
{2}	(2)	¬ ◊ ¬ p	P
{2}	(3)	□ p	2 D
{1, 2}	(4)	(□ p ∧ ¬ □ p)	1, 3 Conj
{1}	(5)	¬ ¬ ◊ ¬ p	4 RAA
{1}	(6)	◊ ¬ p	5 DN

T4   □ ¬ p ├ ¬ ◊ p

Proof

{1}	(1)	□ ¬ p	P
{2}	(2)	¬ ¬ ◊ p	P
{2}	(3)	◊ p	3 DN
{1}	(4)	¬ □ ¬ p	3 D
{1, 2}	(5)	□ ¬ p ∧ ¬ □ ¬ p	1, 3 Conj
{1}	(6)	¬ ¬ ¬ ◊ p	4 RAA
{1}	(7)	¬ ◊ p	6 DN

T5   ◊ □ p ├ p

Proof

{1}	(1)	$\lozenge \square p$	P
{2}	(2)	$\neg p$	P
{2}	(3)	$\lozenge \neg p$	2 $\lozenge$I
{2}	(4)	$\square \lozenge \neg p$	3 $\square\lozenge$
$\varnothing$	(5)	$\square (\lozenge \neg p \supset \neg \square p)$	$\square$I by T2
$\varnothing$	(6)	$\square \lozenge \neg p \supset \square \neg \square p$	5 ND
{2}	(7)	$\square \neg \square p$	4, 6 MP
{2}	(8)	$\neg \lozenge \square p$	7 by T4
{1, 2}	(9)	$\lozenge \square p \wedge \neg \lozenge \square p$	1, 9 Conj
{1}	(10)	$\neg \neg p$	9 RAA
{1}	(11)	p	10 DN

T6 $\lozenge p, \square (p \supset q) \vdash \lozenge q$

Proof

{1}	(1)	$\lozenge p$	P
{2}	(2)	$\square (p \supset q)$	P
$\varnothing$	(3)	$\square ((p \supset q) \supset (\neg q \supset \neg p))$	$\square$I $\vdash ((p \supset q) \supset (\neg q \supset \neg p))$
$\varnothing$	(4)	$(\square (p \supset q) \supset \square (\neg q \supset \neg p))$	3 ND
{2}	(5)	$\square (\neg q \supset \neg p)$	2, 4 MP
{2}	(6)	$(\square \neg q \supset \square \neg p)$	5 ND
{1}	(7)	$\neg \square \neg p$	1 D
{1, 2}	(8)	$\neg \square \neg q$	6, 7 MT
{1}	(9)	$\lozenge q$	8 D

Exercise 4.2   Prove the following:

1. $\square (p \supset q), \neg q \vdash \neg p$
2. $\neg \lozenge (p \wedge q), p \vdash \neg q$
3. $\square (p \equiv \neg p) \vdash q$
4. $\neg \lozenge \neg (p \vee q), \neg q \vdash \neg p$
5. $\lozenge (\square p \wedge \square \neg p) \vdash p \wedge \neg p$
6. $\square (\lozenge p \supset \square q), \square \neg q \vdash \lozenge \neg p$
7. $\square (p \supset q) \vdash \neg \lozenge (p \wedge \neg q)$
8. $\square (p \supset q) \vdash (\lozenge p \supset \lozenge q)$
9. $\square \neg \lozenge \neg p \vdash \square \square p$
10. $\lozenge \neg \square \neg p \vdash \lozenge \lozenge p$
11. $\lozenge \square p \vdash \lozenge \neg \lozenge \neg p$
12. $\square \lozenge \neg \neg p \vdash \square \neg \square \neg p$
13. $\square \lozenge p \vdash \square \neg \square \neg p$
14. $\lozenge \neg \neg p \vdash \lozenge p$
15. $\square \neg \neg p \vdash \square p$
16. $\square \lozenge p \vdash \square \neg \square \neg p$

17. $\Diamond \Diamond p \vdash \Diamond p$ (Hint: use $\Box\Box$)

18. $\Diamond p \vdash \Diamond \neg \neg p$

Exercise 4.3 Show that for any formulas ϕ and ψ: if $\vdash (\Diamond \phi \supset \psi)$ then $\vdash (\phi \supset \Box \psi)$.

S5, S4, T, and B

The syntactic system that has just been given is often called S5. A weaker system than S5 is called S4. S4 is S5 minus the rule $\Box \Diamond$; that is, S4 has all the rules above except

$$\Diamond \phi \rightarrow \Box \Diamond \phi$$

A still weaker system is system T. System T is S4 minus the $\Box\Box$ rule:

$$\Box \phi \rightarrow \Box \Box \phi$$

A fourth system is called B after David Brouwer. It results from system T by the addition of B

$$\phi \rightarrow \Box \Diamond \phi$$

These different systems represent different senses of necessity and possibility.

Exercise 4.4 Prove the following:

$$\Diamond \Box \phi \rightarrow \phi$$

in systems B and S5.

Possible Worlds

Certain features are pretty standard in the semantics for modal logic. Let's take a look at these features.

The general idea is that there are possible worlds and that sentences are true or false *at* possible worlds, so that one and the same sentence may be true *at* one possible world, and false *at* another possible world, and, perhaps, neither true nor false *at* yet another possible world.

It goes with talk of possible worlds to speak of what *exists in* a possible world, so that what *exists in* one possible world may not *exist in* yet another possible world.

Further, it is part of how we speak in terms of possible worlds to say that something may have different properties or stand in different relations in different possible worlds. For example, the sentence "Socrates was married" will be true *at* any possible world such that Socrates *exists in* that world and is married *in* that world, and will be false *at* any possible world such that he *exists in* that world but is unmarried *in* that world.

At a World and In a World

We have spoken of things existing *in* a world and of things having properties *in* a world or being *in* a world in certain relations to other things *in* that world.

Some possible worlds include no dragons but both lions and speakers all of whom speak just as we speakers of English speak. For any such world, the sentence "There are lions" will be true *in* that world. It will be true *in* that world because it is among the true sentences of the language spoken by the speakers in that world. But there also are worlds that include no dragons but both lions and speakers all of whom speak just as we speakers of English speak *except* for using "lion" where we would use "dragon" and conversely. The sentence "There are lions" will not be true *in* that world, since the sentence "There are lions" is among the false sentences of the language spoken by the speakers in that world.

But even though the sentence "There are lions" is false *in* possible worlds of the second type, that sentence is true *at* such worlds. It is true *at* such worlds because there are things that exist in those worlds that are lions in those worlds. That these things are not called "lions" *in* that world is irrelevant. There are lions in that world even if they are not called "lions" in that world.

The primary notion of truth for possible worlds is, then, that of being true *at* a world.

Model Sets and Model Systems

We use Hintikka's paper "The Modes of Modality" as our guide for the study of the variety of systems of modal logic and the philosophically interesting interpretations of them (Hintikka 1969c, pp. 71–86).

Model sets, and model systems, give a method for testing sets of sentences of different systems, such as S5, S4, T, and B, for consistency and hence, indirectly, a method for testing arguments for validity. A model set is a set of well-formed formulas meeting certain conditions that insure that the set is consistent.

Evaluation of modal (epistemic, deontic, temporal, etc.) sentences requires consideration of alternative possibilities. A *model set* can be thought of as a partial description of a possible world, the condition on model sets being designed to insure that what is described is really possible. A *model system* is a set of related model sets. Again, the conditions are intended to insure that the model sets of the model system are related in the appropriate way for the modal notion in question.

Normal form. We say a sentence is in Hintikka normal form (hnf) if and only if the only truth-functional connectives it contains are "$\neg$," "$\wedge$," and "$\vee$," and "$\neg$" is applied only to atomic sentences.

Every sentence is equivalent to a sentence in hnf. For any given sentence ϕ, an equivalent sentence in hnf can be found by repeatedly replacing one well-formed part by its equivalent in the following list of equivalences.

1. $\neg (\phi \supset \psi) \Leftrightarrow (\phi \wedge \neg \psi)$
2. $(\phi \supset \psi) \Leftrightarrow (\neg \phi \vee \psi)$
3. $\neg (\phi \equiv \psi) \Leftrightarrow (\phi \wedge \neg \psi) \vee (\neg \phi \wedge \psi)$
4. $(\phi \equiv \psi) \Leftrightarrow (\phi \wedge \psi) \vee (\neg \phi \wedge \neg \psi)$
5. $\neg (\phi \wedge \psi) \Leftrightarrow \neg \phi \vee \neg \psi$
6. $\neg (\phi \vee \psi) \Leftrightarrow \neg \phi \wedge \neg \psi$
7. $\neg \square \phi \Leftrightarrow \Diamond \neg \phi$
8. $\neg \Diamond \phi \Leftrightarrow \square \neg \phi$

Conditions 1 through 4 eliminate $\supset$ and $\equiv$. The other conditions allow us to move $\neg$ inside until it has smallest scope. Double negations are eliminated as they occur.

A model set is a set of sentences in hnf that satisfies the conditions listed below. A modal system is a set M of model sets, with a binary relation, R, of alternativeness defined on M. (R is a *binary relation defined on* M if and only if R is a binary relation and for each $<x, y> \in R, x \in M$ and $y \in M$.)

A model set can be thought of as a partial description of a possible world. Thus, a model system is a set of descriptions of possible worlds, plus a relation of alternativeness or relative possibility defined on those descriptions, and hence on the worlds described. The following conditions on modal systems represent the basic idea of possible world semantics in model set terms.

1. If $\phi \in m$, then it is not the case that $\neg \phi \in m$. (C $\neg$)
2. If $(\phi \wedge \psi) \in m$, then $\phi \in m$ and $\psi \in m$. (C $\wedge$)
3. If $(\phi \vee \psi) \in m$, then $\phi \in m$ or $\psi \in m$. (C $\vee$)
4. If $\square \phi \in m$, then $\phi \in m$. (C $\square$)
5. If $\lozenge \phi \in m$, then there is at least one model set m_1 that is an alternative to m such that $\phi \in m_1$. (C $\lozenge$)
6. If $\square \phi \in m$ and if model set m_1 is an alternative to m, then $\phi \in m_1$. (C $\square^+$)

We can now define the following semantical notions.

1. A sentence ϕ in hnf is consistent if and only if there is a model system <M, R> and a model set m such that $m \in M$ and $\phi \in m$.
2. A sentence that is not in hnf is consistent if and only if its hnf is consistent.
3. A sentence ϕ is valid if and only if $\neg \phi$ is not consistent.
4. A finite set is consistent if and only if the set consisting of the hnf of each of its members is included in a model set of some model system.
5. An argument, $\phi_1, \ldots, \phi_n \therefore \psi$, is valid if and only if $\{\phi_1, \ldots, \phi_n, \neg\psi\}$ is not consistent. (That is, there is no model set of any model system that contains all of the premises and the negation of the conclusion.)

The system that results from adding the rules (C $\square$) (C $\lozenge$) (C $\square^+$) to the conditions for sentential logic—(C $\neg$) (C $\wedge$) (C $\vee$)—is equivalent to the syntactic system T in that a sentence is valid if and only if it is a theorem of T; an argument, $\phi_1, \ldots, \phi_n \therefore \psi$, is valid if and only if ψ is deducible from $\{\phi_1, \ldots, \phi_n\}$ using only the rules of T; and so on.

A finite set is consistent if and only if the set consisting of the hnf of each of its members is embeddable in a model set of a model system. The conditions on model sets and systems can be viewed as directions for constructing model sets and systems. Each of the conditions other than (C $\neg$) tells us what must be added to a set to make it a model set. (C $\neg$) is a negative condition that tells us what a model set cannot have.

To test a finite set to see if it is consistent, list the hnf of the members of the set, and then attempt to add sentences to the list to satisfy the conditions on model sets. If you can do this, so that every condition is satisfied for every sentence we list, and there are no violations of (C $\neg$), then we have a model set, and the original set of sentences is consistent. If every attempt to add sentences to satisfy the other conditions is blocked by (C $\neg$), then the set is inconsistent.

To test an argument for validity, take the hnf of the premises and the negation of the conclusion and attempt to construct a model set of a model system.

If you succeed, it is not valid. If you must fail, then the argument is valid. Exhibiting a model set that contains the premises and the negation of the conclusion shows that the argument is not valid. Thus, we have a method of disproof, which is one thing you want from a semantics.

We can consider different notions of consistency, and hence, different notions of possibility and necessity, by imposing conditions on the relation, R, of alternativeness, or by adding conditions on model sets related by R. For example,

1. If $\Box \phi \in m$, and m_1 is an alternative to m, then $\Box \phi \in m_1$. (C $\Box\Box^+$)
2. If $\Box \phi \in m$, and m is an alternative to m_1, then $\phi \in m_1$. (C $\Box_+$)
3. If $\Box \phi \in m$, and m is an alternative to m_1, then $\Box \phi \in m_1$. (C $\Box\Box_+$)

(C $\Box$) has the effect of rendering R reflexive. Adding (C $\Box\Box^+$) has the effect of requiring that R be transitive, and hence yields S4. Putting $\Box \phi$ in all alternatives insures that ϕ will be in alternatives of alternatives, which is the effect of transitivity. Adding (C $\Box_+$) is equivalent to requiring that R be symmetrical, and hence yields a system equivalent to B. If (C $\Box\Box^+$) is present, (C $\Box\Box_+$) must be added to get the effect of symmetry. Thus, adding (C $\Box\Box_+$) to S4 is equivalent to requiring that R be an equivalence relation, and hence gives a system equivalent to S5. In general, the strongest condition for adding $\Box$ to alternativeness must be reversed to get the effect of symmetry. Adding (C $\Box_+$) to S4 does not yield a coherent system. This illustrates a danger of model set techniques. Adding (C $\Box\Box_+$) to the semantics of T gives the effect of symmetry. But adding (C $\Box\Box^+$) and (C $\Box_+$) to the semantics of T does not give the effect of transitivity plus symmetry. Also, since (C $\Box$) is equivalent to requiring that R be reflexive, dropping (C $\Box$) is equivalent to allowing R not to be reflective, as would be appropriate if $\Box$ were interpreted as belief or obligation. To sum up:

1. The semantics of $T = $ (C $\neg$), (C $\wedge$), (C $\vee$), (C $\Box$), (C $\Diamond$), (C $\Box^+$).
2. The semantics of $T +$ (C $\Box\Box^+$) = the semantics of $T +$ transitivity of R = the semantics of S4.
3. The semantics of $T +$ (C$\Box_+$) = the semantics of $T +$ symmetry of R = the semantics of B.
4. The semantics of $T +$ (C $\Box\Box^+$) + (C$\Box\Box_+$) = the semantics of $T +$ R is an equivalence relation = the semantics of S5.

Consider

□ (p ∨ q) ∴ □ p ∨ □ q

This can be proven invalid in *T* by the use of model set construction. Let m be a model set belonging to some model system. Now consider

1.	□ (p ∨ q)	∈ m	supposition about premise
2.	◊ ¬ p ∧ ◊ ¬ q	∈ m	supposition about negation of conclusion in hnf
3.	◊ ¬ p	∈ m	from 2 by (C ∧)
4.	◊ ¬ q	∈ m	from 2 by (C ∧)
5.	¬ p	∈ m₁	for some m₁ such that m₁ R m, from 3 by (C ◊)
6.	p ∨ q	∈ m₁	from 1 by (C □⁺)
7.	q	∈ m₁	one of the alternatives provided by 6 and by (C ∨)
8.	¬ q	∈ m₂	for some m₂ such that m₂ R m, from 4 by (C ◊)
9.	p ∨ q	∈ m₂	from 1 by (C □⁺)
10.	p	∈ m₂	one of the alternatives provided by 9 and by (C ∨)

This shows that the argument

□ (p ∨ q) ∴ □ p ∨ □ q

is invalid in system *T*. For there is a model system <M, R> and a model set m belonging to M such that "□ (p ∨ q)" belongs to m while "◊ ¬ p ∧ ◊ ¬ q," which is equivalent to the negation of the conclusion, belongs to the same model set m. Moreover, the only conditions we used were (C ∧), (C ∨), (C ◊), and (C □⁺). That is, we did not use any of the conditions beyond the semantics of *T*. Hence, the original argument is invalid in *T*.

For another example consider:

◊ (p ∨ q) ∴ ◊ p ∨ ◊ q

Is this valid in *T*? Let <M, R> be any modal system. Is there a model set m belonging to M that contains "◊ (p ∨ q)" and "□ ¬ p ∧ □ ¬ q"? No. The following series of steps justifies this answer.

1.	◊ (p ∨ q)	∈ m	supposition about premise
2.	□ ¬ p ∧ □ ¬ q	∈ m	supposition about negation of conclusion in hnf
3.	p ∨ q	∈ m₁	for some m₁ R m, from 1 by (C ◊)
4.	p	∈ m₁	one alternative provided by line 3 by (C ∨)
5.	□ ¬ p	∈ m	line 2 by (C ∧)
6.	¬ p	∈ m₁	line 5 by (C □⁺), since m₁ R m by step 3
7.	q	∈ m₁	the second alternative provided by line 3 by (C ∨)

8. $\square \neg q$ $\in m$ line 2 by (C $\wedge$)
9. $\neg q$ $\in m_1$ line 8 by (C $\square^+$), since m_1 R m by step 3.

On either alternative provided by line 3 we get a contradiction. Thus the suppositions on lines 1 and 2 yield a contradiction. Thus, there is no model set m of any model system such that "$\lozenge$ (p $\vee$ q)" and "$\square \neg$ p $\wedge \square \neg$ q" both belong to m. But "$\square \neg$ p $\wedge \square \neg$ q" is equivalent to the negation of "$\lozenge$ p $\vee \lozenge$ q." So the argument with the premise "$\lozenge$ (p $\vee$ q)" and conclusion "$\lozenge$ p $\vee \lozenge$ q" is valid. Moreover it is valid in T, since we used no rules outside of the semantics of T.

For an example of an $S4$ validity that is not a T validity consider

$\square$ p $\therefore \square\square$ p

The following steps show the $S4$ validity of this argument:

1. $\square$ p $\in m$ supposition about the premise, where <M, R> is a model system and m is a member of M
2. $\lozenge\lozenge \neg$ p $\in m$ supposition about the negation of the conclusion in hnf
3. $\lozenge \neg$ p $\in m_1$ for some m_1 such that m_1 bears R to m, from line 2 by (C $\lozenge$)
4. $\neg$ p $\in m_2$ for some m_2 such that m_2 bears R to m_1, from line 3 by (C $\lozenge$)
5. $\square$ p $\in m_1$ from line 1 and the fact that m_1 bears R to m, by (C $\square^+$)
6. p $\in m_2$ from line 5 and the fact that m_2 bears R to m_1, by (C $\square^+$)

Since line 6 contradicts line 4, it is impossible for "$\square$ p" and "$\lozenge \lozenge \neg$ p" to belong to a model set m belonging to a set of model sets M of a model system <M, R>. Since we only used rules of the semantics for $S4$,

$\square$ p $\therefore \square\square$ p

is $S4$ valid.

For an example of an $S5$ validity that is not a T validity and not a $S4$ validity consider

$\lozenge$ p $\therefore \square \lozenge$ p

Again let m be any model set belonging to a model system <M, R>. The following steps show the $S5$ validity of this argument:

1. $\lozenge$ p $\in m$ supposition about the premise

2. $\Diamond \Box \neg p \in m$ supposition about the negation of the conclusion in hnf

3. $p \in m_1$ for some m_1 which bears R to m, from line 1, (C $\Diamond$)

4. $\Box \neg p \in m_2$ for some m_2 which bears R to m, from line 2, (C $\Diamond$)

5. $\Box \neg p \in m$ from line 4, (C $\Box \Box_+$)

6. $\neg p \in m_1$ lines 5 and 3 (using the fact that in 3 m_1 is said to bear R to m), (C $\Box^+$)

Since line 6 contradicts line 3, it is impossible for "$\Diamond$ p" and "$\Diamond \Box \neg$ p" (which is equivalent to the negation of the conclusion) to belong to a model set m belonging to a set of model sets M of a model system <M, R>. Since we used rules of the semantics for S5,

$\Diamond p \therefore \Box \Diamond p$

is *S5* valid.

Exercise 4.5 *T* is the weakest system of modal logic that we have formulated in *SML*. For each of the following arguments, determine whether it is valid in *T*:

1. $\Diamond p \vee \Diamond q \therefore \Diamond (p \vee q)$
2. $\Box p \vee \Box q \therefore \Box (p \vee q)$
3. $\Diamond (p \supset q) \therefore \Diamond p \supset \Diamond q$
4. $\Box (p \wedge q) \therefore \Box p \wedge \Box q$
5. $\Box p \wedge \Box q \therefore \Box (p \wedge q)$
6. $\Diamond (p \wedge q) \therefore \Diamond p \wedge \Diamond q$
7. $\Diamond p \wedge \Diamond q \therefore \Diamond (p \wedge q)$
8. $\Box (p \vee q) \therefore \Diamond p \vee \Box q$
9. $\Diamond p \vee \Box q \therefore \Box (p \vee q)$
10. $\Box p \supset \Box q \therefore \Box (p \supset q)$
11. $\Box p \equiv \Box q \therefore \Diamond p \equiv \Diamond q$
12. $\Box p \equiv \Box q \therefore \Box (p \equiv q)$
13. $\Box (p \supset q) \therefore \Diamond p \supset \Diamond q$
14. $p \therefore \Box \Diamond p$
15. $\Box \Diamond p \therefore p$

Deontic Logic and Model Sets

We follow Hintikka's paper "Deontic Logic and Its Philosophical Morals" in presenting a semantical treatment of deontic logic (Hintikka 1969d, pp. 184–214).

We now introduce a language *SDL*—a language for *sentential deontic logic*. Syntactically, this is the language that results from the language *SL* for sentential logic by adding the two unary connectives "O" and "P" (for obligations and permissibility), and the three binary operators "∨," "≡," and "⊃" (for disjunctions, biconditionals, and conditionals).

Definition 4.2   Every *SL* sentence is a *SDL* sentence.

If ϕ is an *SDL* sentence, so are $\neg \phi$, O ϕ, and P ϕ.

If ϕ and ψ are *SDL* sentences, so are $(\phi \wedge \psi)$ $(\phi \vee \psi)$, $(\phi \supset \psi)$, and $(\phi \equiv \psi)$.

We continue to omit the outermost parentheses of a sentence, where this omission will create no confusion.

The logic of O and P is similar to the logic of □ and ◊ as set forth in system *T*, with O replacing □ and P replacing ◊. But there are differences.

In system *T* we had as valid rules ◊I

$$\phi \rightarrow \Diamond \phi$$

and □E

$$\Box \phi \rightarrow \phi$$

Whatever is true is possible, and whatever is necessary is true. However, it is **not** true that whatever is true is permissible; and it is **not** true that whatever is obligatory is true.

The system of deontic logic with which we shall operate works like *T*, putting P for ◊ and O for □, and less ◊I and □I.

We shall develop this logic semantically via model sets and model systems.

First, to the conditions defining Hintikka normal form we add:

$$\neg P \phi \Leftrightarrow O \neg \phi$$
$$\neg O \phi \Leftrightarrow P \neg \phi$$

Second, to conditions $(C \neg), (C \vee), (C \wedge)$, we add (where "m" and "m_1" stand for a model sets and "R" stands for deontic alternativeness):

If O φ ∈ m and m₁ R m, then φ ∈ m₁. (C O*)

If O φ ∈ m, and m₁ bears R to some model set belonging to M, then φ ∈ m₁. (C O)rest

If P φ ∈ m, then, for at least one m₁ which bears R to m, φ ∈ m₁. (C P*)

If O φ ∈ m, then, for at least one m₁ which bears R to m, φ ∈ m₁. (C o*)

A model system is a set of model sets together with a relation R (called the alternativeness relation) which jointly satisfy the above conditions.

A finite set of sentences is semantically consistent just in case it is included in a model set of a model system. As usual, an argument

$$\phi_1, \ldots, \phi_n \therefore \psi$$

is valid just in case {φ₁, ..., φₙ, ¬ψ} is semantically consistent. A sentence is a logical truth just in case its negation in hnf belongs to no model set of any model system.

Let us call the world partially described by model set m, W. Then according to (C P*) it is permissible that φ only if φ is true at some deontic alternative to W. A deontic alternative to W is a world W₁ at which all the obligations (duties, norms) of W are satisfied. Relative to W, W₁ is a heaven or a deontically perfect world. (C O*) spells out the idea that a deontic alternative or a heaven relative to W is a world in which all norms in W are satisfied. (C O)rest says that a heaven is a world in which *all* obligations are satisfied, not just the obligations in W. (C o*) insures that for every norm in W, there is a heaven relative to W in which that norm is satisfied. Condition (C O*) would be satisfied vacuously if W had no heavens relative to it.

As a first example, consider the following plausible-looking principle:

> If we are obliged to do A, then if our doing of A implies our obligation to do B, then we ought to do B.

Setting this in the form of an argument, we have:

O p, p ⊃ O q ∴ O q

Setting the premises and the negation of the conclusion into hnf, we have:

1. O p
2. ¬ p ∨ O q
3. P ¬ q

Now we shall assume these three sentences belong to a model set belonging to a set of sets of a model system, and then see if that assumption can be consistently carried out.

1. O p	∈ m	assumption about the first premise
2. ¬ p ∨ O q	∈ m	assumption about the second premise
3. P ¬ q	∈ m	assumption about the negation of the conclusion
4. ¬ p	∈ m	from 2 using (C ∨)
5. ¬ q	∈ m₁	for some m, which bears R to m from 3 using (C P*)
6. p	∈ m₁	from 1 using (C O*)

None of the conditions for model set construction are violated. Thus, the argument is not valid. The invalidity is shown by the model system consisting of the following two model sets:

{O p, ¬ p ∨ O q, P ¬ q, ¬ p}
{p, ¬ q}

of which the latter is assumed to be a heaven relative to the former; that is, the latter bears R to the former.

As a second example, consider

O ((O p ∧ (p ⊃ O q)) ⊃ O q)

Is this a logical truth of *SDL*? Let us negate it and put its negation in hnf:

P ((O p ∧ (¬ p ∨ O q)) ∧ P ¬ q)

Now let us apply a model set analysis to this sentence:

1. P ((O p ∧ (¬ p ∨ O q)) ∧ P ¬ q)	∈ m	assumption
2. (O p ∧ (¬ p ∨ O q)) ∧ P ¬ q	∈ m₁	for some m, which from 1 using (C P*) bears R to m
3. O p ∧ (¬ p ∨ O q)	∈ m₁	from 2 using (C ∧)
4. P ¬ q	∈ m₁	from 2 using (C ∧)
5. O p	∈ m₁	from 3 using (C ∧)
6. ¬ p ∨ O q	∈ m₁	from 3 using (C ∧)
7. p	∈ m₁	from 5 using (C O)rest
8. ¬ p	∈ m₁	from 6 using (C ∨)

This violates (C ¬). So we need to pursue the second alternative provided by step 6:

9.	O q	∈ m₁	from 6 using (C ∨)	
10.	¬ q	∈ m₂	for some m₂ which bears R to m₁	from 4 using (C P*)
11.	q	∈ m₂	from 9 using (C O*)	

Since each alternative provided by step 6 violates (C ¬), we conclude that the sentence

O ((O p ∧ (p ⊃ O q)) ⊃ O q)

is a logical truth.

As a final example, consider the principle:

> If the doing of A and B jointly require the doing of C, then, if we do A and we are obliged to do B, we ought to do C.

Putting this in the form of an argument, we get:

(p ∧ q) ⊃ r, p, O q ∴ O r

Is this argument valid?

To answer this question we go through the following three stages: First, put the premises and the negation of the conclusion in hnf. Second, assume each of these belongs to a model set of a model system. Third, see if the model set can be constructed without violating (C ¬).

1. (¬ p ∨ ¬ q) ∨ r	∈ m	assumption
2. p	∈ m	assumption
3. O q	∈ m	assumption
4. P ¬ r	∈ m	assumption

1–4 complete the first two stages outlined above. The third stage is implemented below by 5–7.

5. r	∈ m	from 2 using (C ∨)	
6. ¬ r	∈ m₁	for some m₁ which bears R to m	from 4 using (C P*)
7. q	∈ m₁	from 3 using (C O*)	

No further steps are forced and (C ¬) is not violated. Thus, the argument is invalid.

Exercise 4.6 Which of the following sentences are logical truths? Use the model set method to justify your answer.

1. O O p ⊃ O p
2. O p ⊃ O O p
3. P P p ⊃ P p
4. P p ⊃ P P p
5. O P p ⊃ O p
6. O p ⊃ O P p
7. P O p ⊃ O p
8. O p ⊃ P O p
9. O p ∨ O ¬ p
10. P p ∨ P ¬ p
11. O (p ∨ ¬ p)
12. P (p ∨ ¬ p)
13. ¬ P (p ∧ ¬ p)

Exercise 4.7 Use the model set method to determine the validity of each of the following arguments:

1. O (p ∧ q) ∴ O p ∧ O q
2. O p, O q ∴ O (p ∧ q)
3. P (p ∧ q) ∴ P p ∧ P q
4. P p, P q ∴ P (p ∧ q)
5. O (p ∨ q), ¬ O p ∴ O q
6. O p ∨ O q ∴ O (p ∨ q)
7. P (p ∨ q), ¬ P p ∴ P q
8. P p ∨ P q ∴ P (p ∨ q)
9. O (p ⊃ q), O p ∴ O q
10. (O p ⊃ O q) ∴ O (p ⊃ q)
11. P (p ⊃ q), P p ∴ P q
12. (P p ⊃ P q) ∴ P (p ⊃ q)
13. O p ∴ P p

Quantification and Modality

If we lump the rules for deduction of quantifier logic to modal logic, we get a system of quantified modal logic. If the modal system is *S5*, then we get quantified *S5*, "*QS5*" for short. The system of derivations for quantified modal logic that is *QS5* results from adding the rules ES, EG, US, and UG to the derivation system for *S5*. The semantics for the system of derivations for quantified modal logic that is *QS5* results from adding the rules (C u), (C ∀), and (C ∃) to the semantics of *S5*. The rules (C u), (C ∀), and (C ∃) are given below.

A *QS5 derivation* is any finite sequence of lines each satisfying one of the following conditions (the letters "φ" and "ψ" are variables of the metalanguage that stand for well-formed formulas [wffs] of the object language; the letters "A" and "B" stand for sets of sentences of the object language; "φ β/α" stands for the result of replacing each occurrence of α in φ by β):

P   For every φ, <{φ}, φ> is a derivation.

Simp If S is a derivation and <A, (φ ∧ ψ)> occurs in S, then S, <A, φ> and S, <A, ψ> also are derivations.

Conj If S is a derivation and both <A, φ> and <B, ψ> occur in S, then S, <A ∪ B, (φ ∧ ψ)> also is a derivation.

Add   If S is a derivation and either <A, φ> or <A, ψ> occurs in S, then S, <A, (φ ∨ ψ)> also is a derivation.

DS If S is a derivation and <A, ¬ ψ> and either <B, (φ ∨ ψ)> or <B, (ψ ∨ φ) occurs in S, then S, <A ∪ B, φ> also is a derivation.

DM If S is a derivation and <A, ¬ (φ ∨ ψ)> occurs in S, then S, <A, (¬ φ ∧ ¬ ψ)> is also a derivation; and if S is a derivation and <A, ¬ (φ ∧ ψ)> occurs in S, then S, <A, (¬ φ ∨ ¬ ψ)> is also a derivation.

MP If S is a derivation and both <A, φ> and <B, (φ ⊃ ψ)> occur in S, then S, <A ∪ B, ψ> also is a derivation.

MI If S is a derivation and <A, (φ ∨ ψ)> occurs in S, then S, <A, (¬ φ ⊃ ψ)> is also a derivation.

C If S is a derivation and <A ∪ {φ}, ψ> occurs in S, then S, <A, (φ ⊃ ψ)> also is a derivation.

RAA If S is a derivation and <A ∪ {φ}, (ψ ∧ ¬ ψ)> occurs in S, then S, <A, ¬ φ> also is a derivation.

DN If S is a derivation and <A, ¬ ¬ φ> occurs in S, then S, <A, φ> also is a derivation.

Biconditional Elimination (BE)

$$\phi \equiv \psi \rightarrow \phi \supset \psi$$
$$\phi \equiv \psi \rightarrow \psi \supset \phi$$

Biconditional Introduction (BI)

$$(\phi \supset \psi) \wedge (\psi \supset \phi) \rightarrow \phi \equiv \psi$$

Dilemma (DI)

$$\phi \vee \psi, \phi \supset \chi, \psi \supset \chi \rightarrow \chi$$

EG If S is a derivation and <A, φ> occurs in S, then, S, <A, ∃α ψ> is also a derivation if ψ results from replacing one or more occurrences of constant β in φ by variable α not in φ.

ES If S is a derivation and <B, ψ>, <A, ∃α φ>, and <{φ β/α}, φ β/α > occur in S, then S, <(A ∪ B) ~ {φ β/α}, ψ> is also a derivation if the constant β occurs neither in φ nor in ψ nor in any sentence in A or B.

UG If S is a derivation and <A, φ β/α> occurs in S and constant β occurs in no sentence in A, then S, <A, ∀α φ> is also a derivation.

US If S is a derivation and <A, ∀α φ> occurs in S, then S, <A, φ β/α> is also a derivation.

D If S is a derivation and <A, □ φ> occurs in S, S, <A, ¬ ◊ ¬ φ> is also a derivation.
  If S is a derivation and <A, ¬ ◊ ¬ φ> occurs in S, S, <A, □ φ> is also a derivation.
  If S is a derivation and <A, ◊ φ> occurs in S, S, <A, ¬ □¬ φ> is also a derivation.

If S is a derivation and <A, ¬ □ ¬ φ> occurs in S, S, <A, ◊ φ> is also a derivation.

ND   If S is a derivation and <A, □ (φ ⊃ ψ)> occurs in S, then S, <A, (□ φ ⊃ □ ψ)> is also a derivation.

◊I   If S is a derivation and <A, φ> occurs in S, then S, <A, ◊ φ> is also a derivation.

□I   If S is a derivation and <∅, φ> occurs in S, then S, <∅, □ φ>is also a derivation.

□E   If S is a derivation and <A, □ φ> occurs in S, then S, <A, φ> is also a derivation.

□□   If S is a derivation and <A, □ φ> occurs in S, then S, <A, □ □ φ> is also a derivation.

□◊   If S is a derivation and <A, ◊ φ> occurs in S, then S, <A, □ ◊ φ> is also a derivation.

Some Derivations

Following is a derivation in *QS5*:

T1   ∃x □ Fx ⊢ □ ∃x Fx

Proof

{1}	(1)	∃x □ Fx	P
{2}	(2)	□ Fa	P
∅	(3)	Fa ⊃ ∃x Fx	QL
∅	(4)	□ (Fa ⊃ ∃x Fx)	3 □ I
∅	(5)	□ Fa ⊃ □ ∃x Fx	4 ND
{2}	(6)	□ ∃x Fx	2, 5 MP
{1}	(7)	□ ∃x Fx	6 ES

In some cases it is convenient to shorten derivations by justifying some lines by previously proven results or by observing that a line can be justified by sentential logic or by quantificational logic. Such is the case in the proof above (line 3) and in the proofs below.

T2   □ ∀x Fx ⊢ ∀x □ Fx

Proof

{1}	(1)	□ ∀x Fx	P
∅	(2)	∀x Fx ⊃ Fa	QL
∅	(3)	□ (∀x Fx ⊃ Fa)	2 □ I

∅	(4)	□ ∀x Fx ⊃ □ Fa	3 ND
{1}	(5)	□ Fa	1, 4 MP
{1}	(6)	∀x □ Fx	5 UG

T3   ∀x □ Fx ⊢ □ ∀x Fx

Proof

∅	(1)	∀x □ Fx ⊃ □ Fa	QL
∅	(2)	◊ ∀x □ Fx ⊃ ◊ □ Fa	1, using 12 of exercise 4.2
∅	(3)	◊ □ Fa ⊃ Fa	using exercise 4.4
∅	(4)	◊ ∀x □ Fx ⊃ Fa	2, 3 SL
∅	(5)	◊ ∀x □ Fx ⊃ ∀x Fx	4 QL
∅	(6)	∀x □ Fx ⊃ □ ∀x Fx	5 using exercise 4.3

Exercise 5.1   Prove the following:

1. □ ∀x (Fx ⊃ Gx) ⊢ □ (∀x Fx ⊃ ∀y Gy)
2. ⊢ □ (◊ ∃x Fx ⊃ ∃y ◊ Fy)
3. ⊢ □ (∃y ◊ Fy ⊃ ◊ ∃x Fx)
4. ◊ ∀x Fx ⊢ ∀x ◊ Fx

Model Sets and Systems

As in Chapters 2, 3, and 5 our semantics will proceed by model set construction. In Chapter 5 this was extended to model system construction. Model sets and systems give a method for testing sentences and sets of sentences for consistency and hence, indirectly, a method for testing arguments for validity. A model set is a set of sentences meeting certain conditions that insure that the set is consistent. We follow Hintikka's ideas put forth in Hintikka 1969b.

As before we say a well-formed formula is in Hintikka normal form (hnf) if and only if the only truth-functional connectives it contains are "¬," "∧," and "∨," and "¬" is applied only to atomic well-formed formulas.

Every well-formed formula is equivalent to a well-formed formula in hnf. For any given well-formed formula φ, an equivalent well-formed formula in hnf can be found by repeatedly replacing one well-formed part by its equivalent in the following list of equivalencies:

a.   ¬ (φ ⊃ ψ) ⇔ (φ ∧ ¬ ψ)
b.   (φ ⊃ ψ) ⇔ (¬ φ ∨ ψ)

c. $\neg(\phi \equiv \psi) \Leftrightarrow (\phi \wedge \neg \psi) \vee (\neg \phi \wedge \psi)$
d. $(\phi \equiv \psi) \Leftrightarrow (\phi \wedge \psi) \vee (\neg \phi \wedge \neg \psi)$
e. $\neg(\phi \wedge \psi) \Leftrightarrow \neg \phi \vee \neg \psi$
f. $\neg(\phi \vee \psi) \Leftrightarrow \neg \phi \wedge \neg \psi$
g. $\neg \exists \alpha \phi \Leftrightarrow \forall \alpha \neg \phi$
h. $\neg \forall \alpha \phi \Leftrightarrow \exists \alpha \neg \phi$
i. $\neg \Box \phi \Leftrightarrow \Diamond \neg \phi$
j. $\neg \Diamond \phi \Leftrightarrow \Box \neg \phi$

Conditions (a) through (d) eliminate $\supset$ and $\equiv$. The other conditions allow us to move $\neg$ inside until it has smallest scope. Double negations are eliminated as they occur.

A model set is a set of sentences in hnf that satisfies the conditions listed below. A modal system is a set M of model sets, with an equivalence relation, R, of alternativeness defined on M. That is, R is a reflexive, symmetric, and transitive relative defined on M.

1. If $\phi \in$ m, then it is not the case that $\neg \phi \in$ m. (C $\neg$)
2. If $(\phi \wedge \psi) \in$ m, then $\phi \in$ m and $\psi \in$ m. (C $\wedge$)
3. If $(\phi \vee \psi) \in$ m, then $\phi \in$ m or $\psi \in$ m. (C $\vee$)
4. If $\exists \alpha \phi \in$ m, then $\phi \, \beta/\alpha \in$ m, for at least one constant β. (C $\exists$)
5. If $\forall \alpha \phi \in$ m, then $\phi \, \beta/\alpha \in$ m, for any constant β that occurs in any formula in m. (C $\forall$)
6. If $\forall \alpha \phi \in$ m, then $\phi \, \beta/\alpha \in$ m, for at least one constant β. (C u)
7. If $\Box \phi \in$ m, then $\phi \in$ m. (C $\Box$)
8. If $\Diamond \phi \in$ m, then there is at least one model set m_1 that is an alternative to m such that $\phi \in m_1$. (C $\Diamond$)
9. If $\Box \phi \in$ m and if model set m_1 is an alternative to m, then $\phi \in m_1$. (C $\Box^+$)

The definitions of semantical notions of consistency and validity are as usual:

1. A sentence ϕ in hnf is consistent if and only if there is a model set m such that $\phi \in$ m.
2. A sentence that is not in hnf is consistent if and only if its hnf is consistent.
3. A sentence ϕ is valid if and only if $\neg \phi$ is not consistent.
4. A finite set is consistent if and only if the set consisting of the hnf of each of its members is included in a model set.
5. An argument, $\phi_1, \ldots, \phi_n \therefore \psi$, is valid if and only if $\{\phi_1, \ldots, \phi_n, \neg \psi\}$ is not consistent. (That is, there is no model set that contains all of the premises and the negation of the conclusion.)

A finite set is consistent if and only if the set consisting of the hnf of each of its members is embeddable in a model set belonging to some model system. To test a finite set to see if it is consistent, list the hnf of the members of the set, and then attempt to add sentences to the list to satisfy the conditions on model sets. If you can do this, so that every condition is satisfied for every sentence we list, then we have a model set, and the original set of sentences is consistent. If every attempt to add sentences to satisfy the other conditions is blocked, the set is inconsistent.

To test an argument for validity, take the hnf of the premises and the negation of the conclusion and attempt to construct a model set. If you succeed, it is not valid. If you must fail, then the argument is valid. Exhibiting a model set that contains the premises and the negation of the conclusion shows that the argument is not valid. Thus, we have a method of disproof.

Consider

T1 (in argument form) $\exists x \,\Box\, Fx \therefore \Box\, \exists x\, Fx$

Here is a proof of the validity of this argument. We suppose a model system M and a model set m such that m ∈ M and such that the hnf of the premise and the hnf of the conclusion belong to m:

1.	$\exists x \,\Box\, Fx$	∈ m	supposition about the premise of T1
2.	$\Diamond\, \forall x \,\neg\, Fx$	∈ m	supposition about the negation of the conclusion of T1 in hnf
3.	$\Box\, Fa$	∈ m	from 1 by (C ∃)
4.	$\forall x \,\neg\, Fx$	∈ m$_1$	for some m$_1$ alternative to m, from 2 by (C ◊)
5.	Fa	∈ m$_1$	from 3 by (C □*)
6.	$\neg\, Fa$	∈ m$_1$	from 4 by (C∀)

Since 1 and 2 cannot be embedded in a model set of any model system, T1 is valid.

The fact that **T1** is valid raises doubts about QS5. For consider what T1 says.

T1 $\exists x \,\Box\, Fx \models \Box\, \exists x\, Fx$

The premise says that there is something in the actual world that is necessarily F. (If F is read as round, say, a wheel might plausibly be said to verify this.)

Are we to conclude, then, that in every possible world there are round things? A tacit assumption of *QS5* is if an object necessarily has a property, then it has that property in every possible world, which implies that the object exists in every possible world. Only if this is assumed does the validity of Barcan type formulas such as **T1** make any sense.

The assumption of *QS5* is actually stronger than this. For consider

T3   ∀x □ Fx ⊢ □ ∀x Fx

Intuitively, ∀x □ Fx says that everything in a given circumstance is necessarily F; and □ ∀x Fx says in every possible circumstance everything is F. The presupposition is that every possible circumstance involves the same individuals. To accommodate this presupposition C ∀ needs to be strengthened to C ∀*:

> If ∀α φ ∈ m, then φ β/α ∈ m, for any constant β that occurs in any formula in any model set in the model system to which m belongs. (C ∀*)

Without strengthening C ∀ to C ∀* T3 turns out to be invalid. That is, without this strengthening *QS5* is unsound.

Exercise 5.2   Determine the validity of the following arguments in *QS5* (use C ∀* rather than C ∀):

  1. ∃x ◊ Fx ∴ ◊ ∃x Fx
  2. □ ∃x Fx ∴ ∃x □ Fx
  3. ◊ ∀x Fx ∴ ∀x ◊ Fx
  4. ∀x ◊ Fx ∴ ◊ ∀x Fx

Exercise 5.3   Show the invalidity of the following arguments in *QS5* (use C ∀* rather than C ∀):

  1. □ ∃x (Fx ∧ Gx) ∴ ∃x (Fx ∧ □ Gx)
  2. ∃x (Fx ∧ □ Gx) ∴ □ ∃x (Fx ∧ Gx)
  3. ◊ ∃x (Fx ∧ Gx) ∴ ∃x (Fx ∧ ◊ Gx)
  4. ∃x (Fx ∧ ◊ Gx) ∴ ◊ ∃x (Fx ∧ Gx)
  5. □ ∀x (Fx ⊃ Gx) ∴ ∀x (Fx ⊃ □ Gx)
  6. ∀x (Fx ⊃ □ Gx) ∴ □ ∀x (Fx ⊃ Gx)
  7. ◊ ∀x (Fx ⊃ Gx) ∴ ∀x (Fx ⊃ ◊ Gx)
  8. ∀x (Fx ⊃ ◊ Gx) ∴ ◊ ∀x (Fx ⊃ Gx)

An Alternative

In this final section of the text we survey one alternative treatment of necessity and quantification, in particular, with respect to the validity of Barcan type formulas. We shall confine our attention to changes in the conditions required for model sets.

Let us take another look at

T1 $\quad \exists x \,\square\, Fx \vdash \square\, \exists x\, Fx$

which we found to be problematic. Let us also take a look at the steps that led us to conclude that it is valid.

We suppose a model system M and a model set m such that m ∈ M and such that the hnf of the premise and the hnf of the conclusion belong to m:

1.	$\exists x \,\square\, Fx$	∈ m	supposition about the premise of T1
2.	$\Diamond \,\forall x \,\neg\, Fx$	∈ m	supposition about the negation of the conclusion of T1 in hnf
3.	$\square\, Fa$	∈ m	from 1 by (C ∃)
4.	$\forall x \,\neg\, Fx$	∈ m₁	for some m₁ alternative to m, from 2 by (C ◊)
5.	Fa	∈ m₁	from 3 by (C □⁺)
6.	$\neg\, Fa$	∈ m₁	from 4 by (C ∀)

Since 1 and 2 cannot be embedded in a model set of any model system, we concluded that T1 is valid. We observed that underlying this proof was the assumption that whatever necessarily possesses a property in one possible state of affairs exists in all alternative states of affairs. This assumption has to be given up.

The presence of a constant (e.g., "a" above) in a model set m is the formal counterpart to the existence of its bearer in the state of affairs described by m. Thus, if we are to give up our assumption (that if an object necessarily has a property, then it has that property in every possible world, which implies that the object exists in every possible world), then when a sentence ϕ is shifted from a model set to one of its alternatives m_1 we have to pay attention to the constants ϕ contains. In our argument above let us interpret "F" as "is round"; let m be an actual state of affairs; and let the value of "a" be an actual wheel. We went from step 3, which says it is necessary this actual wheel is round, to step 5, which says that this actual wheel is round in m_1. How do we know the actual wheel exists in m_1?

A way out of this entanglement is to change (C □⁺), which allows us to go from 3 to 5, as follows:

> If □ φ ∈ m, and if m₁ is an alternative to m, and if each constant in φ occurs in at least one other sentence in m₁, then φ ∈ m₁. (C □*)

Using (C □*), instead of (C □⁺), the steps from 3 to 5 is blocked. In fact, we can now see that

∃x □ Fx ∴ □ ∃x Fx

is invalid. Here is the proof:

1.	∃x □ Fx	∈ m	supposition about the premise of T1
2.	◊ ∀x ¬ Fx	∈ m	supposition about the negation of the conclusion of T1 in hnf
3.	□ Fa	∈ m	from 1 by (C ∃)
4.	∀x ¬ Fx	∈ m₁	for some m₁ alternative to m, from 2 by (C ◊)
5.	¬ Fb	∈ m₁	from 4 by (C u)

we have, by means of these steps, constructed a counterexample to

∃x □ Fx ∴ □ ∃x Fx

Let M consist of m and m₁, where m₁ is an alternative to m:

m = {∃x □ Fx ∧ ◊ ∀x ¬ Fx, ∃x □ Fx, ◊ ∀x ¬ Fx, □ Fa, Fa}

and

m₁ = {∀x ¬ Fx, ¬ Fb}.

It would not be coherent to retain C ∀* in the same system which contains C □*. For C ∀* formulates the assumption that all possible states of affairs contain the same individuals; and C □* goes against this assumption. When we use C □* we have to use C ∀.

So we have two systems. The first, using C □⁺ and C ∀*, assumes that all possible states of affairs involve the same individuals. The second, using C □* and C ∀, does not assume this.

Exercise 5.4 Determine the validity of

∀x □ Fx ∴ □ ∀x Fx

and

□ ∀x Fx ∴ ∀x □ Fx

in the new system (i.e., the system in which C □* and C ∀ replaces C □⁺ and C ∀*, respectively).

Exercise 5.5 Use the new system to determine the validity of the following arguments:

1. ∃x (Fx ∧ Gx), □ ∀x (Gx ⊃ □ Hx) ∴ ∃x (Fx ∧ □ Hx)
2. □ ∀x (Fx ⊃ Gx), □ ∀x (Gx ⊃ Hx) ∴ □ ∀x (¬ Hx ⊃ ¬ Fx)
3. □ ∃x (Fx ∧ Gax), □ ∀x ∀y (◊ Gxy ⊃ □ Gyx) ∴ ∃x (Fx ∧ Gxa)
4. □ ∀x (Fx ⊃ Gx), ∃x ◊ (Fx ∧ Hx) ∴ ∃x ◊ (Gx ∧ Hx)
5. □ ∀x (Fx ⊃ ◊ Gx), □ □ ∀x (Gx ⊃ □ Hx) ∴ ∃x Fx ⊃ ∃x □ Hx

Set Theory

In this chapter we illustrate how one can construct first-order theories, using the resources of the Chapters 2 and 3. We shall propound just enough set theory to prove an important theorem about the power set of a set. The first-order language in which we express our theses about sets utilizes the following symbols: (1) connectives ∨ (*or*), ∧ (*and*), ⊃ (*only if*), ≡ (*if and only if*), ¬ (*it is not the case that*); (2) variables: x, y, . . .; (3) constants a, b, . . .; quantifiers ∀x, ∀y, . . . (*for all*), ∃x, ∃y, . . . (*for some*), ∃!x, ∃!y, . . . (*for exactly one*); (4) the sign for identity = (*is identical with*); (5) predicates: S (*is a set*), ∈ (*is a member of*).

As inference rules for formal derivations we take those of Chapters 2 and 3. With respect to pure set constructions we use "formula" to denote just those formulas whose only non-logical symbols are the names and predicates indicated above together with such symbols as are defined in terms of them.

We start with a definitional schema for the *uniqueness quantifier*:

D1. $\exists! \alpha \; \phi \equiv \exists \alpha \; (\phi \wedge \forall \omega \; (\phi \; \omega/\alpha \supset \omega = \alpha))$.

Definitions for the *subset* and *proper subset* predicates are:

D2. $x \subseteq y \equiv Sx \wedge Sy \wedge \forall z \; (z \in x \supset z \in y)$,
D3. $x \subset y \equiv Sx \wedge Sy \wedge x \subseteq y \wedge x \neq y$.

The members of a set are to be sharply distinguished from the subsets of a set. Subsets are *sets* of *members* of a set, and thus are always themselves sets. The *members* of a set, on the other hand, need not be sets at all.

The Axiom of Extensionality

Our theses about sets correspond to certain axioms or theorems of Zermello-Fraenkel set theory (ZF). The *axiom of extensionality* settles identity for sets.

A1. $\forall x \; \forall y \; (((Sx \wedge Sy) \wedge \forall z \; (z \in x \equiv z \in y)) \supset x = y)$

That is, sets with the same members are the same set. Thus, in particular, from the fact that a pair of set names are formed with distinct formulas it does *not* follow that those set names denote distinct sets.

Axioms of Separation

The *axioms of separation* are all sentences that are instances of the schema

A2. $\forall \alpha \; (S\alpha \supset \exists \beta \; (S\beta \wedge \forall \omega \; (\omega \in \beta \equiv (\omega \in \alpha \wedge \phi))))$

resulting from placing "α," "β," and "ω" by variables and "ϕ" by a formula in which the variable replacing "β" has no free occurrences.

The general idea of this axiom is that for each set x and formula ϕ, ϕ determines a subset of y of x. Thus, for example, relative to the set of humans, the formula "x is female" determines that subset of the set of humans membering all and only female humans. Relative to the set of mammals the same formula determines the subset membering all and only female mammals.

It would be natural at this point to suggest simplifying A2 to

A2*. $\exists \beta \, (S\beta \wedge \forall \omega \, (\omega \in \beta \equiv \phi))$

thereby capturing the idea that each formula free in at most one variable determines a set, not from some set, but simply from whatever there is. But, as Russell showed, this idea is incorrect. For note the following simple derivation, where "z∉z" replaces "ϕ."

{1}	(1)	$\exists x \, (Sx \wedge \forall z \, (z \in x \equiv z \notin z))$	P
{2}	(2)	$(Sa \wedge \forall z \, (z \in a \equiv z \notin z)$	P^{ES}
{2}	(3)	$\forall z \, (z \in a \equiv z \notin z)$	2, sentential logic
{2}	(4)	$a \in a \equiv a \notin a$	3, US
{2}	(5)	$p \wedge \neg p$	4, sentential logic
{1}	(6)	$p \wedge \neg p$	1, 2, 5, ES
Ø	(7)	$\exists x \, (Sx \wedge \forall z \, (z \in x \equiv z \notin z)) \supset (p \wedge \neg p)$	1, 6, C
Ø	(8)	$\neg \, \exists x \, (Sx \wedge \forall z \, (z \in x \equiv z \notin z))$	7 sentential logic

Thus, since the negation of one of the A2* instances is logically false, A2* is not an acceptable axiom schema.

Pairing Axiom and Rule U

A1 and the A2 axioms all are vacuously true if there are no sets. The first set-existential axiom is the *pairing axiom*.

A3. $\forall x \, \forall y \, \exists z \, (Sz \wedge \forall w \, (w \in z \equiv (w = x \vee w = y)))$.

An immediate consequence of A3 is:

T1. $\exists x \, Sx.$

Exercise 6.1   Derive T1 from A3.
From A1 and A3:

T2. $\forall x \, \forall y \, \exists ! z \, (Sz \wedge \forall w \, (w \in z \equiv (w \in x \vee w \in y)))$.

It will be useful to observe the general form of a derivation establishing uniqueness by use of A1.

$$\vdots$$

Δ	(n)	$\exists\alpha\ (S\alpha \wedge \forall\omega\ (\omega \in \alpha \equiv \phi))$	given
$\{n+1\}$	(n + 1)	$S\beta \wedge \forall\omega\ (\omega \in \beta \equiv \phi)$	$P^{ES}\beta$
$\{n+2\}$	(n + 2)	$S\beta' \wedge \forall\omega\ (\omega \in \beta' \equiv \phi)$	P
$\{n+1\}$	(n + 3)	$\forall\omega\ (\omega \in \beta \equiv \phi)$	n + 1 sentential logic
$\{n+2\}$	(n + 4)	$\forall\omega\ (\omega \in \beta' \equiv \phi)$	n + 2 sentential logic
$\{n+1\}$	(n + 5)	$\beta'' \in \beta \equiv \phi$	n + 3 US
$\{n+2\}$	(n + 6)	$\beta'' \in \beta' \equiv \phi$	n + 4 US
$\{n+1, n+2\}$	(n + 7)	$\beta'' \in \beta \equiv \beta'' \in \beta'$	n + 5, n + 6 sentential logic
$\{n+1, n+2\}$	(n + 8)	$\forall\omega\ (\omega \in \beta \equiv \omega \in \beta')$	n + 7 US
$\{A1\}$	(n + 9)	$\forall\alpha\ \forall\alpha'\ ((S\alpha \wedge S\alpha') \supset (\alpha = \alpha' \equiv \forall\omega\ (\omega \in \alpha \equiv \omega \in \alpha')))$	A1
$\{A1\}$	(n + 10)	$(S\beta \wedge S\beta') \supset (\beta = \beta' \equiv\forall\omega\ (\omega \in \beta \equiv \omega \in \beta'))$	n + 9 US
$\{n+1, n+2, A1\}$	(n + 11)	$\beta = \beta'$	n + 1, n + 2, n + 8, n + 10 sentential logic
$\{n+1, A1\}$	(n + 12)	$(S\beta' \wedge \forall\omega\ (\omega' \in \beta' \equiv \phi)) \supset \beta = \beta'$	n + 2, n + 11 C
$\{n+1, A1\}$	(n + 13)	$\forall\alpha'\ (S\alpha' \wedge \forall\omega\ (\omega' \in \alpha' \equiv \phi)) \supset \beta = \alpha'$	n + 12 UG
$\{n+1, A1\}$	(n + 14)	$(S\beta \wedge \forall\omega\ (\omega \in \beta \equiv \phi)) \wedge (\forall\alpha'\ (S\alpha' \wedge \forall\omega\ (\omega' \in \alpha' \equiv \phi)) \supset \beta = \alpha')$	n + 1, n + 13 sentential logic
$\{n+1, A1\}$	(n + 15)	$\exists\alpha\ (S\beta \wedge \forall\omega\ (\omega \in \beta \equiv \phi)) \wedge \forall\alpha'\ ((S\alpha' \wedge \forall\omega\ (\omega' \in \alpha' \equiv \phi)) \supset \beta = \alpha')$	n + 14 EG
$\{A1\} \cup \Delta$	(n + 16)	$\exists\alpha\ (S\beta \wedge \forall\omega\ (\omega \in \beta \equiv \phi)) \wedge \forall\alpha'\ ((S\alpha' \wedge \forall\omega\ (\omega' \in \alpha' \equiv \phi)) \supset \beta = \alpha')$	n, n + 15, ES
$\{A1\} \cup \Delta$	(n + 16)	$\exists!\alpha\ (S\beta \wedge \forall\omega\ (\omega \in \beta \equiv \phi))$	n + 15 D1

$$\vdots$$

On the basis of this derivation form we assert a derived rule of inference.

U ∃!α (Sα ∧ ∀ω (ω ∈ α ≡ φ)) may be entered on a line if ∃α (Sα ∧ ∀ω (ω ∈ α ≡ φ)) appears on an earlier line and α has no free occurrences in φ; as premise members of the new line take all those of that earlier line plus A1.

Using U, the derivation of T2 and A3 is as follows:

{A3}	(1)	∀x ∀y ∃z (Sz ∧ ∀w (w ∈ z ≡ (w = x ∨ w = y)))	
{A3}	(2)	∃z (Sz ∧ ∀w (w ∈ z ≡ (w = a ∨ w = b))	1 US
{A3, A1}	(3)	∃!z (Sz ∧ ∀w (w ∈ z ≡ (w = a ∨ w = b))	2 U
{A3, A1}	(4)	∀x ∀y ∃!z (Sz ∧ ∀w (w ∈ z ≡ (w = x ∨ w = y)))	3 UG

Note that the first line is justified by being axiom 3. For the rest of this chapter we will adopt the convention that lines may be entered in proofs if they are axioms, theorems, or if they are justified by definitions or by U.

Also from A1 and A3:

T3. ∀x ∃!y (Sy ∧ ∀z (z ∈ y ≡ z = x))
T4. ∀x ∀y (x ≠ y ⊃ ∃!z (Sz ∧ ∀w (w ∈ z ≡ (w = z ∨ w = y))))

Exercise 6.2 Prove T3.

The set membering just x is called the *unit set* of x, and the set membering just x and y is call the *pair set* of x and y.

The Restriction on the A2 Axioms

We can now explain the restriction on the A2 axioms specifying that the variable replacing "β" have no free occurrences in the formula replacing φ. Suppose that restriction is not observed. We have the following derivation:

A3	(1)	∀x ∀y ∃z (Sz ∧ ∀w (w ∈ z ≡ (w = x ∨ w = y)))	
A3	(2)	∃z (Sz ∧ ∀w (w ∈ z ≡ (w = a ∨ w = a)))	1 US (twice)
{3}	(3)	Sb ∧ ∀w (w ∈ b ≡ (w = a ∨ w = a))	Pᵉˢb
{3}	(4)	∀w (w ∈ b ≡ (w = a ∨ w = a))	3 sentential logic
{3}	(5)	a ∈ b ≡ (a = a ∨ a = a)	4 US
{3}	(6)	a ∈ b ≡ a = a	5 sentential logic
Ø	(7)	a = a	QLI
{3}	(8)	a ∈ b	6, 7 sentential logic

{9}	(9)	$\forall x\ (Sx \supset \exists y\ (Sy \wedge \forall z\ (z \in y \equiv (z \in x \wedge z \notin y))))$	P
{9}	(10)	$(Sb \supset \exists y\ (Sy \wedge \forall z\ (z \in y \equiv (z \in b \wedge z \notin y))))$	9US
{3, 9}	(11)	$\exists y\ (Sy \wedge \forall z\ (z \in y \equiv (z \in b \wedge z \notin y)))$	3, 10 sentential logic
{12}	(12)	$Sc \wedge \forall z\ (z \in c \equiv (z \in b \wedge z \notin c))$	$P^{ES}c$
{12}	(13)	$\forall z\ (z \in c \equiv (z \in b \wedge z \notin c))$	12 sentential logic
{12}	(14)	$a \in c \equiv (a \in b \wedge a \notin c)$	13 US
{3, 12}	(15)	$a \in c \equiv a \notin c$	8, 14 sentential logic
{3, 12}	(16)	$p \wedge \neg p$	15 sentential logic
{3, 9}	(17)	$p \wedge \neg p$	11, 12, 16 ES
{A3, 9}	(18)	$p \wedge \neg p$	2, 3, 17 ES
{A3}	(19)	$\forall x\ (Sx \supset \exists y\ (Sy \wedge \forall z\ (z \in y \equiv (z \in x \wedge z \notin y)))) \supset (p \wedge \neg p)$	9, 18 C
{A3}	(20)	$\neg\ \forall x\ (Sx \supset \exists y\ (Sy \wedge \forall z\ (z \in y \equiv (z \in x \wedge z \notin y))))$	19 sentential logic

Now, the sentence at line (20) is the negation of what would be an A2 axiom where the above noted restriction waived. Thus, A2 is consistent with A3 only if that restriction is observed.

It proves convenient to have a bracket notation for sets. We introduce this notation as an operation symbol. To that end we first state our rule for defining set-theoretic operation symbols.

> A biconditional introducing a new n-place operation symbol (n $\geqq$ 0) is a proper definition if and only if it is of the form
>
> $$o\ (\alpha_1, \ldots, \alpha_n) = \omega \equiv \phi$$
>
> and the following four conditions hold: (i) $\alpha_1, \ldots, \alpha_n$, ω are distinct variables; (ii) no variables other than $\alpha_1, \ldots, \alpha_n$, ω are free in ϕ; (iii) ϕ is a formula the only no-logical constants of which are "$\in$," "S," and previously defined symbols; and (iv) the formula $\forall \alpha_1 \ldots \forall \alpha_n\ \exists! \omega\ \phi$ is derivable from axioms and preceding definitions.

The ordering of definitions provides for the eliminability of defined terms. Condition (iv) must be met to insure a unique referent for each complex term constructed with the defined operation symbol. The sentence required by (iv) for the definition of o is called the *enabling theorem* for o.

Given the enabling theorem T2, we define:

D4. $\{x, y\} = z \equiv Sz \wedge \forall w\ (w \in z \equiv (w = x \vee w = y))$

We next prove an elementary theorem about sets in the bracket notation.

{T2}	(1)	$\{a, b\} = \{a, b\}$	QLI
{T2}	(2)	$S\{a, b\} \wedge \forall w\ (w \in \{a, b\} \equiv (w = a \vee w = b))$	1, D4
{T2}	(3)	$\forall w\ (w \in \{a, b\} \equiv (w = a \vee w = b))$	2 sentential logic
{T2}	(4)	$\forall x\ \forall y\ \forall w\ (w \in \{x, y\} \equiv (w = x \vee w = y))$	3 UG

Thus, from T2 and D4:

T5. $\forall x\ \forall y\ \forall w\ (w \in \{x, y\} \equiv (w = x \vee w = y))$.

Note that T2 is listed as a premise at line (1) of the above derivation despite the fact that the sentence on that line is entered by QLI. The reason is that it is by no means true just by identity that $\{a, b\} = \{a, b\}$, since it is only in virtue of T2 that a referent is assured for "$\{a, b\}$" given referents for "a" and "b." In general, any sentence employing defined operation symbols depends on the theorems enabling the definitions, and through them on zero or more axioms. This point becomes clear if we consider how, for example, the sentence

(1) $a \in \{a, b\}$

yields to a sentence free of the bracket notion. First note that

(2) $\exists x\ (x = \{a, b\} \wedge a \in x)$

is logically equivalent to (1). Then applying D4 to (2) we obtain

(3) $\exists x\ (Sx \wedge \forall w\ (w \in x \equiv (w = a \vee w = b)) \wedge a \in x)$

which is void of brackets. (3) makes explicit the assertion of the existence of a set membering just a and b.

In general, definitions of operation symbols are not "axiom free" since, in general, their enabling theorems derive from axioms and thus are not purely logical.

Also from T2 and D4:

T6. $\forall x \, \forall y \, S \, \{x, y\}$.

From A1, T5, and T6:

T7. $\forall x \, \forall y \, \{x, y\} = \{y, x\}$

From A1, T5, and T6, the useful theorem:

T8. $\forall x \, \forall y \, \forall z \, \forall w \, (\{x, y\} = \{z, w\} \equiv ((x = z \wedge y = w) \vee (x = w \wedge y = z)))$.

With T3 as enabling theorem we further define:

D5. $\{x\} = y \equiv Sy \wedge \forall z \, (z \in y \equiv z = x)$.

From D5 and T3,

T9. $\forall x \, \forall y \, (x \in \{y\} \equiv x = y)$;
T10. $\forall x \, S \, \{x\}$;
T11. $\forall x \, \forall y \, (\{x\} = \{y\} \equiv x = y)$.

From A1, T5, T6, and T9,

T12. $\forall x \, (\{x\} = \{x, x\})$.

The Null Set

We now show the existence of exactly one memberless set, the *empty* or *null set*.

{A2}	(1)	$\forall x \, (Sx \supset \exists y \, (Sy \wedge \forall z \, (z \in y \equiv$ $(z \in x \wedge z \neq z))))$	
{T1}	(2)	$\exists x \, Sx$	
{3}	(3)	Sa	$^{\text{PES}}a$
{A2}	(4)	$Sa \wedge \exists y \, (Sy \wedge \forall z \, (z \in y \equiv (z \in a \wedge z \neq z)))$	1 US
{3, A2}	(5)	$\exists y \, (Sy \wedge \forall z \, (z \in y \equiv (z \in a \wedge z \neq z)))$ 3, 4 sentential logic
{6}	(6)	$Sb \wedge \forall z \, (z \in b \equiv (z \in a \wedge z \neq z))$	$^{\text{PES}}b$

{6}	(7)	$\forall z\,(z \in b \equiv (z \in a \land z \neq z))$	6 sentential logic
{6}	(8)	$c \in b \equiv (c \in a \land c \neq c)$	7 US
Ø	(9)	$c = c$	QLI
{6}	(10)	$c \notin b$	8, 9 sentential logic
{6}	(11)	$c \in b \equiv (p \land \neg p)$	10 sentential logic
{6}	(12)	$\forall y\,(y \in b \equiv (p \land \neg p))$	11 UG
{6}	(13)	$Sb \land \forall y\,(y \in b \equiv (p \land \neg p))$	6, 12 sentential logic
{6}	(14)	$\exists x\,(Sx \land \forall y\,(y \in x \equiv (p \land \neg p)))$	13 EG
{3, A2}	(15)	$\exists x\,(Sx \land \forall y\,(y \in x \equiv (p \land \neg p)))$	5, 6, 14 ES
{T1, A2}	(16)	$\exists x\,(Sx \land \forall y\,(y \in x \equiv (p \land \neg p)))$	2, 3, 15 ES
{T1, A1, A2}	(17)	$\exists!x\,(Sx \land \forall y\,(y \in x \equiv (p \land \neg p)))$	16 U
{T1, A1, A2}	(18)	$\exists!x\,(Sx \land \forall y\,(y \notin x))$	17 sentential logic and quantificational logic with identity

Thus, from T1, A1, and A2:

T13. $\exists!x\,(Sx \land \forall y\,(y \notin x))$.

With T13 as enabling theorem, we define:

D6. $\varnothing = x \equiv (Sx \land \forall y\,(y \notin x))$

Immediately from D6:

T14. $S\varnothing$,
T15. $\forall x\,(x \notin \varnothing)$.

Exercise 6.3   Prove T14.

T13 asserts the existence of a memberless set. This suggests the possibility of deriving the existence of an all-membering set. But in fact the opposite is derivable.

{1}	(1)	$\exists x\,(Sx \land \forall y\,(y \in x))$	P
{A2}	(2)	$\forall x\,(Sx \supset \exists y\,(Sy \land \forall z\,(z \in y \equiv (z \in x \equiv z \notin z))))$	P

{3}	(3)	Sa ∧ ∀y (y ∈ a)	P^{ES}a
{A2}	(4)	Sa ⊃ ∃y (Sy ∧ ∀z (z ∈ y ≡ (z ∈ a ≡ z ∉ z)))	2 US
{3, A2}	(5)	∃y (Sy ∧ ∀z (z ∈ y ≡ (z ∈ a ≡ z ∉ z)))	3, 4 sentential logic
{6}	(6)	Sb ∧ ∀z (z ∈ b ≡ (z ∈ a ≡ z ∉ z))	P^{ES}b
{6}	(7)	∀z (z ∈ b ≡ (z ∈ a ≡ z ∉ z))	6 sentential logic
{6}	(8)	b ∈ b ≡ (b ∈ a ≡ b ∉ b)	7 US
{3}	(9)	∀y (y ∈ a)	3 sentential logic
{3}	(10)	b ∈ a	9 US
{3, 6}	(11)	p ∧ ¬ p	8, 10 sentential logic
{3, A2}	(12)	p ∧ ¬ p	5, 6, 11 ES
{1, A2}	(13)	p ∧ ¬ p	1, 3, 12 ES
{A2}	(14)	∃x (Sx ∧ ∀y (y ∈ x)) ⊃ (p ∧ ¬ p)	1, 13 C
{A2}	(15)	¬ ∃x (Sx ∧ ∀y (y ∈ x))	14 sentential logic

Thus, from A2,

T16. ¬ ∃x (Sx ∧ ∀y (y ∈ x)).

T16 establishes

T17. ¬ ∃x (Sx ∧ ∀y (y ∈ x ≡ y = y)).

Exercise 6.4 Prove T17.

It is worth noting that the derivation for T16 employs the A2 axiom which results from replacing "φ" by "z ∉ z," the very replacement which Russell used to establish the incorrectness of A2*. If there were a universal set then each specification of an A2 axiom to that universal set would yield a conditional with a consequent the same in force as the corresponding instance of the A2* schema. Thus, A2 avoids the inconsistency of A2* only if there is no universal set. This is, as it were, part of the sense of the derivations of T16 and T17.

Further developments require an axiom corresponding to a theorem of ZF and ZF being built up on a basis that takes just "∈" and "∅"as undefined.

A4. ∀x (¬ Sx ⊃ ∀y (y ∉ x))

That is, all non-sets are memberless.

Now, the truth of axioms 1–4 together insure the existence of the empty set and on one- and two-membered sets, but no more.

We can see this by remarking that A1 and A4 do not imply the existence of sets, that A3 implies only the existence of at most two-membered sets, and that A2 yields only subsets of sets already established.

An Interpretation

It is possible to construct an interpretation, satisfying each of A1, A3, A4, under which, for each element m of the interpretation, there are at most two elements n_1 and n_2 in the interpretation such that n_1 and m, and n_2 and m, in that order, satisfy "∈" under that interpretation.

Let I be the interpretation. Then the values of the variables "x," "y," and so on, under I are just the numbers $n \geq 1$. "S" under I is a predicate true of just those numbers which are prime or are the product of just two distinct primes neither of which is 1. "∈" under I is a predicate true of numbers n and m, in that order, just in case m = the n + 1st prime or m = the product of the n + 1st prime and the k + 1st prime, for some $k \neq n$.

To see that this interpretation yields the desired results note that for each number n there is exactly one n + 1th prime for any n and is not the product of any two primes. Thus, there is no number n such that n and 1, in that order, satisfy "∈" under I.

More Axioms

The problem at this point is, then, to determine a further axiom or axioms sufficient for establishing the existence of sets of more than two members. One possibility would be to replace A3 by an axiom schema.

A3*. $\forall \alpha_1, \ldots, \forall \alpha_n \exists \beta (S\beta \wedge \forall \omega (\omega \in \beta \equiv \omega = \alpha_1 \vee \ldots \vee \omega = \alpha_n))$

By A3* we could then establish not only the existence of unit sets and pair sets, but the existence of sets $\{a_1, \ldots, a_n\}$, for any number n. Further, given any set $\{a_1, \ldots, a_n\}$ where each of the a_i has some m elements, by repeated applications of A3 we can obtain a set A membering just the elements of each of the $a_1, \ldots, a_n$. This indicates that instead of A3* we could instead use this axiom:

A5*. $\forall x \exists y (Sy \wedge \forall z (z \in y \equiv \exists w (w \in x \wedge z \in w)))$

under the *restriction* that if x is a set then x has finitely many members which are sets all of which again are sets with finitely many members. (Note that, by A4, if x is not a set, then y = ∅ and that if x is a set membering only non-sets, then again y = ∅.) That is, A5*, *under that restriction*, will provide for just the sets provided for by schema A3*.

The Union Axiom

The axiom we shall adopt is A5* less that restriction, the *union axiom*.

A5.   ∀x ∃y (Sy ∧ ∀z (z∈ y ≡ ∃w (w ∈ x ∧ z ∈ w)))

The union axiom is a "decomposition" axiom since it provides, for each set A of sets, a set membering just the members of members of A. Thus, given ∅, {∅}, and {{∅}}, by A3 we obtain {∅, {{∅}}}, and thus also {{{∅, {∅}}, {{∅}}}} and then, by A5, {∅, {∅}, {{∅}}}. A5 also "decomposes" sets with infinitely many members each of which is again a set with infinitely many members. Thus, A5 is an unlimited "decomposition" axiom.

From A5 by A1:

T18.   ∀x ∃!y (Sy ∧ ∀z (z ∈ y ≡ ∃w (w ∈ x ∧ z ∈ w)))

With T18 as an enabling theorem we define the union operation:

D7.   ∪x = y ≡ Sy ∧ ∀z (z ∈ y ≡ ∃w (w ∈ x ∧ z ∈ w))

From T18 and D7:

T19.   ∀x S∪x;
T20.   ∀x ∀y (y ∈ ∪x ≡ ∃w (w ∈ x ∧ y ∈ w));
T21.   ∪∅ = ∅.

From D7 and A4:

T22.   ∀x (¬ Sx ⊃ ∪x = ∅);
T23.   ∀x (∀y (y ∈ x ⊃ ¬ Sy) ⊃ ∪x = ∅).

Exercise 6.5   Prove T22.

We also derive:

T24. $\forall x \forall y \exists! z (Sz \wedge \forall w (w \in z \equiv (w \in x \wedge w \notin y)))$

from A1, T20, and the following A2 axiom

$\forall x (Sx \supset \exists y (Sy \wedge \forall z (z \in y \equiv (z \in x \wedge (z \in a \wedge z \notin b)))))$.

The key point in the derivation is to apply US to T20 to obtain

$S \cup \{a, b\}$.

With T24 as enabling theorem we define the *difference* of x and y:

D8. $x \sim y = z \equiv Sz \wedge \forall w (w \in z \equiv (w \in x \wedge w \notin y))$.

Note that if x is a non-set than $x \sim y = \emptyset$ and that if y is a non-set and x is a set, then $x \sim y = x$. That is, from D8 and A4:

T25. $\forall x \forall y (\neg Sx \supset x \sim y = \emptyset)$;
T26. $\forall x \forall y ((Sx \wedge \neg Sy) \supset x \sim y = x)$;

and from D8:

T27. $\forall x \forall y Sx \sim y$;
T28. $\forall x \forall y \forall z (z \in x \sim y \equiv (z \in x \wedge z \notin y))$.

Exercise 6.6   Prove T25.

General Intersection Operation

We want next to define a general intersection operation. To do so we must first establish a theorem somewhat more difficult to derive than any thus far met. We thus write out the derivation in full. The methods to be used are characteristic of those employed in the derivations for several later theorems.

{T19}	(1)	$\forall x S \cup x$
{A2}	(2)	$\forall x (Sx \supset \exists y (Sy \wedge \forall z (z \in y \equiv (z \in x \wedge \exists w$
		$(Sw \wedge w \in a) \wedge \forall u ((Su \wedge u \in a) \supset z \in u)))))$

{T19}	(3)	$S \cup a$	1 US
{A2}	(4)	$S \cup a \supset \exists y\,(Sy \wedge \forall z\,(z \in y \equiv$ $(z \in \cup a \wedge \exists w\,(Sw \wedge w \in a) \wedge$ $\forall u(Su \wedge u \in a) \supset z \in u))))$	2 US
{A2, T19}	(5)	$\exists y\,(Sy \wedge \forall z\,(z \in y \equiv (z \in \cup a \wedge \exists w$ $(Sw \wedge w \in a) \wedge \forall u\,((Su \wedge u \in a)$ $\supset z \in u))))$	3, 4 sentential logic
{6}	(6)	$Sb \wedge \forall z\,(z \in b \equiv (z \in \cup a \wedge \exists w$ $(Sw \wedge w \in a) \wedge \forall u\,((Su \wedge u \in a)$ $\supset z \in u)))$	$P^{ES}b$
{6}	(7)	$\forall z\,(z \in b \equiv (z \in \cup a \wedge \exists w$ $(Sw \wedge w \in a) \wedge \forall u\,((Su \wedge u \in a)$ $\supset z \in u)))$ 6 sentential logic	
{6}	(8)	$c \in b \equiv (c \in \cup a \wedge \exists w$ $(Sw \wedge w \in a) \wedge \forall u\,((Su \wedge u \in a) \supset c \in u))$	7 US
{6}	(9)	$c \in b \supset [\exists w\,(Sw \wedge w \in a)$ $\wedge \forall u\,((Su \wedge u \in a) \supset c \in u)]$	8 sentential logic
{10}	(10)	$\exists w\,[(Sw \wedge w \in a) \wedge \forall u$ $((Su \wedge u \in a) \supset c \in u)]$	P
{11}	(11)	$(Sd \wedge d \in a) \wedge \forall u$ $((Su \wedge u \in a) \supset c \in u)$	$P^{ES}d$
{11}	(12)	$\forall u\,((Su \wedge u \in a) \supset c \in u)$	11 sentential logic
{11}	(13)	$(Sd \wedge d \in a) \supset c \in d$	12 US
{11}	(14)	$d \in a \wedge c \in d$	11, 13 sentential logic
{T20}	(15)	$\forall x\,\forall z\,(z \in \cup x \equiv \exists w\,(w \in x \wedge z \in w))$	T20
{T20}	(16)	$c \in \cup a \equiv \exists w\,(w \in a \wedge c \in w)$	15 US
{11}	(17)	$\exists w\,(w \in a \wedge c \in w)$	14 EG
{11, T20}	(18)	$c \in \cup a$	16, 17 sentential logic
{10, T20}	(19)	$c \in \cup a$	10, 11–18, ES
{6, 10, T20}	(20)	$c \in b$	19, 10, 8 sentential logic
{6, T20}	(21)	$\exists w\,(Sw \wedge w \in a) \wedge \forall u\,((Su \wedge u \in a)$ $\supset c \in u) \supset c \in b$	10, 20 C
{6, T20}	(22)	$c \in b \equiv \exists w\,(Sw \wedge w \in a)$ $\wedge \forall u\,((Su \wedge u \in a) \supset c \in u)$	9, 21 sentential logic
{6, T20}	(23)	$\forall z\,(z \in b \equiv \exists w\,(Sw \wedge w \in a) \wedge \forall u$ $((Su \wedge u \in a) \supset z \in u))$	22 UG
{6, T20}	(24)	$Sb \wedge \forall z\,(z \in b \equiv \exists w\,(Sw \wedge w \in a)$ $\wedge \forall u\,((Su \wedge u \in a) \supset z \in u))$	6, 23 sentential logic

{6, T20}	(25)	$\exists y\,(Sy \wedge \forall z\,(z \in y \equiv \exists w\,(Sw \wedge w \in a)$	
		$\wedge\,\forall u\,((Su \wedge u \in a) \supset z \in u)))$	24 EG
{A2, T19, T20}	(26)	$\exists y\,(Sy \wedge \forall z\,(z \in y \equiv \exists w$	
		$(Sw \wedge w \in a) \wedge \forall u\,((Su \wedge u \in a) \supset z \in u)))$	5, 6, 25, ES
{T19, A2, T20}	(27)	$\exists! y\,(Sy \wedge \forall z\,(z \in y \equiv \exists w$	
		$(Sw \wedge w \in a) \wedge \forall u\,((Su \wedge u \in a) \supset z \in u)))$	26 U

Generalizing on "a" yields the enabling theorem:

T29. $\forall x\,\exists! y\,(Sy \wedge \forall z\,(z \in y \equiv \exists w\,(Sw \wedge w \in x) \wedge \forall u\,((Su \wedge u \in x) \supset z \in u)))$.

On the basis of T29 we define an *intersection* operation:

D9. $\cap x = y \equiv Sy \wedge \forall z\,(z \in y \equiv \exists w\,(Sw \wedge w \in x) \wedge \forall u\,((Su \wedge u \in x) \supset z \in u)))$

From D9 and A4:

T30. $\forall x\,(\neg Sx \supset \cap x = \emptyset)$;
T31. $\forall x\,(\forall y\,(y \in x \supset \neg Sy) \supset \cap x = \emptyset)$.

From D9:

T32. $\forall x\,(\exists y\,(Sy \wedge y \in x) \supset \forall z\,(z \in \cap x \equiv \forall w\,(Sw \wedge w \in x) \supset z \in w))$.

Order and Relations

We now turn to the notion of *order*. The basic theorem, from T8, T11, and T12, is:

T33. $\forall x\,\forall y\,\forall z\,\forall w\,(\{\{x\}, \{x, y\}\} = \{\{z\}, \{z, w\}\} \equiv (x = z \wedge y = w))$.

Thus, $\{\{x\}, \{x, y\}\}$ signally differs from $\{x, y\}$ in that even if $x \neq y$, $\{x, y\} = \{y, x\}$, but if $x \neq y$, then $\{\{x\}, \{x, y\}\} \neq \{\{y\}, \{y, x\}\}$. We call $\{\{x\}, \{x, y\}\}$ and *ordered pair* and define:

D10. x is an ordered pair $\equiv \exists y\,\exists z\,(x = \{\{y\}, \{y, z\}\})$.

As convenient and standard notion for ordered pairs we use corners. First, as enabling theorem, from D4, D5, and A1:

T34. x ∀y ∃!z z = {{x}, {x, y}}.

Then:

D11. <x, y> = z ≡ z = {{x}, {x, y}}.

From D11 and T6:

T35. ∀x ∀y S<x, y>.

The standard law for ordered pairs now emerges from T33 and D11:

∀x ∀y ∀z ∀w (<x, y> = <z, w> ≡ (x = z ∧ y = w)).

Further important notions of order now easily emerge. We first define *relations*:

D12. Rx ≡ (Sx ∧ ∀y (y ∈ x ⊃ y is an ordered pair)).

Note in particular, from T14, T15, and D12:

T36. R∅.

Exercise 6.7   Prove T36.

We call ∅ the *null relation*. Next note the theorem

T37. ∀x ∃!y (Sy ∧ ∀z (z ∈ y ≡ ∃w <z, w> ∈ x)).

which can be derived using A1, T21, D5, and the following A2 axiom:

∀x (Sx ⊃ ∃y (Sy ∧ ∀z (z ∈ y ≡ ∃w <z, w> ∈ a)))

and the specification

S ∪ ∪ a

from T19. The general method of proof is that illustrated in the derivation for T29. With T39 as enabling theorem we define the notion of a *domain*:

D13. $\mathbf{d}x = y \equiv Sy \wedge \forall z\ (z \in y \equiv \exists w <z, w> \in x)$.

From D13:

T38. $\forall x\ S\mathbf{d}x$.

The basic application of the notion of a domain is to relations. From D12 and D13:

T39. $\forall x\ (Rx \supset (S\mathbf{d}x \wedge \forall z\ (z \in \mathbf{d}x \equiv \exists w <z, w> \in x)))$.

By a derivation similar to that for T37, we obtain:

T40. $\forall x\ \exists! y\ (Sy \wedge \forall z\ (z \in y \equiv \exists w <w, z> \in x))$.

On the basis of T40 we define the notion of *range*.

D14. $\mathbf{r}x = y \equiv (Sy \wedge \forall z\ (z \in y \equiv \exists w <w, z> \in x))$.

From D14:

T41. $\forall x\ S\mathbf{r}x$.

From D12 and D14:

T42. $\forall x\ \forall z\ (z \in \mathbf{r}x \equiv \exists w <w, z> \in x)$.

The notion of *field* is next defined:

D15. $\mathbf{f}x = \cup \{\mathbf{d}x, \mathbf{r}x\}$.

Functions

We next define the notion of a *function*:

D16. $Fx \equiv (Rx \wedge \forall y\ \forall z\ \forall w\ ((<y, z> \in x \wedge <y, w> \in x) \supset z = w))$.

A relation satisfying the second conjunct in D16 is called a *many-one* relation. Thus, functions are many-one relations. The notion of being *1-1* is next defined:

D17.   x is 1-1 ≡ (Fx ∧ ∀y ∀z ∀w ((<z, y> ∈ x ∧ <w, y> ∈ x) ⊃ z = w)).

We define next some further useful terminology:

D18.1.   x is a function of y to z ≡ (Fx ∧ Sy ∧ Sz ∧ **d**x = y ∧ rx ⊆ z);
D18.2.   x is a function from y into z ≡ x is a function on y to z;
D18.3.   x is a function from y onto z ≡ (Fx ∧ Sy ∧ Sz ∧ **d**x = y ∧ rx = z);
D18.4.   x maps y into z ≡ (x is 1-1 ∧Sy ∧ Sz ∧ **d**x = y ∧ rx ⊆ z);
D18.5.   x maps y onto z ≡ (x is 1-1 ∧ Sy ∧ Sz ∧ **d**x = y ∧ rx = z).

Sizes of Sets

We now return to the idea of the comparative "sizes" of sets. The intuitive notion of sameness of "size" for sets is this: sets with *equally many members* are the same in set size. Such sets are called *equinumerous* or *equipolent*. This intuitive notion can be made formally precise through the notion of 1-1 functions. Briefly, sets are equally many membered just in case there exists a 1-1 function which maps one set *onto* the other. We thus define:

D19.   x ≈ y ≡ ∃z (z is 1-1 ∧ **d**z = x ∧ rz = y).

Thus, no non-sets are equinumerous and no non-set is equinumerous with any set. From T38, T41, and D19:

T43.   ∀x ∀y (x ≈ y ⊃ (Sx ∧ Sy)).

From D16 and T15:

T44.   FØ.

From D17, T15, T39, T42, and T44:

T45.   (Ø is 1-1 ∧ **d**x = Ø ∧ rØ = Ø).

From T45 and D19:

T46.   Ø ≈ Ø.

The next question is whether every non-empty set is equinumerous with itself. To devise a theorem to this effect it is necessary to establish that for each set A there exists a 1-1 function with A as both its domain and range. The natural candidate would be the identity function for A. Thus, for example, if A ={Ø, {Ø}}, then the identity function for A = {<Ø, Ø>, <{Ø}, {Ø}>}. But is there such a function? It would be natural at this point to introduce a unary operation symbol "[**i** x]" as notion for the identity function for object x. The definition of this operator would be:

[**i** x] = y ≡ (Sx ∧ ∀z (z ∈ y ≡ ∃w (z = <w, w> ∧ w ∈ x))).

The enabling theorem would thus be:

∀x ∃!y (Sy ∧ ∀z (z ∈ y ≡ ∃w (z = <w, w> ∧ w ∈ x))).

This theorem would in turn be derived from A1 and the A2 axiom

∀x (Sx ⊃ ∃y (Sy ∧ ∀z (z ∈ y ≡ (z ∈ x ∧ ∃w (z = <w, w> ∧ w ∈ a))))).

But what is to be the specification for "x"? Plainly, for each set A the specification for "x" must be a set membering ordered pairs of elements of A. This is, for each set A the selection set for the A2 axiom above must be a set of ordered pairs from A. Thus, if A = {a, b, . . .}, then the specification of "x" must be to a set A* = {. . . <a, a>, . . . , <b, b>, . . .} = {. . . , {{a}}, . . . , {{b}}, . . .}. Now, A3 asserts that for each x ∈ A there is the set {{x}} = <x, x>. But it does not assert or imply that there is any *set* of *all* such sets {{x}}. Our other set-existential axiom is A5, which is a "decomposition" axiom and thus not suited to prove the existence of {. . . , {{a}}, . . . , {{b}}, . . .} from {a, b, . . .}. Rather, a new "composition" axiom is needed. That is, the axioms thus far laid down do not provide even for the existence of identity functions and thus do not provide for a proof of the assertion that sets are self-equinumerous.

The Power Set Axiom

A simple choice for a new axiom would be:

∀x ∃y (Sy ∧ ∀z (z ∈ y ≡ ∃w (w ∈ x ∧ z = {w}))).

This would be an axiom serving the current need, but it leaves us unprepared for the development of, say, {... <a, b>, ..., <b, a>, ...} from {a, b, ...}. And such a construction will be needed for functions needed for further proofs. An axiom sufficient for this construction would be:

$$\forall x\, \exists y\, (Sy \land \forall z\, (z \in y \equiv \exists w\, \exists u\, (w \in x \land u \in x \land (z = \{w\} \lor z = \{w, u\}))))).$$

The idea involved in each of these possible axioms is this: there are sets of subsets of sets. Generalizing on this idea yields the *power set axiom*:

A6. $\forall x\, \exists y\, (Sy \land \forall z\, (z \in y \equiv z \subseteq x)).$

From A6 by A1, the enabling theorem:

T47. $\forall x\, \exists! y\, (Sy \land \forall z\, (z \in y \equiv z \subseteq x)).$

For the definition of the power set operator:

D20. $\wp x = y \equiv (Sy \land \forall z\, (z \in y \equiv z \subseteq y)).$

From A4, D4, D5, D6, and D20:

T48. $\forall x\, (\neg Sx \supset \wp x = \varnothing);$
T49. $\wp \varnothing = \{\varnothing\};$
T50. $\forall x\, \forall y\, (x \in y \supset \{x\} \in \wp y);$
T51. $\forall x\, \forall y\, \forall z\, ((x \in z \land y \in z) \supset \{x, y\} \in \wp z);$
T52. $x\, S\, \wp x.$

We now proceed to our theorem for the definition of "[i]." Note that by T52:

$$S\, \wp\, \wp a$$

We then specify our A2 axiom to the above to obtain:

$$S\, \wp\, \wp a \supset \exists y\, (Sy \land \forall z\, (z \in y \equiv (z \in \wp\, \wp a \land \exists w\, (z = <w, w> \land w \in a)))).$$

Now, by T50 we have:

$$b \in a \supset \{b\} \in \wp a;$$
$$\{b\} \in \wp a \supset \{\{b\}\} \in \wp\, \wp a.$$

Thus, following the general method of the derivation of T29, we arrive at:

T53. $\forall x \exists! y (Sy \wedge \forall z (z \in y \equiv \exists w (z = <w, w> \wedge w \in x)))$.

We now define:

D21. $[i\ x] = y \equiv (Sy \wedge \forall z (z \in y \equiv \exists w (z - <w, w> \wedge w \in x)))$.

From D11, D16, D17, D21, and T33:

T54. $\forall x [i\ x]$ is 1-1.

From D13, D14, D21, and T54:

T55. $\forall x \forall y \forall z (\{x, y\} \in z \supset (x \in \cup z \wedge y \in \cup z))$;

and thus, by D19:

T56. $\forall x (Sx \supset x \approx x)$.

Some simple theorems that prove useful are the following, from T5:

T57. $\forall x \forall y\ x \in \{x, y\}$;
T58. $\forall x \forall y\ y \in \{x, y\}$;

and, from T20, T57, and T58:

T59. $\forall x \forall y \forall z (\{x, y\} \in z \supset (x \in \cup z \wedge y \in \cup z))$.

From A1 and T5, 19, 49, 50, 51, and 57–59 we can use the A2 axiom

$\forall x (Sx \supset \exists y (Sy \wedge \forall z (z \in y \equiv (z \in x \wedge \exists w \exists u (z = <w, u> \wedge <u, w> \in a)))))$,

with

$\cup \cup\ a,$

as specification for "x," derive:

T60. $\forall x \exists! y \, (Sy \wedge \forall z \, (z \in y \equiv \exists w \, \exists u \, (z = <w, u> \wedge <u, w> \in x)))$,

and thus define a *converse* operation:

D22. $cx = y \equiv (Sy \wedge \forall z \, (z \in y \equiv \exists w \, \exists u \, (z = <w, u> \wedge <u, w> \in x)))$.

At this point we shall no longer list all definitions and theorems entering into derivations of new theorems. From D22 and the definitions and theorems for relations, functions, and 1-1 functions:

T61. $\forall x \, \forall y \, (y \in cx \equiv \exists w \, \exists u \, (y = <w, u> \wedge <u, w> \in x))$;
T62. $\forall x \, (Rx \supset ccx = x)$;
T63. $\forall x \, ((Fx \wedge Fcx) \supset x \text{ is } 1\text{-}1)$;
T64. $\forall x \, (x \text{ is } 1\text{-}1 \equiv cx \text{ is } 1\text{-}1)$.

From T64, T38, and T41:

T65. $\forall x \, \forall y \, \forall z \, ((x \text{ is } 1\text{-}1 \wedge dx = y \wedge cx = z) \equiv (cx \text{ is } 1\text{-}1 \wedge dcx = z \wedge rx = y))$.

From T65 and D19:

T66. $\forall x \, \forall y \, (x \approx y \equiv y \approx x)$.

For suppose that $a \approx b$. Then for some function f, f is 1-1 and $df = a \wedge rf = b$. But then, by T65, f is 1-1 and $dcf = b$ and $rcf = a$. Thus, there is a 1-1 function with b as its domain and a as its range. Thus, $b \approx a$.

Using the following A2 axiom,

$\forall x \, (Sx \supset \exists y \, (Sy \wedge \forall z \, (z \in x \equiv (z \in x \wedge \exists w \, \exists u \, (z = <w, u> \wedge \exists t \, <w, t> \in a \wedge \exists v$
$<v, u> \in b)))))$,

and specifying "x" to

$\cup \cup \cup \{a, b\}$,

we can establish

T67. $\forall x \, \forall y \, \exists! z \, (Sz \wedge \forall s \, (s \in z \equiv \exists w \, \exists u \, (s = <w, u> \wedge \exists t \, <w, t>$
$\in x \wedge \exists v \, <v, u> \in y)))$.

We can thus define an operation for *composition*:

D23. x o y = z ≡ (Sz ∧ ∀s (s ∈ z ≡ ∃w ∃u (s = <w, u> ∧ ∃t <w, t>
∈ x ∧ ∃v <v, u> ∈ y))).

The primary application of composition is to functions. Thus, where f is a function from set A onto set B and g is a function from set B onto set C, f o g is a function from set A onto set C. The theorem is:

T68. ∀x ∀y ∀z ∀w ∀u ((Fx ∧ dx = z ∧ rx = w) ∧ (Fy ∧ dy = w ∧ ry = u)
⊃ Fx o y ∧ dx o y = z ∧ rx o y = u).

From D23 and T68 we can establish the further theorem:

T69. ∀x ∀y ∀z ((x ≈ y ∧ y ≈ z) ⊃ x ≈ z).

Theorems T56, T66, and T69 together establish that the set relationship of being equally many membered is reflexive, symmetric, and transitive. We next turn to the notion of being *more membered*:

D24. x > y ≡ (¬ x ≈ y ∧ ∃z (z is 1-1 ∧ dz ⊆ x ∧ rz = y)).

The left conjunct of the defining conjunction asserts that there is no 1-1 function correlating the members of x and y. The right conjunct asserts that there is a 1-1 function that maps a subset of x onto y. Combining D24 with D19 yields the notion of being equally or more membered:

D25. x ≥ y ≡ (x > y ∨ x ≈ y).

Thus the theorem:

T70. ∀x ∀y (x ≥ y ≡ (x ≈ y ∨ ∃z (z is 1-1 ∧ dz ⊆ x ∧ rz = y))).

Further definitions are:

D26. x < y ≡ y > x
D27. x ≥ y ≡ y ≥ x

We next introduce a standard form of notation for functions. The enabling theorem, which has a lengthy derivation from A1, A2, A3, and D16, is:

> T71. ∀x ∀y ∃!z (Fz ∧∃w (<y, w> ∈ x ∧ z = w) ∨ (¬ Fx ∨ ¬ ∃w <y, w> ∈ x ∨ z = ∅)).

Thus,

> D28. f (y) = z ≡ (Ff ∧∃w (<y, w> ∈ f ∧ z = w) ∨ (¬ Ff ∨ ¬ ∃w <y, w> ∈ f ∨ z = ∅)).

Thus also:

> T72. ∀f (Ff ⊃ ∀y ∀z (<y, z> ∈ f ≡ f (y) = z)).

So, if f is a function then <a, b> ∈ f just in case f (a) = b. (We shall typically use lowercase letters "f," "g," "h," and so on, for functions, as accords with standard practice.)

We want next to establish that for any set A there is a 1-1 function which maps a subset of ℘A onto A. The basic idea is that for each set A and a ∈ A, {a} ∈ ℘A. Thus there is a 1-1 function from the set A* of unit sets of members of ℘A onto A. Thus, since the set A* is a subset of ℘A, that function is a mapping from a subset of ℘A onto A. The basic theorem is:

> T73. ∀x ∃!y (Sy ∧ ∀z (z ∈ y ≡ ∃u (z = <{u}, u> ∧ u ∈ x))).

We use the A2 axiom

> ∀x (Sx ⊃ ∃!y (Sy ∧ ∀z (z ∈ y ≡ (z ∈ x ∧ ∃u (z = <{u}, u> ∧ u ∈ a)))))

and specify "x" to

> ∪ {℘a, a}.

With T73 as enabling theorem:

> D29. [Kx] = y ≡ (Sy ∧ ∀z (z ∈ y ≡ ∃u (z = <{u}, u> ∧ u ∈ x))).

It is now fairly easy to establish:

T74. $\forall x \, (Sx \supset \exists y \, ([Kx] \text{ is } 1\text{-}1 \land \mathbf{d} \, [Kx] \subseteq \wp x \land \mathbf{r} \, [Kx] = x \,))$,

and thus also:

T75. $\forall x \, (Sx \supset \exists y \, (y \text{ is } 1\text{-}1 \land \mathbf{d}y \subseteq \wp x \land \mathbf{r}y = x))$.

A Basic Theorem

We now turn to a fundamental theorem about power sets, namely, that the power set of a set is more membered than that set.

Proof

Suppose that, for set A, it is not the case that $\wp A > A$. Then, from D23, either

(1) $A \approx A$

or

(2) $\neg \exists x \, (x \text{ is } 1\text{-}1 \land \mathbf{d}x \subseteq \wp A \land \mathbf{r}x = A)$.

Since A is a set, (2) is false by T75. Now, from (1) by T66,

(3) $A \approx \wp A$

in which case, by D19,

(4) $\exists x \, (x \text{ is } 1\text{-}1 \land \mathbf{d}x = A \land \mathbf{r}x = \wp A)$.

Let f be this function. By A2 there is the axiom

(5) $\forall x \, (Sx \supset \exists y \, (Sy \land \forall z \, (z \in y \equiv (z \in x \land z \notin f \, (z)))))$.

Specifying "x" to the set A, and setting "*B*" as "y" we have:

(6) SB

(7) $\forall z\, (z \in B \equiv (z \in A \land z \notin f(z)))$.

By (7), set B is a subset of A. Thus, by sentential logic and D20,

(8) $B \in \wp A$.

Now, since f is 1-1 and $f = \mathbf{d}A$ and $\mathbf{r}\, f = \wp A$ and (8),

(9) $B \in \mathbf{r}\, f$.

Thus also, by (3), for some a $\in$ A,

(10) $f(a) = B$.

Now suppose that

(11) $a \in B$.

Then, by (7),

(12) $a \in B \supset a \notin f(a)$.

Thus, from (11) and (12),

(13) $a \notin f(a)$.

Thus, from (10) and (13),

(14) $a \notin B$.

Thus, if a $\in$ B, then a $\notin$ B. Thus

(15) $a \notin B$.

From (10) and (15),

(16) $a \notin f(a)$.

But since a ∈ A, we have by (7)

(17)   a ∉ f (a) ⊃ a ∈ B.

Thus, from (16) and (17),

(18)   a ⊂ B.

and thus, from (15) and (18),

(19)   p ∧ ¬ p

Thus, the assumption that, for set A, it is not the case that ℘ A > A leads to a contradiction. Thus our theorem:

T76.   ∀x (Sx ⊃ ℘x > x).

That is, for any set A, the power set of A is more membered than A.

7

Incompleteness

In this chapter we provide a non-technical account of some of the ideas involved in Gödel's incompleteness proof.

The Language of Arithmetic

In the following discussion we adopt as the language for arithmetic the language which includes just the following basic expressions: the variables "x," "y," ..., the universal quantifiers "∀x," "∀y," ..., the existential quantifiers "∃x," "∃y," ..., the connectives "∨," "⊃," "≡," "¬," and "∧," the binary operators "×" and "+," the unary operator "s," the identity predicate "=," the individual constant "0," and the left and right parentheses. We assume familiarity with the usual formation rules and rules of inferences. We will denote this language by "L."

L is the arithmetical object language (the "language of arithmetic") for our account of Gödel's proof. That account itself proceeds in English supplemented by the usual symbols of arithmetic and set theory. We will denote this language by "E." E is the metalanguage within which we will present an account of Gödel's proof.

It will also prove useful to have variables indexed to specific numerals of L. To this end we use the ordinary numerical variables "n," "m," and so on in boldface type. Thus, such a sentence as

For every n, **n** = 0 is a formula of L

is to be read as follows:

For every n, the expression consisting of the numeral of L consisting of prefixing n occurrences of "s" to "0" followed by "=" followed by "0" is a formula of L.

Finally, we will use expressions like "Q (x, y)"and "t (x, y)" as metalinguistic variables ranging over formulas and functional expressions of L in which exactly the two variables "x" and "y" have free occurrences. Thus, for example, we would read

∀x ¬ Q (x, **n**)

as

the result of prefixing "∀x ¬" to the result of replacing each free occurrence of "y" in the formula Q (x, y) by numeral **n**

The most fundamental axioms for arithmetic can be formulated in L as follows:

A1. ∀x (0 ≠ sx)
A2. ∀x ∀y (sx = sy ⊃ x = y)
A3. ∀x (x + 0 = x)
A4. ∀x ∀y ((x + sy) = s(x = y))
A5. ∀x (x × 0 = 0)
A6. ∀x ∀y (x × sy = (x × y) + x)

Axioms A1 and A2 fix certain properties of the series of natural numbers: s0 ≠ 0 (by axiom 1); ss0 ≠ 0 and ss0 ≠ s0 (by axioms 1 and 2), and so forth.

Axioms A3 and A4 fix the sums: By axiom 3, 0 + 0 = 0, s0 + 0 = s0, . . .; and by axioms 3 and 4, 0 + s0 = s0, s0 + s0 = ss0, ss0 + s0 = sss0, . . . , and so forth.

Axioms A5 and A6 do the same for products.

We call these the *Elementary Axioms* and call the theory based on these axioms *Elementary Arithmetic.*

The Elementary Axioms *decide* the simple equations of arithmetic (the sentences void of quantifiers) in the sense that for any such equation S, either it or its negation ¬ S will be derivable from the axioms. We will say that a set of axioms for arithmetic that agrees with these axioms on the elementary equations has at least *elementary power*.

Now, supposing these axioms to be consistent, they do not in general decide the quantifications of L.

In particular, there are many cases in which it is possible to derive from the axioms *every instance* of some universal quantification but not possible to derive the quantification itself. For example, these axioms (A1–A6) provide for the proof of

$$(0 = 0 \lor \exists y \, (0 = sy))$$
$$(s0 = 0 \lor \exists y \, (s0 = sy))$$
$$(ss0 = 0 \lor \exists y \, (ss0 = sy))$$

•
•
•

but not for a proof of

$$\forall x \, (x = 0 \lor \exists y \, (x = sy))$$

Now, a set of axioms is said to be ω-*incomplete* if, for some universal quantification, each of its instances is derivable from those axioms but the quantification is not thus derivable. The Elementary Axioms are, then, ω-incomplete. (We shall also say that a generalization not provable from axioms sufficient to establish all its instances is *underdetermined* by those axioms.)

It is worth noting also the further possibilities of a set of axioms from which each instance of a universal quantification is derivable along with the negation of that quantification. A set of axioms of that sort is said to be ω-*inconsistent*.

The obvious response to ω-incompleteness is to add further axioms. The traditional course was to add infinitely many new axioms: the *induction* axioms.

A7. All sentences of the following form:
$$(A \, (0) \land \forall x \, (A \, (x) \supset \forall x \, A \, (sx)) \supset \forall x \, A \, (x)$$

The A7 axioms immensely strengthen axioms 1–6 and with them provide for the derivation of enormously many more sentences of pure arithmetic, including enormously many generalizations underdetermined by the Elementary Axioms.

We shall call axioms A1–A6 plus the A7 axioms the *Peano Axioms*, after the Italian mathematician Giuseppe Peano. The theory based on these axioms is called *Peano Arithmetic*. Peano Arithmetic is a development of elementary arithmetic providing a powerful general theory of the natural numbers.

Gödel's argument shows (to a near approximation) that Peano Arithmetic, like Elementary Arithmetic, is, if consistent, incomplete in the strong sense that if those axioms are consistent there is at least one arithmetic sentence such that neither it nor its negation is derivable from the Peano Axioms. Further, his method of proof allows for its generalization to *any* consistent axiom set of at least elementary power.

What Gödel showed, then, is that the addition of the induction axioms does not essentially change the situation in respect to incompleteness. Just as the Elementary Axioms leave many generalizations underdetermined, so also the Peano Axioms leave certain generalizations underdetermined. Thus, Gödel showed that there is no strengthening of the Elementary Axioms sufficient to provide a proof of *each* generalization all of whose instances are provable.

Three Key Concepts

Gödel proceeded by first defining a function (a "Gödel function"), here denoted by "g," which assigns distinct numbers to distinct formulas and to distinct finite sequences of formulas of L.

It is critical to his proof that the function g is so defined that (i) given any number we can determine whether g assigns it to some formula or sequence, and if so just which formula or sequence, and (ii) given any formula or sequence of formulas we can determine which number g assigns to it. There are functions satisfying these conditions because the set of formulas and sequences of formulas of L is decidable.

Next, we shall say that a sequence S terminating in a formula F is a *Peano Proof* of F if and only if S is a derivation of F from the Peano Axioms. Now, there are certain pairs of numbers <n, m> such that for some sequence S which is a Peano Proof of formula F, g (S) = n and g (F) = m. For the concise expression of this condition we introduce a "proof predicate" "P" by the following definition:

D1. Pnm if and only if for some sequence of formulas S and formula F, S is a Peano
Proof of F and g (S) = n and g (F) = m.

Further, there are certain triples of numbers <n, m, k> such for some formula F, g (F) = n and for some G which results from F by replacing each free
occurrence of variable "y" in F by the numeral of L consisting of "0" prefixed
by m occurrences of "s," g (G) = k. Again, for conciseness of expression we
introduce a function symbol "f" by the following definition:

D2. f (n, m) = k if and only if : (i) there are formulas F and G such that G results from
F by replacing the free occurrences of "y" in F by occurrences of **m** (i.e., the
numeral which results from prefixing "0" by m occurrences of "s") and g (F) =
n and g (G) = k; otherwise (ii) k = 0

An example will help clarify the "substitution function" f. Consider the following sentences of L:

(y = 0 ∨ ∃x (y = sx))
(ss0 = 0 ∨ ∃x (ss0 = sx))

and note that the second sentence results from the first by replacing each
free occurrence of "y" by the numeral "ss0." This is the numeral that results
from prefixing "0" by 2 occurrences of "s." Now suppose that g ("(y = 0 ∨ ∃x
(y = sx))") = 3. Then f (3, 2) = g ("(ss0 = 0 ∨ ∃x (ss0 = sx))").

Three Key Theorems

Next, recall that there is an effective specification of the admissible inference
sequences of L and an effective specification of the Peano Axioms. Thus there
is an effective specification of the Peano Proofs (i.e., the derivations from the
Peano Axioms). Further, we recall that the formulas of L are effectively specified and that there is an effective procedure associated with function g. These
circumstances make possible proofs of the following key points in respect to
the predicates defined above:

T1. For some binary formula A (x, y) of L and for any numbers n and m, (i) there is
a Peano Proof of A (**n, m**) if and only if Pnm and (ii) there is a Peano Proof of
¬A (**n, m**) if and only if not Pnm.

(An n-ary predicate K of the metalanguage is said to be numeral-wise
represented by a degree-n formula F of the language L of arithmetic if and only

if F (k_1, ..., k_n) has a Peano Proof if K holds of the numbers k_1, ..., k_n and ¬ F (k_1, ..., k_n) has Peano Proof if K does not hold of k_1, ..., k_n. Put in these terms, T1 says that some binary formula A of L numeral-wise represents the predicate "P" of the metalanguage.)

> T2. For some binary functional expression t of L and for any numbers n, m, and k, there is a Peano Proof of t (**n**, **m**) = **k** if and only if f (n, m) = k and there is a Peano Proof of ¬ t (**n**, **m**) = **k** if and only if not f (n, m) = k.

(We also say that there is some function symbol of L that numeral-wise represents the function symbol "f" of the metalanguage.)

From T1 and T2 Gödel showed:

> T3. For some degree-2 formula Q of L and for any numbers n and m, there is a Peano Proof of Q (**n**, **m**) if and only if Pnf (m, m) and there is a Peano Proof of ¬ Q (**n**, **m**) if and only if not Pnf (m, m).

We are now in a position to give the gist of the Gödel proof.

The Core Argument

Let Q be a degree-2 of L satisfying T3. Then, since ¬ Q (x, y) is a formula of L and g is defined for the formulas of L,

> 1. For some m, g ($\forall$x ¬ Q (x, y)) = m.

let m be a number satisfying g ($\forall$x ¬ Q (x, y)) = m, that is,

> 2. g ($\forall$x ¬ Q (x, y)) = m.

We now make the following assumptions:

> C   The Peano Axioms are consistent, that is, there is no sentence such that both it and its negation have Peano Proofs.
>
> W   The Peano Axioms are ω-consistent, that is, there is no universal quantification such that there are Peano Proofs for each of its instances and a Peano Proof of its negation.

and consider the following supposition in relation to m:

> S   There is a Peano Proof of $\forall$x ¬ Q (x, **m**).

Then, by D1

    3. For some n, Pnm and g ($\forall$x $\neg$ Q (x, y)) = m.

Next note that

    4. f (m, m) = g ($\forall$x $\neg$ Q (x, **m**)).

Thus, from 3 and 4,

    5. For some n, Pnf (m, m).

But in that case, by T3,

    6. For some n there is a Peano Proof of Q (**n**, **m**).

But then,

    7. There is a Peano Proof of $\exists$x Q (x, **m**).

Hence also,

    8. There is a Peano Proof of $\neg\forall$x $\neg$ Q (x, **m**).

Thus, from this and supposition S,

    9. There are Peano Proofs of both $\forall$x $\neg$ Q (x, **m**) and $\neg$ $\forall$x $\neg$ Q (x, **m**),

which contradicts the assumption of consistency, Thus,

    10. There is no Peano Proof of $\forall$x $\neg$ Q (x, **m**).

Thus, by D1

    11. For each n, not Png ($\forall$x $\neg$ Q (x, **m**)).

From this and 4 above,

    12. For each n, not Pnf (m, m).

So, by T3,

> 13. For each n, there is a Peano Proof of $\neg Q$ (**n**, **m**).

Thus, by the assumption of ω-consistency,

> 14 There is no Peano Proof of $\neg \forall x \neg Q$ (x, **m**)

By conditionalizing on assumption C in respect to the conclusion at line 10,

> 15. There is no Peano Proof of $\forall x \neg Q$ (x, **m**) if the Peano Axioms are consistent.

By conditionalizing on assumption W in respect to the conclusion at line 14,

> 16. There is no Peano Proof of $\forall x \neg Q$ (x, **m**) if the Peano Axioms are ω-consistent.

So, by conjoining 15 and 16 and applying existential generalization,

> 17. There is some m such that there is no Peano Proof of $\forall x \neg Q$ (x, m) if the Peano Axioms are consistent and there is no Peano Proof of $\neg \forall x \neg Q$ (x, **m**) if the Peano Axioms are ω-consistent.

And also, since $\forall x \neg Q$ (x, **m**) is an arithmetical sentence,

> 18. There is some arithmetical sentence S such that there is no Peano Proof of S if the Peano Axioms are consistent, and no Peano Proof of $\neg$ S if the Peano Axioms are ω-consistent.

Concluding Observations

As was first shown by Rosser, it is possible to establish in respect to a somewhat more complex sentence than the one considered by Gödel that it is neither provable nor disprovable if the Peano Axioms are consistent.

We thus will drop the reference to ω-consistency in the following discussion and speak just in terms of consistency.

Let A be some set of axioms providing for derivations of the Peano theorems. There will then be definitions paralleling definitions D1 and D2 above (just substitute "A Proof " for "Peano Proof ") for which there will be provable *T* principles like T1 and T2 above. It will then be possible to carry out a proof strictly analogous to the proof sketched above which shows that there is a sentence of arithmetic undecidable by A (if these axioms are consistent).

We can think of the predicate "P" as a *Peano Proof Predicate.* If we add to our axioms to arrive at a new axiom set A, then the predicate "P" (which now will hold for different pairs of numbers) is an *A Proof* predicate. Each new axioms set yields a new proof predicate. And each new proof predicate provides for the identification of a new sentence which can be shown to be undecided by the new axioms set.

Thus the following generalized incompleteness result:

> For any consistent set of axioms for arithmetic of at least elementary strength, there is an arithmetical sentence such that neither it nor its negation is derivable from those axioms.

Since the Peano Axioms will be a subset of infinitely many distinct axioms sets, there will be infinitely many sentences not decided by the Peano Axioms (for any sentence not decided by a set of axioms is also not decided by any of its subsets). The same will hold for each of the axioms sets built up from the Peano Axioms.

That there are infinitely many different sentences undecided by the Peano Axioms is also evident from the fact that there are infinitely many Gödel functions satisfying the conditions noted above and each of these yields a new Peano Proof predicate sufficient to identify a new undecidable sentence.

Finally, Gödel did not identify an arithmetical sentence that says of itself that it is unprovable. Arithmetical sentences do not speak of proof. Rather, Gödel identified a sentence S of L which, relative to a particular numbering of the formulas and formula sequences of L, numeral-wise represents a metalinguistic sentence K which says that S has no Peano Proof.

An Introduction to Term Logic

8

Chapter Outline

Syllogistic

We use Sommers (1970, 1982, 1990), Englebretsen (1996), and Sommers and Englebretsen (2000) for the study of term logic.

The building and study of formal logic began with Aristotle. His investigations concerning rhetoric, the use of persuasive language (especially in the practice of public contentious debate), led him to investigate more closely the use of language to construct arguments the effect of which was due not to style but to reason alone. He began his logical studies holding a view of sentence structure derived from his teacher Plato. That view was that every simple declarative sentence consists of a noun and a verb. A sentence is more than just a list of words; it is a linguistic unit itself, because nouns and verbs are *grammatically* fit for one another; they naturally combine pair-wise to form sentences. Soon, however, Aristotle realized that in an argument there are words that shift about, occupying different positions in different sentences. He replaced the Platonic noun-verb account of logical syntax with a *copular* account. According to this new theory, a simple declarative sentence consists of a pair of *terms* bound together logically (not necessarily grammatically) by a *logical copula*. Any expression, noun, pronoun, verb, adjective, noun phrase, verb phrase, and so on, is a term. A copula is not a term. It is a formal device for uniting pairs of terms to form a sentence: it binds, connects the two terms and stands between them (thus the terms are literally *termini*, ends points of sentences). Any term can occupy any term position, any terminus. There were four logical copulae for Aristotle. English versions of each are "belongs to every," "belongs to no," "belongs to some," and "does not belong to some." Let A and B be any two terms, then there are but four kinds of sentences: "A belongs to every B," "A belongs to no B," "A belongs to some B," and "A does not belong to some B." These are the four so-called *categorical* forms.

Having in hand an account of logical syntax, Aristotle went on to build his logic—*syllogistic*. He took logical arguments to consist, fundamentally, of a pair of categorical premises and a categorical conclusion. Syllogistic was a *formal* logic because it defined such concepts as validity in terms of the form of an argument. The form of any argument was determined by the forms of its three sentences, and for each of these the terms were replaced by variable letters (as we just did above). The introduction of such variables for non-formal expressions makes Aristotle not only the first logician but the first "symbolic" logician as well. An argument consisting of a pair of categorical premises and a categorical conclusion is a syllogism. A standard, classical, syllogism involves, then, three sentences and three different terms. Two of these terms will appear in the conclusion (and each will have occurred in a premise); the third term (called the *middle* term) will occur in each premise but not in the conclusion. Since there are four possible categorical forms and each standard syllogism consists of three categorical sentences, there are 4^3 (= 64) possible arrangements of two premises and a conclusion. Moreover, there are, for each of these arrangements four ways of arranging the three terms. The 64 arrangements of categorical forms for premises and conclusion are known as *moods*. The four ways of arranging the three terms of a syllogism are known as *figures*. The decision about whether a given syllogism is valid or invalid depends on discerning whether or not it has certain characteristics that all valid syllogisms (perfect as well as imperfect) share. Aristotle was cognizant of these validity conditions. But to see them most clearly it's easier to step ahead several centuries to logicians of the scholastic thirteenth and fourteenth centuries. Aristotle had formulated categoricals with the logical copula standing between the two terms. He would say, for example, "Rational belongs to every man." This is as awkward in English as it was in Greek (and later Latin). The scholastic logicians rendered categoricals more natural by (i) splitting the copula into two parts, (ii) attaching the first part to the first term and the second part to the second term, (iii) reversing the order of the two (now augmented) terms, and (iv) adjusting the results for grammatical rectitude. Aristotle's "Rational belongs to every man" became, in order, "Rational belongs to / every man," "Every man/rational belongs to," "Every man is rational." The two parts of the split copula became the *quantifier* and the *qualifier* (still called, by itself, the copula). The term with quantifier is known as the *subject*; the qualified term is the *predicate*. The quantity and quality of a categorical are determined by the quantity of the subject and the quality of the predicate. Quantity is either *universal* or *particular*; quality is either *affirmative* or *negative*. When the quality is negative the sentence is said to be a *denial*. Before continuing it must be emphasized that quantifiers and qualifiers are not logical formatives; they are fragments of a split logical formative—a copula. They may appear sometimes as orthographically separate entities, but from the point of view of logical syntax they always work in tandem (in this they are like the "either . . . or . . ." of sentential logic). We can now state four of the necessary conditions for syllogistic validity: *at least one premise is universal; at least one premise is affirmative; if one of the premises is particular so is the conclusion; if one of the premises is negative so is the conclusion.* There are two more necessary conditions. Taken together with the first four these constitute necessary and sufficient conditions for syllogistic validity (thus can be used as a decision procedure).

The two additional conditions depend on the scholastic logicians theory (in truth there were many theories) of *distribution*. Commonsense tells you that if I say that all dogs are canines I give you information about all dogs but not about all canines. Were I to say that some canines are foxes you would have been given no information either about all canines or about all foxes. The scholastics noted this distinction, calling any term used in a sentence in such a way that information is given (perhaps implicitly) about all the things satisfying that term distributed; terms not used in a sentence in that way are undistributed. Notice that terms are only distributed/undistributed (have a distribution value) relative to the various sentences in which they occur. In our two examples above "canine" was distributed in the first and undistributed in the second. Quantity is obviously a good guide for determining distribution for subject terms. But what about predicate terms? The doctrine of distribution holds that a term is distributed in a sentence if and only if it is universally quantified either in that sentence itself or in a sentence logically following from it. The doctrine also holds that when a term is distributed/undistributed its negation is undistributed/distributed. Thus, inside a negation, terms reverse their distribution values. The final two necessary conditions for syllogistic validity are: *the middle term is distributed at least once; any term distributed in the conclusion is distributed in the premises.*

Proof for syllogistic depends on the Aristotelian notion of a perfect syllogism, one immediately recognized as valid by any rational person. Recall that there are four syllogistic figures (ways in which the three terms of a syllogism can be arranged). In the so-called *first figure* the middle term is the subject term of the first premise and the predicate term of the second premise, the predicate term of the first premise is the predicate term of the conclusion, and the subject term of the second premise is the subject term of the conclusion (in a standard syllogism the premise with the predicate term of the conclusion is placed first). As it happens, only four moods in this figure are valid, and these are Aristotle's four perfect syllogisms. The forms of these (along with their scholastic names) are as follows:

> Barbara: Every M is P; every S is M; so every S is P
> Celarent: No M is P; every S is M; so no S is P
> Darii: Every M is P; some S is M; so some S is P
> Ferio: No M is P; some S is M; so some S is not P

The proof of any other (i.e., imperfect) valid syllogism is either direct or indirect. A direct proof is a proof by *reduction*; an indirect proof is a proof by *reductio ad absurdum*. In the first case the proof is achieved by replacing one or more of the syllogism's sentences by logically equivalent sentences (or in special cases by sentences that are merely entailed by them) and reordering the premises (if necessary) so that the final result is a syllogism in one of the perfect forms. Needless to say, not just any change in the form of a sentence will yield a logically equivalent (or entailed) sentence. This can only be guaranteed by making the change in form according to certain clearly formulated rules. Such rules are called rules of *immediate inference*. Three of the most important of these are (*simple*) *conversion*—the two terms of a universal negative, or the two terms of a particular affirmative, can exchange positions; *obversion*—any negative categorical is equivalent to an affirmation whose predicate term is the negation of the predicate term of the original; *subalternation*—a universal entails its corresponding particular. Here are examples of each such immediate inference. Conversion: No logicians are fools = No fools are logicians; Obversion: Some men are not wise = Some men are unwise; Subalternation: Every philosopher is wise ⇒ Some philosopher is wise.

As one might expect, indirect proof for syllogistic relies on the fact that no valid argument can have all true premises but a false conclusion. Thus the set consisting of the premises and the negation of the conclusion (called the *counterset* of the argument) of a valid syllogism must be inconsistent. Proof that the counterset of syllogism is inconsistent amounts to an indirect proof of the syllogism. This is achieved by applying the rules of immediate inference to one or more of the members of the counterset so that at least one pair of the resulting members are negations of one another (contradictory, thus the counterset has been reduced to a contradiction—*reductio ad absurdum*.

It has often been claimed (e.g., by Leibniz) that a single rule governs all syllogistic validity. The rule goes by its scholastic Latin title, *dictum de omni et nullo* (it says: *Quod de aliquo omni dicitur/negatur, etiam de qualibet eius parte*). In other words: What is affirmed/denied of any whole is affirmed/denied of any part of that whole. This might be paraphrased as: what is affirmed or denied of all S is affirmed or denied of whatever S is affirmed of. A close inspection of the four perfect syllogistic forms shows that in each case the term affirmed or denied of all M in the first premise, namely P, is affirmed or denied in the conclusion of what P is affirmed of in the second premise, namely all or some S. Since the dictum characterizes all perfect syllogisms, and since all valid imperfect syllogisms are reducible to perfect forms, the dictum characterizes all valid syllogisms.

The Limits of Syllogistic

In spite of rivals from time to time, Aristotle's logic, or at least a closely related version of it (all of it referred to today as *traditional formal logic*), dominated logical studies from ancient times until the late nineteenth century. That is a very long time. That such traditional logic has been (almost) thoroughly replaced by a quite different formal logic (the one so far presented in this book) is due to a variety of historical, technical, and philosophical factors. One factor contributing to the demise of the old logic was its very limited scope. The Aristotelian system could provide a good account of arguments that could be put into the syllogistic mold. But can all, or even most, arguments be so treated? They can if all sentences can be construed as categoricals. But can even this be done? At least three fairly common and ordinary kinds of sentences seem not to be categorical at all. Notice that the terms of a genuine categorical are always *general*. They are terms such as "dog," "canine," "logician," and so on; they are terms meant to apply to many things. There are lots of dogs and even many logicians. None of the terms in a categorical is *singular*, meant to apply to just one thing (unlike "Mars," "Obama," or "2"). For a variety of philosophical reasons Aristotle chose to limit categorical treatment to sentences making no use of singular terms. Later scholastic logicians tried to incorporate such sentences into syllogistic, but their usual method of doing so was *ad hoc* and unnatural.

A second kind of sentence that appears immune to categorical treatment consists of those making use of *relational* terms. A genuine categorical always consists of a single subject (quantified term) and a single predicate (qualified term). Relational sentences such as "Every painter owns some brushes" and "Some logician wrote some books" seem to have too many subjects. No logician before the nineteenth century was able to give a clear, systematic, satisfactory account of the logical treatment of such relational sentences (though Leibniz gave it a good shot).

Finally, there are sentences that are compounds of other sentences. Conjunctions, disjunctions, conditionals, and so on, have components which are themselves sentences. These component sentences might very well be categorical, but it's hard to see that the compound sentences are categorical in any way. What is required in order to provide a logical home for inferences involving such sentences is a sentential logic such as the one presented in Chapter 2. Aristotle mentions that he could do something like this, later Stoic logicians did (but were soon forgotten), and Leibniz outlined a program for incorporating sentential logic into syllogistic. Still, only in the late nineteenth century was a system of well-formulated sentential logic achieved.

From the time of Aristotle to the nineteenth century, with a few notable exceptions, most scholars who pursued an interest in logic were philosophers. Early in that century a number of mathematicians (especially, for example, Boole and De Morgan in England) began looking at logic as a kind of mathematics—an algebra (hence they are known as *algebraic* logicians). Soon after, spurred on by developments in mathematics, such as the formation of non-Euclidean geometries, that seemed to undermine mathematical footing, a number of mathematicians began seeking ways of shoring up the foundations of mathematics. One way, the way followed by Frege, was to build a logic strong enough to serve as this foundation. This idea, that mathematics could rest on logic was known as *logicism*. The resulting system of formal logic is generally known as *modern mathematical logic*. It is the logic presented in the other chapters of this book. This new logic, compared with the old traditional logic, is powerful and impressive. It faces none of the limits of the old logic. It incorporates into one system not only the logic of general terms but the logic of singular terms, relational terms, and compound sentences. Moreover, while the old logic symbolized general terms using letters as variables, the new logic is fully symbolic, using special symbols for all formative expressions. Like any mathematical system, modern logic enjoys the advantages of a fully symbolized language. Since for any element of the language there are recursive rules governing its behavior (i.e., it is algorithmic) calculation is mechanical. Having said all this, it might seem that there is no hope for anything like traditional logic in face of the advantages enjoyed by modern mathematical logic. Nonetheless, in the rest of this chapter we will present the outlines of a system of logic that is, in many of its fundamentals, similar to traditional logic, yet enjoys the same advantages (and maybe more) as the new logic.

Term Functor Logic

Traditional formal logic, in particular syllogistic, is a *term logic*. A term logic takes all non-formative expressions to be fit for any logical role in a sentence. Unlike the standard modern logic, term logic does not place logical weight on distinctions such as noun/verb, singular/general, and so on. Such distinctions are taken to be matters of semantics rather than syntax. Modern logic takes all negation to be logically sentential (thus the only formative symbol for negation is "$\neg$"). In contrast, a term logic takes all negation to be term negation. We've seen that while modern logic analyzes simple sentences without requiring any logical copula, traditional logic analyzes such sentences as pairs of copulated terms. Thus term logic (only the basics of which are introduced below) shares with traditional logic the notion that simple sentences are pairs of copulated terms. As we will now see, the copulae in this new logic are binary functors on terms.

We begin with a formal language, *TFL*, based on a vocabulary of non-formative expressions, symbolized by uppercase letters (A, B, C, . . .) and two formative expressions, called *term functors*. The two functors are symbolized as "–" (minus) and "+" (plus). We define a *term* as follows:

Definition 8.1 (i) any letter is a simple term of *TFL*;
(ii) any expression consisting of a term prefixed by a minus is a negative term of *TFL*;
(iii) any expression consisting of a pair of terms flanking a plus is a compound term of *TFL*.

Parentheses will be used in the usual way for grouping and disambiguation. Thus, for example, – A + B is to be distinguished from – (A + B). The negative term functor is unary, applying to terms one at a time; the term functor for compounding is binary. Term negation, by definition 4.1 (ii), can be reiterated. The result of negating a negated term is logically equivalent to that term (e.g., – – A = A). The binary functor has the important feature of symmetry (but it is neither reflexive nor transitive). For example, A + B = B + A. It is also associative (e.g., A + (B + C) = (A + B) + C).

One might well note that a natural language such as English has a number of expressions that often behave in ways reflected by our *TFL* functors. Thus, for example, "not," "it is not the case that," "isn't," "non ...," "... less," "un ...," and so on, act as term negators; "and," "both ... and," "some ... are ...," Aristotle's "belongs to some," and so on, act as symmetric and associative compounders. Here are some examples of English expressions and their symbolizations in *TFL*.

unmarried	– M
not responsible	– R
fat and happy	F + H
Albert and Bob	*A + B*
Some logicians are wise (Wise belongs to some logicians)	*W + L*

Our formal language, *TFL*, must be extended if we are to reflect more of natural language. To that end we make use of the following definitions for a unary plus and a binary minus.

Definition 8.2 (i) for any term A, the expression consisting of A prefixed by a plus is a positive term of TFL (+ A = df – – A)
(ii) for any term consisting of a pair of terms flanking a minus is a compound term of *TFL* (A – B) = df – (– A + – B)

Note first that both our new unary plus and binary minus are defined in terms of our more basic unary minus and binary plus. One needn't worry that these unary and binary versions of each formative will be confused. As in algebra and arithmetic, position will always distinguish the two versions. Consider, for example, the equation 2 − 7 = − 5, where the first minus is the binary sign of subtraction and the second minus is the unary sign for negative numbers. As well, note that just as in algebra and arithmetic we will tend to suppress unary pluses when convenient (just as we did on the 2 and 7 in the equation above). Also note that our definition for the binary minus depends on the distribution of a unary minus into a compound term and then the replacement of a binary plus followed immediately by a unary minus with a binary minus. The new binary minus is reflexive and transitive, but not symmetric. English examples of expressions corresponding to our new formatives are:

massive	+ M
Wise belongs to every philosopher	W − P

We now make a further important modification. Our two binary functors can be viewed as logical copulae (e.g., "belongs to some" and belongs to every"). But such expressions are not always natural. We say "Some logicians are wise" rather than "Wise belongs to some logicians." The new modification in *TFL* follows the scholastic logicians procedure for *splitting* copulae. The following definitions introduce split versions of our two copulae, our two binary functors.

Definition 8.3   (i) + A + B = df B + A
                      (ii) − A + B = df B − A

In English we make use of both split and unsplit versions of many functor-like expressions (e.g., It's cold and sunny vs. It's both cold and sunny; Sleepy characterized every juror vs. Every juror was sleepy). Finally, notice that, once split, the two fragments of the copula can often be construed as quantifier and qualifier respectively. We can now formulate such English sentences as the following:

Every logician is wise	− L + W
Some philosophers are unwise	+ P + − W
Some philosophers are not wise	+ P − W
Some logicians are rich and famous	+ L + (R + F)
Some logicians are both rich and famous	+ L + (+ R + F)

Exercise 8.1   Translate each of the following into the language of *TFL*:

1. Every dog is friendly
2. No gourmet is fat

3. Every gourmet is fat and happy
4. Some wise logicians are philosophers
5. Not all jewels are valuable
6. Some actors are neither modest nor shy
7. It is not the case that every logician is a mathematician
8. Whatever is not extended is thinking
9. Whatever is either extended or thinking is a substance
10. No philosopher is both poetic and unmusical
11. Every man who is not both ambitious and talented is sad and lonely
12. Some men who are brave are neither fools nor cowards

Singular Terms and Identity in TFL

Our formal language, *TFL*, is now far more expressive in that we can more easily and naturally formulate a wide range of natural language expressions. Still it is far from an adequate formal model for natural language. Recall that traditional logic was unclear about the logic of singular terms. In modern formal systems definite descriptions are analyzed (à la Russell) in terms of existential quantifiers and bound variables, proper names are treated as free variable constants, and pronouns are treated as bound variables. As well, simple ("atomic") sentences of *QL* are construed (à la Plato and Frege) as pairs consisting of a verb ("function expression" or "predicate") and an appropriate number of names ("argument expressions"). The distinction between singular terms and predicates is syntactic and fundamental in *QL*. Quite appropriately, then, it is marked by the use of different kinds of symbols (lowercase/uppercase). In *TFL* the distinction between singulars and general terms, predicates, is not syntactic. But it is semantic. Singular terms denote exactly one individual; general terms can denote one or more individuals. This means that singular terms, such as names, are treated on a par with any other kind of term in *TFL*. It also means that any inference that depends upon the singularity of a term is not formal.

Since singular terms are terms they can occur anywhere a term can occur in *TFL*. In particular, in a sentence with a split copula a singular term could be in either the subject term position (thus quantified) or in the predicate term position (thus qualified). Suppose I say "Socrates is wise." In formulating this we want to know the quantity. The scholastics tended to take such a sentence to be universal (since its subject term must be distributed, saying something about everything that is Socrates). Later logicians held that the quantity must be particular. Still later, Leibniz argued that the quantity was both universal and particular. Our version takes the quantity of such sentences to be particular—but, it takes such sentences to always materially, non-formally imply their corresponding universals. Singular subjects are said to have *wild* quantity. Since, in general, when S is singular: + S + P = − S + P, we will mark the wild quantity of singular subjects using ±. "Socrates is wise" would be formulated as ∀S + W.

Consider the perfectly valid inference: "Some Greek philosopher was Socrates; Socrates was wise; hence, some Greek philosopher was wise." Two things should be noted. First, the middle term of this syllogistic inference is "Socrates" so it must be distributed (given universal quantity) in the second premise. Second, "Socrates" is the predicate term in the first premise. The fact that singular subject terms have wild quantity, along with the fact that singular terms can appear as predicate terms (i.e., be qualified), means that *TFL* requires no special "identity theory." A sentence like "Twain is (identical to) Clemens" is simply formulated as ∀T + C. For those looking for the reflexivity, symmetry, and transitivity of identity, *TFL* offers, given the wild quantity of singular subjects, the reflexivity of the split binary negative (i.e., universal affirmations like "Every Twain is Twain"), the symmetry of the binary plus (split or unsplit) (i.e., the equivalence of "Some Twain is Clemens" and "Some Clemens is Twain"), and the transitivity of the split binary minus (i.e., "Every Twain is Clemens; every Clemens is the author of *Huckleberry Finn*; so every Twain is the author of *Huckleberry Finn*"). Since the quantity of singular subjects is wild (when we use a name to refer to an individual we know that there is something being referred to and we know that in using the term we are referring to anything that is so referred to), in using a natural language such as English we virtually always leave the quantity tacit. We don't say "Every Twain is Clemens" or "Some Twain is the author of *Huckleberry Finn*, or even "Some/every Twain is . . .," we simply use the name alone.

Exercise 8.2   Translate into *TFL*:

1. Romeo is not Don Juan
2. Clay is Ali
3. Claire is a girl who is not a fool
4. No living composer is Mozart
5. Mars is not Phosphorus
6. Woody is not Pitt and he's not Clooney
7. Ed is not a man who worries
8. Bacon isn't Shakespeare
9. Max is everywhere
10. It isn't the case that Nixon was noble

Relationals in TFL

It is important to realize that every sentence in *TFL* is a term (called a *sentential term*). Moreover, every term is either negative (e.g., "massless" – M) or positive ("massive" + M). As well, every sentence is a compound term, where every compound term is a concatenation of a pair of copulated (via a split or unsplit binary functor) terms (simple or compound). Thus, we can display a general ("omnibus") form in *TFL* for all sentences.

–/+ (–/+ (–/+ X) –/+ (–/+ Y))

The first functor (either minus or plus) is unary and applies to the sentence as a whole; since every term is either negative or positive, so is every sentential term. The third and fifth functors are also unary, each applying to one of the constituent terms. The second and fourth functors constitute a split copula. The second is the quantifier (either minus for universal or plus for particular) and the fourth is the (negative or positive) qualifier. An English paraphrase of our omnibus formula might read (suppressing the unary pluses on component terms):

It is / isn't the case that every / some non X / X is / isn't non Y / Y

A sentence such as "Not everyone who is unmarried is unhappy" could be formulated in *TFL* as – (– (– M) + (– H)).

Consider now a relational expression like "missing" in "Some girl is missing some boy." As with any sentence, this one is a pair of copulated terms. The first term is simple, "girl," while the second is compound. This compound term itself consists of a pair of copulated terms, "missing" and "boy." Note that while the copula for the entire sentence is split, "Some . . . is . . .," the copula for the compound predicate term is unsplit, "some." And this is the norm for relational terms; they consist of a pair of terms copulated by an unsplit functor (e.g., "some" or "every"). This means that words such as "every" and "some" play two distinct logical roles. They are sometimes quantifiers (fragments of a split copula) and other times they are entire unsplit copula. Suppressing unnecessary unary pluses, our sentence can be formulated in *TFL* as + G + (M + B). Here are some other examples involving relational terms.

Romeo loves Juliet	± R + (L ∀ J)
Every boy loves some girl	– B + (L + G)

Some philosophers who write a book are logicians	$+ (+ P + (W + B)) + L$
Whoever draws a circle draws a figure	$- (D + C) + (D + F)$

Something important must be added to our account of the logical form of relationals in *TFL*. Look back at our sentence "Some girl is missing some boy." We will soon see that a necessary condition for two sentences to be logically equivalent is that their *TFL* forms be algebraically equal. But surely "Some girl is missing some boy" is not logically equivalent to "Some boy is missing some girl" $(+ B + (M + G))$. An essential feature of relational expressions is that they have a "direction." The *missing* relation in these two sentences goes in two different directions (from the girl to the boy vs. from the boy to the girl). The order of the relata of a relation matters. We know that in *QL* this notion of direction or order is indicated by the order of the individual variables and constants that follow the predicate term (so that "Romeo loves Juliet" has the form Lrj while "Juliet loves Romeo" has the form Ljr). In *QL* the (singular term) arguments of function expressions (predicates) indicate both the adicity and the order of the predicate. How can these features be exhibited in *TFL*?

In *TFL* we want to keep track of pairs of terms that are copulated to form a compound pair. We do this by subscribing to each term of such a pair an arbitrarily chosen common numeral. A sentence such as "Every logician is rational" could be formulated as $- L_1 + R_1$ ($-L_5 + R_5$ would have worked just as well). Our sentence "Some girl is missing some boy" might be formulated initially as $+ G + (M + B)_1$. But in this case the predicate term is itself a compound of two terms. We can now add new subscripts to indicate this (sub)copulation: $+ G_1 + (L_2 + B_2)_1$. We now introduce a pair of conventions to simplify the use of subscripts. Subscripts may be eliminated when relational order is not a factor (thus the subscripts in our formula $- L_1 + R_1$ can safely be dropped) or when the final subscript has been "amalgamated." A second convention is more useful. When a compound term is relational the subscript on that term may be amalgamated with the subscript on the relational term to indicate the order of the relation. To see amalgamation at work consider, once more, our sentence "Some girl is missing some boy." Applying our conventions allows us to formulate this as $+ G_1 + (M_{12} + B_2)$, indicating that "missing" is a two-place relation and that some girl is the agent and some boy is the object of that relation. A sentence such as "Some girl is missed by some boy" would be formulated in *TFL* as $+ G_1 + (M_{21} + B_2)$, and "Some boy is missed by some girl" (the "passive transformation" of the first sentence) would have the form $+ B_2 + (M_{12} + G_1)$. Finally, consider a slightly more complex example, "Some man gave a rose to every contestant." We will amalgamate (and eliminate unnecessary) subscripts in the following series of steps:

1. $+\dot{M}_1 + ((G_3 + R_3)_2 - W_2)_1$
2. $+M_1 + ((G_3 + R_3)_{12} - W_2)$
3. $+M_1 + ((G_{132} + R_3) - W_2)$

One final note for now concerning relationals. In any compound term of *TFL* the pair of terms involved must share at least one (possibly suppressed) subscript. This restriction will play an important role in deductions.

Exercise 8.3   Translate into *TFL*:

1. There are lawyers who send all judges a bribe
2. Every gourmet loves some dish
3. Every cat has some fleas
4. Descartes doubted all experiences
5. A logician who knew Plato admired Socrates
6. Not all men are kind and gentle, but some women love all men who are kind
7. Max chases every cat that looks at him
8. A boy who kissed Jean lied to Nelly
9. No number is bigger than every number
10. A man who gave a rose to a woman received a summons from a judge

Letting S = student, G = gave, A = apple, and T = teacher, translate each of the following *TFL* sentences into ordinary English

1. $+S_1 + ((G_{123} + A_2) - T_3)$
2. $-T_1 + ((G_{321} + A_2) + S_3)$
3. $-T_1 + ((G_{123} + A_2) + S_3)$
4. $+S_1 + (G_{12} + A_2)$
5. $+A_2 + G_{12}$
6. $-T + S$
7. $+S_1 + ((G_{123} + A_2) - S_3)$
8. $+S_1 + (G_{121} + A_2)$
9. $+T_1 - ((G_{123} + A_2) + S_3)$
10. $-S_1 - ((G_{123} + A_2) - T_3)$

The Logic of Sentences in TFL

As we have seen, *TFL* takes sentences to be compound terms (i.e., copulated pairs of terms). Obviously, sentences, like any terms, can be compounded to form more complex sentences. We have also seen that each of our logical copulae (whether split or unsplit) has certain formal features. The binary plus is symmetric and associative; the binary minus is reflexive and transitive. Importantly, we noted that various natural language expressions also exhibit just such features. Some of these are used to form compounds of sentential terms; others are used to form compound non-sentential terms. All of this means that for *TFL* a logic for compound sentences (the *SL* of modern mathematical logic) is simply a special part of the logic of terms. The logic of (unanalyzed) sentences is simply the logic of sentential terms.

To illustrate the logic of sentences not analyzed down to the level of their non-sentential component term (but, at best, only to the level of their sentential term components) we adopt a handy, simplifying convention. We will use lowercase letters in the middle of the alphabet as variables for sentential terms. The following examples show how various English expressions can be formulated in *TFL* as (split) copulae for either sentential or non-sentential terms.

rich and famous	+ R + F
Some logicians are wise	+ L + W
It's cold and it's raining	+ p + q
Every logician is wise	− L + W
If it's cold then it's raining	− p + q

Just as a universal denial has been defined in terms of the logically more primitive particular affirmation and term negation, we could define the conditional form of sentences in terms of conjunction and negation. We could define the disjunctive form of a sentence in terms of conjunction and negation as well. Since a disjunction is equivalent to the negation of a conjunction of negations, we have: $- - p - - q = df - (+ - p + - q)$. The sentence "Either it's cold or it's raining" would then be formulated in *TFL* as $- - p - - q$. As one might expect, the symmetry of our binary plus guarantees the commutability of both conjunctions and disjunctions; the transitivity of our binary minus guarantees the transitivity of conditionals.

A final note is in order concerning the logic of sentences in *TFL*. Some careful thought will reveal just how the logic of compound sentences (conditional sentences, conjunctions of sentences, etc.) is a *special* part of *TFL*. What will be revealed is a pair of apparent disanalogies between the general logic of terms and the logic of sentential terms. Consider first the fact that a pair of sentence such as "Some logicians are married" and "Some logicians are unmarried" are logically compatible (constitute a consistent set). In general, then, we want to say that any pair of sentences of the forms $+ X + Y$ and $+ X - Y$ are compatible.

However, if X and Y are sentential terms such a pair would not be compatible (consider the two conjunctive sentences "(Both) it's cold and it's raining" and "(Both) it's cold and it's not raining"). So the first apparent disanalogy: + X + Y and + X − Y are compatible when X and Y are non-sentential terms but not when they are sentential terms. Next consider the fact that a conjunction of two sentences logically entails its corresponding conditional (e.g., "(Both) it's cold and it's raining" entails "If it's cold then it's raining"). We are tempted then to say that, in general, sentences of the form + X + Y entail corresponding sentences of the form − X + Y. However, if X and Y are non-sentential terms such an implication would not hold (consider the two sentences "Some logician is married" and "Every logician is married"). So the second apparent disanalogy: + X + Y entails − X + Y when X and Y are sentential terms but not when they are non-sentential terms. How are these apparent disanalogies to be accounted for so that the logic of sentences is a part of the logic of terms rather than a special appendage to that logic? The full answer goes beyond the limits of this book, involving a broad, rich semantic theory. But there is a short answer: *sentential terms are always singular.*

Exercise 8.4

1. Translate into *TFL*:
   a. If it's raining, Tom is reading a book
   b. Either Tom is reading a book or it's not raining
   c. No men are both kind and gentle, but some women love all men who are kind
   d. It is not the case that every girl loves Adonis
   e. Tom is neither reading a book nor sleeping

2. Show why the singularity of sentential terms allows for *TFL* to accommodate the two apparent disanalogies.

Rules of Inference for Derivations in TFL

We begin our discussion of derivation by introducing the notion of *sentential valence*. Recall our omnibus formula: +/− (+/− (+/− S)+/− (+/− P)). The valence of any sentence is determined by the first two signs in its omnibus formulation (remember that the first sign was a unary functor applying to the entire sentence (sentential term) and the second was a quantifier). *A sentence has positive valence if and only if these two signs are the same (both minus or both plus); otherwise the sentence has negative valence.* A bit of thought shows that particular sentences, negations of universal sentences, conjunctions and negations of conditionals or disjunctions have positive valence; universal sentences, negations of particular sentences, conditionals, and disjunctions have negative valence. Often one must restore some or even all of the signs suppressed from the sentences omnibus formula in order to determine valence. The notion of valence allows us to formulate the principle of equivalence for *TFL*.

Principle of Equivalence (PEQ)

Two sentences are equivalent if and only if they have the same valence and are algebraically equal.
Examples of equivalent pairs are:

(i) Not a creature was stirring, $-(+ C + S)$ = Every creature was unstirring, $- C + (- S)$ = No creature was stirring, $- C - S$.
(ii) All men are fools, $- M + F$ = All non-fools are non-men, $-(- F) + (- M)$.

However, the pair $-(- A) + B$ and $+ A + B$, though algebraically equal, are not equivalent since they do not have the same valence (keep in mind that the initial unary plus of their omnibus versions have been suppressed but must be considered in determining valence).

Exercise 8.5 Which of these pairs are equivalent? In each case, say why the others are not equivalent.

1. $+ (- S) + P$ and $+ P - S$
2. $+ S + (- R + P)$ and $- (R - P) + S$
3. $- S + (- P + Q)$ and $- (+ (- Q) + P) + (- S)$
4. $+ (A_1 + (R_{12} - B_2)) + (Q_{13} + C_3)$ and $+ ((- B_2 + R_{12}) + A_1) + (Q_{13} + C_3)$
5. $+ (A_1 + (R_{12} - B_2)) + (Q_{13} + C_3)$ and $- (B_2 + (- R_{12} - A_1)) + (C_3 + Q_{13})$

Next we introduce the definition of tautology. *A sentence is a tautology if and only if it is negative valence and is algebraically equal to 0.* Since the negation of a tautology is a contradiction we have: *A sentence is a contradiction if and only if it is positive in valence and is algebraically equal to 0.* We can then add: *A set of sentences is inconsistent if and only if the conjunction of any subset of its members is a contradiction.* We can now provide the necessary and sufficient conditions for argument validity in a variety of ways:

> (i) An argument is valid if and only if its corresponding conditional formula (with the conjunction of the premises as antecedent and the conclusion as consequent) is a tautology.
>
> (ii) An argument is valid if and only if its counterset (the set of premises and the negation of the conclusion) is inconsistent. We will formulate a third way.

Validity

An argument is valid if and only if the number of premises with positive valence equals the number of conclusions with positive valence (i.e., either 1 or 0) and the sum of the premises algebraically equals the conclusion.

Application of **Validity** to an argument amounts to a decision procedure. In practice this decision procedure is simple and fast. Once an argument is formulated in the language of *TFL* inspect it to see if the number of premises with positive valence equals the number of conclusions with positive valence; if that condition is satisfied (i.e., either all the premises and the conclusion are negative in valence or the conclusion and exactly one of the premises are positive in valence), then algebraically determine the sum of the premises; if that sum is algebraically equal to the conclusion then the argument is valid (if not then it is invalid).

Exercise 8.6 Valid or invalid?

1. $- A_1 + (R_{12} + B_2)$
   $- (R_{13} + C) + D$
   $- B + D$
   $\therefore - C - A$

2. $- p + (- - q - - r)$
   $- (+ q + s)$
   $+ s + p$
   $\therefore + r$

3. $\pm A + B$
   $C_2 + (R_{21} \pm A_1)$
   $\therefore C_2 + (R_{21} + B_1)$

4. $- p + (+ q + (- - r + s))$
   $- (+ r + q) + p$
   $\therefore + s$

5. $+ M_1 + (L_{12} + S_2)) + (K_{13} + (B + D)_3)$
   $+ S_2 + (L_{23} - (B + D)_3)$
   $\therefore - (B + D)_3 + (K_{13} + M_1)$

We saw in our brief look at syllogistic that traditional logicians formulated both immediate rules of inference and a mediate rule of inference (the *dictum de omni et nullo*). The former apply to a single sentence to yield a second sentence that is either equivalent to the first or logically entailed by it. A mediate rule applies to a pair of sentences to yield a new sentence logically entailed by them. (**Taut** could be construed as a rule for deriving a sentence from no sentence—not even from itself). Every *proof* (of the validity of an argument or the inconsistency of a set of sentences) is a *derivation*. A derivation is finite series of lines (each of which is a sentence of *TFL*), such that every member of the series is justified by one or more rules of inference and the last line is the conclusion, if the derivation is a proof of argument validity, or a contradiction, if the derivation is a proof of set inconsistency. As always, an *indirect* proof of a valid argument is a proof of the inconsistency of its counterset. An important note: while every line in a derivation is a (sentential) term of *TFL*, not every (compound) term in a derivation is a line. We begin with a small number of rules of immediate inference for use in derivations.

Premise (P)

Any premise can be a line in a proof of validity; any member of a set of sentences can be a line in a proof of inconsistency.

Tautology (T)

Any tautology can be added as a line in a proof unless it is the corresponding conditional of an argument being proven.

Commutation (Com)

If + X + Y is a term in a line (or an entire line), then a new line can be added which differs from that line by replacing that term with + Y + X.

Association (Assoc)

If + X + (Y +/– Z) is a term in a line (or an entire line), then a new line can be added which differs from that line by replacing that term with + (+ X + Y) +/– Z; if + (+ X + Y) +/– Z is a term in a line (or an entire line), then a new line can be added which differs from that line by replacing that term with + X + (+ Y +/– Z).

Iteration (It)

If +/– X is a term in a line (or an entire line), then a new line can be added which differs from that line by replacing that term with + (+/– X) + (+/– X); if + (+/– X) + (+/– X) is a term in a line (or an entire line), then a new line can be added which differs from that line by replacing that term with +/– X.

Double Negation (DN)

If + X is a term in a line (or an entire line), then a new line can be added which differs from that line by replacing that term with − − X; if − − X is a term in a line (or an entire line), then a new line can be added which differs from that line by replacing that term with + X.

External Negation (EN)

If − (+/− X +/− Y) is a line, then a new line can be added which differs from that line by replacing it with −/+ X −/+ Y; if −/+ X −/+ Y is a line, then a new line can be added which differs from that line by replacing it with − (+/− X +/− Y).

Internal Negation (IN)

If +/− X − (+/− Y) is a line, then a new line can be added which differs from it by replacing it with +/− X + (−/+ Y); if +/− X + (−/+ Y) is a line, then a new line can be added which differs from it by replacing it with +/− X − (+/− Y). (Note that IN allows distribution of a negative qualifier into a predicate expression; nothing allows a universal quantifier to distribute into a subject expression, thus, for example, "Every nonA is B" is not logically equivalent to "Some A is B," that is, − (− A) + B ... + A + B, since the two do not share a common valence).

Exercise 8.7 What is the missing premise needed for these to be valid?

1. $-S + P, + Q + R \therefore + Q - S$
2. $+ A_1 + (R_{12} + B_2) \therefore + A_1 + (R_{12} + C_2)$
3. All logicians are scholars; so, whoever admires a logician admires a scholar
4. $-p + q, -(-r) + p \therefore q$
5. $T_1 + C_1, -(A_1 - (A_{12} - B_2) + D \therefore T_1 + D_1$

Exercise 8.8 Show why $-(-A) + B$ and $+ A + B$ must have different valences.

Universal Distribution (UD)

If − X + (+ Y + Z) is a line, then new line can be added which differs from it by replacing it with + (− X + Y) + (− X + Z); if + (− X + Y) + (− X + Z) is a line, then a new line can be added which differs from it by replacing it with − X + (+ Y + Z). (In effect, UD is a rule allowing the distribution of universal subjects into conjunctive predicates—to yield conjunctions of universal sentences—or out of such conjunctive sentences—to yield universals with conjunctive predicates.)

Particular Distribution (PD)

If + X + (– – Y – – Z) is line, then a new line can be added which differs from it by replacing it with – – (+ X + Y) – – (+ X + Z); if – – (+ X + Y) – – (+ X + Z) is a line, then a new line can be added which differs from it by replacing it with + X + (– – Y – – Z). (In effect, PD is a rule allowing the distribution of particular subjects into disjunctive predicates—to yield disjunctions of particular sentences—or out of such disjunctive sentences—to yield particulars with disjunctive predicates.)

Wild Quantity (WQ)

If X is singular subject term of a line (or of a sentential term in a line), then a new line can be added which differs from that line by replacing the quantifier of that subject term with any other quantifier. (Note that this is not a formal rule since it depends on the semantic distinction between singular and general terms.)

Simplification (Simp)

If a conjunction of terms is a term (or an entire line), then a new line can be added which differs from it by replacing that term with one of its conjuncts.

There are two rules of mediate inference (i.e., rules that apply to two lines to yield a new line.

Conjunction (Conj)

If there are two lines, then a new line can be added which differs from them by being the conjunction of those two lines.

[Several points are in order concerning our next rule, DON, the key rule of inference for derivations in *TFL*. An inspection of any sentence in *TFL* will show that each simple (non-compound) term is in the range of either no minuses or an even number of minuses or an odd number of minuses. A term of a sentence in the range of an odd number of minuses is *distributed*, otherwise it is *undistributed*. Any universally quantified term will be distributed (and if that term happens to be negative then the unnegated term in such a case will be undistributed). In effect, DON permits us to cancel "middle" terms. For *TFL* such terms are those that appear in premises but not conclusions. DON preserves the syllogistic requirements that middle terms be distributed at least once and that any (non-middle) term distributed in a premise does not appear undistributed in the conclusion.]

Dictum de Omni et Nullo (DON)

If X is a term universally quantified in a line and X is undistributed at least once in a different line, then a new line can be added which differs from that second line by replacing at least one occurrence of the term X there by the entire first line minus its universally quantified X.

Derivation in TFL

As we have seen, a derivation is a finite sequence of lines, each line is a sentence of *TFL*, each line is justified by at least one rule of inference, and the last line is either the conclusion of the valid argument being proven or a contradiction if what is proved is the inconsistency of a set of sentences. Here are some examples of derivations.

Example 1   Prove: $- A + B, + C + A \therefore + B + C$

1. $- A + B$	P
2. $+ C + A$	P
3. $+ C + B$	1, 2, DON
4. $+ B + C$	3, Com

Example 2   Prove: "Every circle is a figure, so every drawer of a circle is a drawer of a figure" that is, $- C + F \therefore - (D + C) + (D + F)$ (here all subscripts are unnecessary and suppressed)

1. $- C + F$	P
2. $- (D + C) + (D + C)$	T
3. $- (D + C) + (D + F)$	1, 2, DON

Line 2 is the formulation of the logically innocuous "Every drawer of a circle is a drawer of a circle"

Example 3 Prove: "Some boy loves some girl, every girl adores some cat, all cats are mangey, whoever adores something mangey is a fool, hence, what some boy loves is a fool"

1. $+ B_1 + (L_{12} + G_2)$ P
2. $- G_2 + (A_{23} + C_3)$ P
3. $- C_3 + M_3$ P
4. $- (A_{23} + M_3) + F_2$ P
5. $- G_2 + (A_{23} + M_3)$ 2, 3, DON
6. $- G_2 + F_2$ 4, 5, DON
7. $+ B_1 + (L_{12} + F_2)$ 1, 6, DON
8. $+ (+ B_1 + L_{12}) + F_2$ 7, Assoc

Example 4 Prove: Some logician is reading a book, so some book is being read by a logician.
(This kind of inference is a case of *passive transformation*)

1. $+ L_1 + (R_{12} + B_2)$ P
2. $+ (R_{12} + B_2) + L_1$ 1, Com ("Some reader of a book is a logician")
3. $+ (+ B_2 + R_{12}) + L_1$ 2, Com ("Some book being read is so by a logician")
4. $+ B_2 + (R_{12} + L_1)$ 3, Assoc

In cases involving relationals it is important to keep in mind the restriction mentioned at the end of our discussion of relationals in *TFL*. Any compound term of *TFL* the pair of terms must share at least one (possibly suppressed) subscript. Thus, for example, given the *TFL* sentence $+ A_1 + (R_{12} + B_2)$, each of the following can be derived (making use of Com, Ass, and Simp): $+ A_1 + R_{12}$, $+ R_{12} + B_2$, $+ R_{12} + A_1$, and $+ B_2 + R_{12}$. However, one could not derive, for example, $+ A_1 + B_2$.

Example 5 Prove: "Twain is Clemens, so Clemens is Twain"

1. $\forall T + C$ P
2. $+ T + C$ 1, WQ
3. $+ C + T$ 2, Com
4. $\forall C + T$ 3, WQ

Example 6 Prove: "Twain wrote a novel, Twain is Clemens, hence Clemens wrote a novel"

1. ∀ T1 + (W12 + N2)   P
2. ∀ T1 + C1   P
3. + T1 + (W12 + N2)   1, WQ
4. − T1 + C1   2, WQ
5. + C1 + (W12 + N2)   3, 4, DON
6. C1 + (W12 + N2)   5, WQ

Example 7   Prove *modus ponens*

1. − p + q   P
2. + p   P
3. + q   1, 2, DON

Exercise 8.9   Prove *modus tollens* using *TFL*.

Example 8   Prove the inconsistency of the set: + A + B, − A − C, − B + (+ D + E)

1. + A + B   P
2. − A − C   P
3. − B + (+ C + D)   P
4. + A + (+ C + D)   1, 3, DON
5. + (+ C + D) + A   4, Com
6. + (+ C + D) − C   2, 5, DON
7. + (+ D + C) − C   6, Com
8. + D + (+ C − C)   7, Assoc
9. + C − C   8, Simp

Exercise 8.10   Prove:

1. − A + B, − B − G, − F + G, − R + F ∴ − R − A
2. + A1 + (L12 ∀ B2), ∀ B2 + (L23 ∀ C3), − (L12 ∀ B2) + (L13 − (L23 ∀ B2)) ∴ ∀ A1 + (L13 ∀ C3)
3. − A1 + (R12 + B2), − (+ A1 + (R12 + B2)) + C1 ∴ − A1 + C1
4. 2 < 3, the square root of 4 = 2 ∴ the square root of 4 < 3
5. Every circle is a figure, therefore, whoever draws a circle draws a figure.
6. The Dean gave a student a pass; the Dean is a logician; no one who gave a pass to a student is competent; so some logician is incompetent.
7. − P1 + (Q12 − T2), + (R12 + T2) + K1 ∴ + (R12 + K1) + (Q12 − P1)
8. Some artists are writers; every writer reads some novels; whoever reads a novel reads a book; so, some of those who read books are artists.
9. Whoever reads Quine avoids Heidegger; therefore, whoever studies with someone who reads Quine studies with someone who avoids Heidegger.

10. The man who loved Juliet killed himself, so, Juliet was loved by a man who killed himself.

The Bridge to TFL

TFL is relatively simple and it is natural in the sense that its syntax is designed to be a close approximation to that of natural language. By contrast, *QL* (including *SL*) was generated by a program aimed at establishing a foundation for mathematics. Nevertheless, it is important to realize that term logic is not a rival to modern logic. Each has its own history, inspiration, and motivation, but both are (qua formal systems) to be judged by such common features as soundness, completeness, and expressive and inferential power. They are two different ways of giving a formal treatment to the kinds of inferences carried out normally in the medium of a natural language. Indeed, as it happens, one can, with little effort, translate back and forth between the two formal languages. Such translation is a matter of applying certain "bridging rules" to the task.

In order to prepare a sentence in *TFL* for translation one needs first to reformulate it in "normal form." In a normal form *TFL* sentence each compound term is written with its subject first and its predicate second, and each simple term is given an explicit subscript. Recall that often such subscripts are omitted when not needed. Also note that in many cases subjects already precede predicates. A normal form sentence can then be translated directly into a *QL* sentence by replacing all *TFL* quantifiers by *QL* quantifiers, all *TFL* qualifiers by appropriate SL signs of conjunction or implication and all subscripts by variables. Those are the bridging rules; note that they allow for translation in either direction. Here are some examples of translations from *TFL* to *QL*.

Example 9

Every apple is red
TFL form: − A + R
Normal form: − A_1 + R_1
QL form: ∀x (Ax / Rx)

Example 10

Some snakes are poisonous
TFL: + S + P
NF: + S_1 + P_1
QL: ∃x (Sx ω Px)

Example 11

Every princess loves herself
TFL (NF): $- P_1 + L_{11}$
QL: $\forall x \, (Px \mid Lxx)$

Example 12

Some philosopher taught a logician who admired him
TFL: $+ P_1 + (T_{12} + (+ L_2 + A_{21}))$
NF: $+ P_1 + ((L_2 + A_{21}) + T_{12})$
QL: $\exists x \, (Px \, \varpi \, (\exists y \, (Ly \, \varpi \, Ayx) \, \varpi \, Txy))$

Example 13

Every brother of a girl is skeptical of her friends
TFL: $- (B_{12} + G_2) + (S_{13} - F_{32})$
NF: $- (+ G_2 + B_{12}) + (- F_{32} + S_{13})$
QL: $\forall x \, \exists y \, (Gy \, \varpi \, Bxy) \mid \forall z \, (Fzy \mid Sxz))$

Example 14

Twain wrote some comedies
TFL: $\pm T_1 + (W_{12} + C_2)$
NF: $+ C_2 + (\forall T_1 + W_{12})$
QL: $\exists x \, (Cx \wedge Wtx)$

Example 15

Twain is Clemens
TFL: $\forall T + C$
NF: $\forall T_1 + C_1$
QL: $t = c$

Exercise 8.11   Translate from *TFL* to *QL*:

1. $- (- A + (- B))$
2. $- (S_{12} + (B_{23} + M_3)) + C_1$
3. A man gave a rose to a woman who hated all flowers
4. Twain wrote no tragedies

5. No student who is not diligent and attentive will have any success
6. Socrates taught a teacher of Aristotle
7. $+ (X + (+ Y + Z)) + (+ Q + - R)$
8. Helen admired herself
9. $- [- A_1 + B_1] + [- (R_{21} + A_1) + (R_{21} + B_1)]$
10. If Romeo loved Juliet then Juliet was loved by Romeo

9 The Elements of a Modal Term Logic

We have seen that the formal study of logic began with Aristotle. His version of term logic, the syllogistic, marked the beginning of formal logic. Having examined a number of aspects of modern formal logic, as well as a new version of term logic, we have explored the ways in which modern logic can be extended and modified in order to accommodate the operators meant to reflect such ordinary modal expressions as "possibly" and "necessarily." As it happens, Aristotle not only began the systematic study of logic, he also initiated the study of formal systems of modal logic. His modal syllogistic was *the* modal logic for most of the next two millennia. Modern systems of modal logic owe little to that traditional theory. Moreover, controversy, arising from technical formalities such as worries about the referential opacity of modal contexts) or from philosophical concerns (such as the avoidance of essentialism), has often accompanied work in modal logic. In this chapter we will set much of that aside in order to present the bare outline of a modal term logic, one based on the system TFL and inspired by (but not dictated by) a number of insights from traditional logic.

Syntax

Traditional modal logicians made a distinction (meant to reflect one seen in ordinary language) between modal expressions as applied to entire statements and modal expressions as applied to just a term used in a statement. We say such things as "It's possible that men will walk on Mars" and also such things as "Mars is possibly inhabited." In the first case, the modal expression "it's possible that" applies to the sentence "men will walk on Mars"; in the second case, the modal expression "possibly" applies to the term "inhabited." Logicians refer to the modality that characterizes entire sentences as *de dicto* modality; modality characterizing a term is known as *de re* modality. Also, sentences making use of expressions of necessity are called *apodeictic*; those making use of expressions of possibility are *problematic*. So there are four types of modal statements: *de dicto* apodeictic, *de re* apodeictic, *de dicto* problematic, and *de re* problematic. Examples of each are: "It is necessarily the case that every prime greater than 2 is odd," "Every man must have a mate," "It could be that all men are fools," "Some cats might talk."

The system of modal term logic introduced here is an extension of TFL. To our formal vocabulary we introduce a new (primitive) unary term functor: □. Given that any term A (including where A is a sentential term) can be charged either positively (+) or negatively (−), + A, − A, □ + A, □ − A, − □ + A, and − □ − A are all terms. Again, since in practice unary + signs can be suppressed, these become simply: A, − A, □ A, □ − A, − □ A, and − □ − A. Since □ is a unary term functor, it can apply even to terms already "modalized" to yield: □□ A and □□ − A. Thus, like our other unary functor (−), □ can be reiterated. But there are important differences between them. *Pairs* of the minus functor can be added or subtracted any time. Thus: − − A = A. As for the □ functor, we can add or subtract it *one at a time* for any term already modalized. Thus □□ A = □ A (but: □□A □ A). We can think of this as the

Axiom of Modal Reduction: / □□ X = □ X

We now define a new unary term functor:

Def. ~: ~ X = df − □ − X

Exercise 9.1   Show that ~ ~ X = ~ X.

Exercise 9.2 Which of the following equivalences are true?

1. $\Box - \Box - X = - \sim \Box - X$
2. $\sim \Box \sim \Box X = \Box \sim \Box \sim X$
3. $- \Box\Box \sim - X = - \sim \sim \Box X$

Axioms of *de re* Term Replacement

Two axioms govern the replacement of *de re* modal terms:

(1) $/ - \sim S + S$
(2) $/ - S + \Box S$

Many theorems can be derived from these. Examples are:

(i) $/ + S + \sim P \rightarrow + S + P$
(ii) $/ - S + \sim P \rightarrow - S + P$
(iii) $/ + S + P \rightarrow + S + \Diamond P$
(iv) $/ - S + P \rightarrow - S + \Box P$
(v) $/ + S + \sim P \rightarrow + S + \Box P$
(vi) $/ - S + \sim P \rightarrow - S + \Box P$

An obvious theorem derived from the axioms is the

De re Theorem: $/ - \sim S + \Box S$

Exercise 9.3

1. Using basic TFL, prove Theorems (i)–(vi).
2. Is $- \sim S + P \rightarrow - S + P$ a theorem?
3. Prove the following:
   a. $- \Box S - \Box P \Box - S - \Box P$
   b. $- S + \sim P, - P + \Box Q \Box - S + \Box Q$
   c. $- \Box S - \Box P, + S + \sim R \Box + \sim R - P$

We saw in our examination of TFL that any sentence is itself a (complex) term, a *sentential term*. This means that *de dicto* modality, just like *de re* modality, is the result of applying a modal functor to a term. Thus, all modality is term modality, and if the term is sentential the modality is called *de dicto*.

Axioms of *de dicto* Modality

The following axioms hold for *de dicto* modality:

Axiom 3: / ~ p → p
Axiom 4: / p → □ p

From these the following theorem can be derived:

De dicto Theorem: / ~ p → □ p

Exercise 9.4 Prove the following:

1. − S + □ P, ~ [− □ P + ~ R] □□ [− S + ~ R]

Semantics with Domains of Discourse

A statement is a sentence used to make (usually implicitly) a truth claim. Every statement is made relative to some specifiable *domain of discourse*. A domain of discourse (from now on just "domain") can be *fixed* or *variable*. A fixed domain is constituted by a given and permanent number of individual things. Sets are fixed domains. A variable domain is constituted by a given, but not permanent, number of individual things. Variable domains are sometimes called *worlds*. Any collection of things can be a domain relative to which a statement is made. A domain can be as large or small as required by the speaker. The entire universe can serve as a domain. Some determinable part of the universe (say the earth and its flora and fauna during the past million years) can be a domain. The items in my garage, the customers in the corner store, the ingredients in the soup I ate for lunch—all can be domains. As we said, statement-making is truth-claiming. And every statement is made relative to some domain. Every truth claim is a claim that some thing(s) are present in or absent from the domain relative to which the statement making that claim is made. So, every statement made relative to a given domain is a claim that some thing(s) is or isn't in that domain.

If I tell you that Native Dancer was a filly, it is clear that my domain is the actual world (or at least the equine part of it). If I tell you that Pegasus had wings, my domain is the world of Greek mythology. If I tell you that 2 is even, my domain is (at least) the set of natural numbers. Consider now the domain that has as its constituents all other domains. This "domain of domains" is, of course, variable. Next consider all the domains relative to some thing(s) that is a common constituent (e.g., all the domains that contain horses, all the domains that contain dragons, all the domains that contain the earth). Let d be such a domain. Let ∪d be the union of domains containing common constituent(s), and ∩d be the intersection of such domains.

While non-modal statements are made relative to some domain of individual things, modal statements are always made relative to some domain of domains. *De dicto* apodeictic statements, made relative to a domain d, make a truth claim about ∩d. *De dicto* problematic statements make a truth claim about ∪d.

Unlike statements of *de dicto* modality, statements of *de re* modality are made relative to a specifiable domain such as the actual world. For example, made relative to the actual world, the statement "Some cats might talk" claims that the world has among its constituents some cats that possibly talk. It doesn't claim that talking cats are present in the world. Rather, it claims that such cats are in *some* domain—and those cats are the very ones referred to in the statement. Generally, a statement of the form "+ S + □ P," made relative to d, claims that the Ss referred to are present in some domain and they are P. Which other domain are we talking about? Let us call a domain that has the constituents referred to in a statement made relative to d, d*. We will say that d* is *accessible* from d. Thus, to say that I am possibly a billionaire is to claim that there is a world that contains me (i.e., a world accessible from this actual one), in which I *am* a billionaire.

The accessibility relation is reflexive and transitive, but, since there is no guarantee that d is accessible from d*, it is not symmetric. We can say: d ⊆ d*. Let ∪d* be the union of domains accessible from d and let ∩d* be the intersection of domains accessible from d.

To say, relative to a given domain, that some S is possibly P is to claim that some domain accessible from that domain has an S that is P. To say, relative to a given domain, that every S is possibly P is to claim that some domain accessible from that domain has no thing(s) that are S but not P. In other words, a *de re* problematic statement made relative to a domain d implicitly claims that ∪d* has or lacks some specified thing(s).

To say, relative to a given domain, that some S is necessarily P is to claim that every domain accessible from that domain has an S that is P. To say, relative to a given domain, that every S is necessarily P is to claim that every domain accessible from that domain has no thing(s) that are S but not P.

In other words, a *de re* apodeictic statement made relative to a domain d implicitly claims that ∩d* has or lacks some specified thing(s).

There are eight *de re* categorical forms of statements (relative to d). Let [S + P] be the set of things (in d) that are both S and P, and let [S – P] be the set of things (in d) that are S but not P. The letters a, e, i, and o, followed by a modal sign will indicate modalized versions of the four standard categorical forms.

Formula	Truth Claim
a ~: – S + ~ P	[S – P] ⊄ ∩d*
e ~: – S + ~ – P	[S + P] ⊄ ∩d*
i ~: + S + ~ P	[S + P] ⊆ ∩d*
o ~: + S + ~ – P	[S – P] ⊆ ∩d*
a □ : – S + □ P	[S – P] ⊄ ∪d*
e □ : – S + □ – P	[S + P] ⊄ ∪d*
i □ : + S + □ P	[S + P] ⊆ ∪d*
o □ : + S + □ – P	[S – P] ⊆ ∪d*

Since in general A ⊆ A ∪ B and A ∩ B ⊆ A, we know that ∪d* ⊆ ∪d and ∩d ⊆ ∩d*. It follows that all *de dicto* apodeictic statements entail their corresponding *de re* apodeictic statements and that all *de re* problematic statements entail their corresponding *de dicto* problematic statements.

Apodeictic Theorem: / ~ p → □ p ~
Problematic Theorem: / p □ → □ p

Exercise 9.5   Prove the following:

1. ~ [+ □ S + P] □□ [+ ~ P + S]
2. ~ [– S – P] □ – [+ S + □P]
3. ~ [+ S – P], – □ R + P □ + S – □ R

Modal Term Logic

The number of syllogistic forms is quite large. But as we saw, only about two dozen are actually valid. When we allow for the modalization of terms (including sentential terms) these numbers increase quite dramatically. Restricting ourselves to syllogisms consisting only of sentences that are either assertoric or of *de dicto* modality, the number of syllogisms for each mood is 27. This is also the number when the modality is restricted to *de re*. Thus the total number of kinds of syllogisms for each mood is 53. Of these several hundred syllogistic forms fewer than half are actually valid. Even more syllogistic forms could be generated by permitting a mixture of both types of modality within the same syllogism. Ockham claimed that doing so would countenance thousands of forms, about a thousand of which would be valid. Fear not; we will not even glance at all these forms.

Here we will examine modalized versions of just one classic syllogistic form. It is a standard syllogism whose three statements are all universal affirmations. Traditionally, it goes by the name Barbara. Barbara has the form: $- M + P, - S + M, \Box - S + P$. Introducing modal functors generates an entire sorority of Barbaras. We will look at some of these new Barbaras, specify some rules of proof, prove some of the valid ones, and, finally, spell out the conditions of validity for modal syllogisms. Given the large numbers alluded to above, we will restrict ourselves further here by concentrating first on just Barbaras that contain *de re* modal functors. Of these 12 are valid. They are:

1r $- M + \sim P$	2r $- M + \sim P$	3r $- M + \sim P$
$-S + \sim M$	$- S + \sim M$	$-S + \sim M$
$\Box -S + \sim P$	$\Box - S + P$	$\Box - S + \Box P$
4r $- M + \sim P$	5r $- M + \sim P$	6r $- M + \sim P$
$- S + M$	$- S + M$	$- S + M$
$\Box - S + \sim P$	$\Box - S + P$	$\Box - S + \Box P$
7r $- M + \Box P$	8r $- M + P$	9r $- M + P$
$- S + \sim M$	$- S + \sim M$	$- S + \sim M$
$\Box - S + P$	$\Box - S + P$	$\Box - S + \Box P$
10r $- M + P$	11r $- M + P$	12r $- M + \Box P$
$- S + M$	$- S + M$	$- S + M$
$\Box - S + P$	$\Box - S + \Box P$	$\Box - S + \Box P$

Notice that 10r is classical Barbara.

Proofs of the validity of each of these 12 moods requires the usual rule of syllogistic inference—the *dictum de omni et nullo*—and our Axioms. Here are proofs for the first three moods above:

Proof of 1.	1. $- M + \sim P$	premise
	2. $- S + \sim M$	premise
	3. $- \sim M + M$	Axiom 1
	4. $- S + M$	2, 3, by the *dictum*
	5. $- S + \sim P$	1, 3, by the *dictum*

Proof of 2.	1. – M + ~ P	premise
	2. – S + ~ M	premise
	3. – ~ M + M	Axiom 1
	4. – S + M	2, 3, by the *dictum*
	5. – S + ~ P	1, 4, by the *dictum*
	6. – ~ P + P	Axiom 1
	7. – S + P	5, 6, by the *dictum*

Proof of 3.	1. – M + ~ P	premise
	2. – S + ~ M	premise
	3. – ~ M + M	Axiom 1
	4. – S + M	2, 3, by the *dictum*
	5. – S + ~ P	1, 4, by the *dictum*
	6. –~ P + P	Axiom 1
	7. – S + P	5, 6, by the *dictum*
	8. – P + □ P	Axiom 2
	9. – S + □ P	7, 8, by the *dictum*

It is easy to see that the logic of syllogisms containing one or more *de re* sentences is a simple extension (viz., the addition of Axioms 1 and 2) of the standard syllogistic logic. However, the admission of *de dicto* modality requires a slightly more substantial extension.

Of the 27 Barbaras with sentences that are either assertoric or *de dicto* only 9 are valid. They are:

1d ~ (– M + P)	2d ~ (– M + P)	3d ~ (– M + P)
~ (– S + M)	~ (– S + M)	~ (– S + M)
□~ (– S + P)	□ – S + P	□ □ (– S + P)
4d ~ (– M + P)	5d ~ (– M + P)	6d – M + P
– S + M	– S + M	~ (– S + M)
□ – S + P	□□ (– S + P)	□ – S + P
7d – M + P	8d – M + P	9d – M + P
~ (– S + M)	– S + M	– S + M
□□ (– S + P)	□ – S + P	□□ (– S + P)

Notice that 8d = 10r (the classical Barbara).

In addition to the *dictum*, proofs for valid *de dicto* syllogisms require Axioms 3 and 4. They also require the following rule:

Rule d: If ~ p and ~ q are lines in a proof, then a new line, ~ (+ p + q) can be added.

Here are proofs of the first three of these moods:

Proof of 1d.	1. ~ (− M + P)	premise
	2. ~ (− S + M)	premise
	3. ~ (+ [− M + P] + [− S + M])	1, 2, by Rule d
	4. ~ (− S + P)	3, by the dictum
Proof of 2d.	1. ~ (− M + P)	premise
	2. ~ (− S + M)	premise
	3. − M + P	1, by Axiom 3
	4. − S + M	2, by Axiom 3
	5. − S + P	3, 4, by the dictum
Proof of 3d.	1. ~ (− M + P)	premise
	2. ~ (− S + M)	premise
	3. ~ (+ [− M + P] + [− S + P])	1, 2, by Rule d
	4. ~ (− S + P)	3, by the dictum
	5. − S + P	4, by Axiom 3
	6. □(− S + P)	5, by Axiom 4

Exercise 9.6 Prove 4d through 9d.

We have already seen that valid syllogisms with mixed modal statements (at least one *de re* and at least one *de dicto*) can be proved as well. For example, we can easily prove:

~ (− M + P)
− S + M
□ − S + □ P

Proof	1. ~ (− M + P)	premise
	2. − S + M	premise
	3. − M + P	1, by Axiom 1
	4. − S + P	2, 3, by the dictum
	5. − S + □ P	4, by Axiom 4

Validity Conditions

It can be seen that apodeictic conclusions follow only from pairs of apodeictic premises. Indeed, we can think of our general forms of statements as arranged in order of "strength" (where one statement is stronger than a second if and only if the first entails the second but the second does not entail the first). Our four axioms guarantee the following list of forms in descending order of strength:

~ p
p ~
p
p □
□p

This suggests that a necessary condition for validity is that the conclusion cannot exceed any premise in strength. The scholastic logicians called this the *peiorem* rule (*peiorem semper sequiter conclusio partem*).

Another necessary condition is suggested by the fact that no syllogism with both premises *de dicto* problematic or one premise and the conclusion *de dicto* problematic is valid.

Adding these conditions to those we already formulated for TFL in general yields the following five conditions, individually necessary and jointly sufficient, for validity:

1. The middle term must be distributed at least once.
2. Any term distributed in the conclusion must be distributed in the premises.
3. The number of particular conclusions must not be exceeded by the number of particular conclusions.
4. The conclusion must not exceed any premise in strength (*peiorem*).
5. The number of *de dicto* problematic statements in a syllogism must not exceed one.

References

Englebretsen, G. (1996). *Something to Reckon With: The Logic of Terms.* Ottawa: University of Ottawa Press.

Leblanc, H. (1968). "A simplified account of validity and implication for quantificational logic." *Journal of Symbolic Logic* **33**: 231–235.

Leblanc, H. (1976). *Truth-Value Semantics.* North Holland: Amsterdam.

Hintikka, J. (1969a). *Modes of Modality.* Dordrecht, Holland: Reidel.

Hintikka, J. (1969b). "Modality and quantification." In Hintikka, J. (1969a), 57–70.

Hintikka, J. (1969c). "The modes of modality." In Hintikka, J. (1969a), 71–86.

Hintikka, J. (1969d). "Deontic logic and its philosophical morals." In Hintikka, J. (1969a), 184–214.

Sommers, F. (1970). "The calculus of terms." *Mind* **79**: 1–39. Reprinted in *The New Syllogistic,* ed. G. Englebretsen, New York: Peter Lang (1987).

Sommers, F. (1982). *The Logic of Natural Language.* Oxford: Clarendon.

Sommers, F. (1990). "Predication in the logic of terms." *Notre Dame Journal of Formal Logic* **31**: 106–126.

Sommers, F. (1993). "The world, the facts, and primary logic." *Notre Dame Journal of Formal Logic* **34**: 169–182.

Sommers, F. and G. Englebretsen (2000). *An Invitation to Formal Reasoning.* Aldershot: Ashgate.

Rules, Axioms, and Principles

Sentential Logic (SL)

Premise (P)

$$\phi \rightarrow \phi$$

Conjunction (Conj)

$$\phi, \psi \rightarrow \phi \wedge \psi$$

Conjunctive Simplification (Simp)

$$\phi \wedge \psi \rightarrow \phi$$
$$\phi \wedge \psi \rightarrow \psi$$

Double Negation (DN)

$$\neg \neg \phi \rightarrow \phi$$
$$\phi \rightarrow \neg \neg \phi$$

Reductio ad Absurdum (RAA)

$$\psi \wedge \neg \psi \rightarrow \neg \phi$$
where ϕ is among the premises of $\psi \wedge \neg \psi$. As premises of the new line take all those of the earlier line less ϕ

Disjunctive Addition (Add)

$$\phi \rightarrow \phi \vee \psi$$
$$\psi \rightarrow \phi \vee \psi$$

Disjunctive Syllogism (DS)

$$\neg\,\phi,\phi\vee\psi\rightarrow\psi$$
$$\neg\,\psi,\phi\vee\psi\rightarrow\phi$$

Modus Ponens (MP)

$$\phi,\phi\supset\psi\rightarrow\psi$$

Modus Tollens (MT)

$$\neg\,\psi,\phi\supset\psi\rightarrow\neg\,\phi$$

Conditionalization (C)

$$\psi\rightarrow\phi\supset\psi$$
where ϕ is among the premises of ψ. As premises of the new line take all those of the earlier line less ϕ

Biconditional Elimination (BE)

$$\phi\equiv\psi\rightarrow\phi\supset\psi$$
$$\phi\equiv\psi\rightarrow\psi\supset\phi$$

Biconditional Introduction (BI)

$$(\phi\supset\psi)\wedge(\psi\supset\phi)\rightarrow\phi\equiv\psi$$

Quantificational Logic (QL)

The rules of SL plus the following:

Existential Generalization (EG)
If S is a derivation and $<A, \phi>$ occurs in S, then, S, $<A, \exists\forall\psi>$ is also a derivation if ψ results from replacing one or more occurrences of constant β in ϕ by variable α not in ϕ.

Existential Specification (ES)

If S is a derivation and $<B, \psi>$, $<A, \exists\forall\phi>$, and $<\{\phi\ \exists/\forall\}, \phi\ \exists/\forall>$ occur in S, then S, $<(A \cup B) \sim \{\phi\ \exists/\forall\}, \psi>$ is also a derivation if the constant β occurs neither in ϕ nor in ψ nor in any sentence in A or B.

Universal Specification (US)

$\forall \forall\, \phi \to \phi\, \exists/\forall$ where $\exists$ is any constant

Universal Generalization (UG)

$\phi\, \exists/\forall \to \forall \forall\, \phi$ where $\exists$ is not in ϕ nor in any premise of $\phi\, \exists/\forall$

Quantifier Negation (QN)

$\neg\, \exists\forall\, \phi \to \forall\forall\, \neg\, \phi$
$\neg\, \forall\forall\, \phi \to \exists\forall\, \neg\, \phi$
$\exists\forall\, \neg\, \phi \to \neg\, \forall\forall\, \phi$
$\forall\forall\, \neg\, \phi \to \neg\, \exists\forall\, \phi$

Quantificational Logic with Identity (QLI)

Identity Elimination (IE)
If S is a derivation and <A, ϕ> occurs in S and <B, $\exists = \gamma$> occurs in S, where ϕ is like ψ except that $\exists$ and γ have been exchanged at one or more places, then S, <A $\cup$ B, ψ> is a derivation.

Identity Introduction (II)
For every name β, the line <$\varnothing$, $\exists = \exists$> is a derivation.

Modal Logic

D	$G\,\phi \to \neg\, \square\, \neg\, \phi$	$\neg\, G\, \neg\, \phi \to \square\, \phi$	
	$\phi \to \neg\, G\, \neg\, \phi$	$\neg\, \square\, \neg\, \phi \to G\, \phi$	
ND	$\square G\, (\phi \supset \psi) \to (G\,\phi \supset G\,\psi)$		
$\square$I	$\phi \to \square\, \phi$		
GI	$/\, \phi \to G\,\phi$		
GE	$G\,\phi \to \phi$		
GG	$G\,\phi \to G\,G\,\phi$		
G$\square$	$\square\phi \to G\,\square\,\phi$		

Set Theory

Axiom of Extensionality

$$\forall x\,\forall y\,(((Sx \wedge Sy) \wedge \forall z\,(z \in x \equiv z \in y)) \supset x = y)$$

Axioms of Separation
The *axioms of separation* are all sentences that are instances of the schema
$\forall\forall\,(S\exists \supset \exists\exists\,(S\exists \wedge \forall\omega\,(\omega \in \exists \equiv (\omega \in \forall \wedge \phi))))$, resulting from placing "$\forall$," "$\exists$," and "ω" by variables and "ϕ" by a formula in which the variable replacing "$\exists$" has no free occurrences.

Pairing Axiom

$$\forall x\,\forall y\,\exists z\,(Sz \wedge \forall w\,(w \in z \equiv (w = x \vee w = y)))$$

Axiom of Non-Sets

$$\forall x\,(\neg\,Sx \supset \forall y\,(y \notin x))$$

Union Axiom

$$\forall x\,\exists y\,(Sy \wedge \forall z\,(z \in y \equiv \exists w\,(w \in x \wedge z \in w)))$$

Power Set Axiom

$$\forall x\,\exists y\,(Sy \wedge \forall z\,(z \in y \equiv z \subseteq x))$$

Term Functor Logic (TFL)

Association (Assoc)
If $+X + (+Y +/- Z)$ is a term in a line (or an entire line) in a proof, then a new line can be added which differs from that line by replacing that term with $+(+X+Y) +/- Z$; if $+(+X+Y) +/- Z$ is a term in a line (or an entire line), then a new line can be added which differs from that line by replacing that term with $+X + (+Y +/- Z)$.

Commutation (Com)
If +X+Y is term in a line (or the entire line) in a proof, then a new line can be added which differs from that line by replacing that term is +Y+X.

Conjunction (Conj)
If there are two lines is a proof, then a new line can be added which differs from them by being the conjunction of those two lines.

Dictum de Omni et Nullo (DON)
If X is a term universally quantified in a line in a proof and X is distributed at least once in a different line, then a new line can be added which differs from that second line by replacing at least one occurrence of the term X there by the entire first line minus its universally quantified X.

Double Negation (DN)
If +X is a term in a line (or an entire line) in a proof, then a new line can be added which differs from that line by replacing that term is – – X; if – – X is a term in a line (or an entire line), then a new line can be added which differs from that line by replacing that term with +X.

External Negation (EN)
If – (+/– X +/– Y) is a line in a proof, then a new line can be added which differs from that line by replacing it with –/+ X –/+ Y; if –/+ X –/+ Y is a line, then a new line can be added which differs from that line by replacing it with – (+/– X +/– Y).

Internal Negation (IN)
If +/– X – (+/– Y) is a line in a proof, then a new line can be added which differs from it by replacing it with +/– X + (–/+ Y); if +/– X + (–/+ Y) is a line, then a new line can be added which differs from it by replacing it with +/– X – (+/– Y).

Iteration (It)
If +/– X is a term in a line (or an entire line) in a proof, then a new line can be added which differs from that line by replacing that term with + (+/– X) + (+/– X); if + (+/– X) + (+/– X) is a term in a line (or an entire line), then a new line can be added which differs from that line by replacing that term with +/– X.

Particular Distribution (PD)

If +X + (– – Y – – Z) is a line in a proof, then a new line can be added which differs from it by replacing it with – – (+X+Y) – – (+X+Z); if – – (+X+Y) – – (+X+Z) is a line, then a new line can be added which differs from it by replacing it with +X + (– – Y – – Z).

Premise (P)

Any premise can be a line in a proof of validity; any member of a set of sentences can be a line in a proof of inconsistency.

Principle of Equivalence (PEQ)

Two sentences are equivalent if and only if they have the same valence and are algebraically equal.

Principle of Validity

An argument is valid if and only if the number of premises with positive valence equals the number of conclusions with positive valence (i.e., either 1 or 0) and the sum of the premises algebraically equals the conclusion.

Simplification (Simp)

If a conjunction of terms is a term (or an entire line) in a proof, then a new line can be added which differs from it by replacing that term with one of its conjuncts.

Tautology (Taut)

Any tautology can be added as a line in a proof unless it is the corresponding conditional of the argument.

Universal Distribution (UD)

If –X + (+Y+Z) is a line in a proof, then a new line can be added which differs from it by replacing it with + (–X+Y) + (–X+Z); if + (–X+Y) + (–X+Z) is a line, then a new line can be added which differs from it by replacing it with –X + (+Y+Z).

Wild Quantity (WQ)

If X is a singular subject term of a line (or of a sentential term in a line) in a proof, then a new line can be added which differs from that by replacing the quantifier of that subject term with any other quantifier.

Modal Term Logic

Apodeictic Theorem

/ G p → p G

Axiom of de re Term Replacement

1. / – G S + S
2. / – S + □ S

Axiom of Modal Reduction

□□X = □ X

Axioms of de dicto Modality

3. / G p → p
4. / p → □ p

De re *Theorem*

/ – G S + □ S

Problematic Theorem

/ p □ → □ p

Rule d

If G p and G q are lines in a proof, then a new line, G (+ p + q), can be added.

Glossary

χd: the union of domains containing common constituent(s) with a domain, d.

χd*: the union of domains accessible from a domain, d.

1d: the intersection of domains containing common constituent(s) with a domain, d.

1d*: the intersection of domains accessible from a domain, d.

Accessible: for any domain, d, d* is said to be accessible from d.

Apodeictic: an expression in the range of a necessity modal operator.

Argument: a set of statements such that one member of the set is what is being claimed to be true and the rest of the members are meant to establish that claim.

Assertoric Statement: any statement not in the range of a modal operator.

Axiom of Extensionality: sets A and B are identical if they have the same members.

Axioms of Separation: all sentences that are instances of the schema

$$\forall\forall\ (S\forall \supset \exists\exists\ (S\exists \wedge \forall\omega\ (\omega \in \exists \equiv (\omega \in \forall \wedge \phi))))$$

resulting from placing "∀," "∃," and "ω" by variables and "φ" by a formula in which the variable replacing "∃" has no free occurrences.

Barcan Formula: ∃x G Fx / G ∃x Fx

Bound (Free) Variable: in QL, an occurrence of a variable in a formula φ is *bound in* φ if and only if it is a variable and is in a part of φ which, for some formula ψ, is a formula ∃∀ ψ or ∀α ψ; otherwise, that occurrence of variable ∀ is *free in* φ.

Categorical: the logical form of a statement consisting of a subject and a predicate. The four classical categorical forms are:

> **A:** All X are Y
> **E:** No X are Y
> **I:** Some X are Y
> **O:** Some X are not Y

Completeness (Incompleteness): in SL, the derivation system is complete because for any *SL* sentence ϕ and set A of *SL* sentences, if ϕ is a semantical consequence of A, then ϕ is derivable from A; in arithmetic, the Peano axioms are incomplete because, for some sentence ϕ of arithmetic, neither ϕ nor $\neg\,\phi$ are derivable from those axioms.

Compound Term: in TFL, a term formed from a pair of terms by means of a binary functor.

Conclusion: in an argument, the statement being claimed to be true.

Consistent (Inconsistent): in SL, a set of sentences that is included in a truth set; in QL, a set of sentences of which each finite subset is included in a truth set; a set of sentences is inconsistent if, and only if, it is not consistent.

Constant: in QL, letters that go in for singular (non-general) terms.

Constructivist Logic: a system of logic that employs the notions of defense and refutation, rather than the notions of truth and falsity.

Contingent: in SL, a sentence that is neither a tautology nor a contradiction.

Contradiction: in SL and QL, a sentence which belongs to no truth set.

Converse Operation: $cx = y \equiv (Sy \wedge \forall z\ (z \in y \equiv \exists w\, \exists u\ (z = <w, u> \wedge <u, w> \in x)))$

Copula: in traditional logic, a qualifier; in TFL, a binary functor.

Counterset: the set of statements consisting of the premises and the negation of the conclusion of a given argument.

d*: any domain containing constituent(s) referred to in some statement made relative to a domain, d.

d-Consistent: in SL, a set of *SL* sentences B such that for no *SL* sentence ψ is it the case that $\psi \wedge \neg\,\psi$ is derivable from B

De dicto **Modality:** the application of a modal operator to a sentence.

De re **Modality:** the application of a modal operator to a non-sentential term.

Deontic Alternativeness: the relation R of a model system appropriate for deontic logic.

Deontic Logic: a system of logic that uses the two unary connectives "O" and "P" (for obligations and permissibility).

Derivation: a finite sequence of lines each satisfying one of various conditions; in SL, the conditions are P, Simp, Conj, RAA, DN; in QL, the conditions are P, Simp, Conj, RAA, DN, ES, EG, QN; in QLI, the conditions are those of QL plus II IE; in T they are those of SL plus D, ND, I, GI, GE; in S4, they are those of T plus GG; in S5, they are those of S4 plus G□; in B, they are those of T plus φ G □ φ; in QS5, the conditions are those of QS5 plus those of QT plus those of S5.

Disjoint: a pair of sets is disjoint if nothing is a member of both.

Distributed (Undistributed): in TFL, a term used in a given statement is distributed (undistributed) if it is in the range of an even number (odd number) of negation signs.

Distributed (Undistributed) Term: in traditional logic, a term used in a given statement is distributed (or undistributed) if from that statement one can (or cannot) infer a statement making a claim about all the things that term is true of. The subject term of universal categoricals (A and E) and the predicate terms of denials (E and O) are distributed. The subject terms of particular categoricals (I and O) and the predicate terms of affirmations (A and I) are undistributed.

Distribution Laws: in traditional logic, necessary conditions for the validity of a syllogism. They are the middle term must be distributed at least once; any term undistributed in the premise must be undistributed in the conclusion; any term distributed in the conclusion must be distributed in the premise.

Domain of Discourse: any totality of objects relative to which a statement is made.

Elementary Arithmetic: the theory based on the axioms of arithmetic less the induction axioms.

Elementary Axioms: those axioms of arithmetic less the induction axioms.

Elementary Power: a set of axioms for arithmetic that agrees with the elementary axioms on the elementary equations.

Enabling Theorem: in set theory, the formula $\forall_1 \ldots \forall\forall_n \exists!\omega\ \phi$ derivable from axioms and preceding definitions that enables a definition of the form $o\ (\forall_1, \ldots, \forall_n) = \omega \equiv \phi$.

Equinumerous (or Equipolent) Sets: sets with equally many members.

Existential Quantifier: in QL, the symbol "$\exists$."

Figure: the arrangement of the terms of a syllogism. There are four possible figures in traditional logic.

Fixed Domain: a domain of discourse whose number of constituents is unchanging.

Form: the logical structure of a statement, independent of its matter.

Formal Validity: take the hnf of the premises and the negation of the conclusion of an argument and attempt to construct a model set; if you succeed, it is not valid; if you must fail, then the argument is valid.

Formative: in a statement, an expression determining (in part) the form of the statement.

Formula: an expression (in a formal language) displaying the logical form of a statement.

Free Variable: an individual variable not in the range of a quantifier applying to it.

Function: x is a function $\equiv$ (x is a relation $\wedge\ \forall y\ \forall z\ \forall w\ ((<y, z> \in x \wedge <y, w> \in x) \supset z = w))$.

General Term: a term that purports to apply to more than one thing.

Gödel Function: a function that assigns distinct numbers to distinct formulas and to distinct finite sequences of formulas of the language of arithmetic.

Gödel's Proof: an argument that shows (to a near approximation) that Peano Arithmetic, like Elementary Arithmetic, is, if consistent, incomplete in the strong sense that if those axioms are consistent there is at least one arithmetic sentence such that neither it nor its negation is derivable from the Peano Axioms; further, his method of proof allows for its generalization to *any* consistent axiom set of at least elementary power.

Grouping: a method of avoiding the kind of ambiguity of multiple readings which arise from being unable to determine the scope of a quantifier or scope.

Hintikka Normal Form (hnf): in SL, a sentence is in Hintikka normal form (hnf) if and only if the only truth-functional connectives it contains are "¬," "∧," and "∨," and "¬" is applied only to atomic sentences; in QL, to the conditions defining Hintikka normal form are added:

$$\neg \exists \alpha \, \phi \Leftrightarrow \forall \alpha \, \neg \phi$$
$$\neg \forall \alpha \, \phi \Leftrightarrow \exists \alpha \, \neg \phi$$

Identity: =

Immediate Inference: in traditional logic, a derivation using only one premise.

Indirect Proof: a proof of an argument's validity by deriving a contradiction from the argument's counterset.

Induction Axioms: all sentences of the following form: $(A (0) \land \forall x (A (x) \supset \forall x \, A (sx)) \supset \forall x \, A (x)$

Interpretation (see **Model**):

Intersection: for any sets A and B, the intersection of those sets is the set whose members are common to both A and B.

Line: a pair the first element of which is a finite set of sentences and the second element of which is some sentence.

Major Premise: in a syllogism, the premise containing the major term.

Major Term: the predicate term of the conclusion of a syllogism.

Many-One Relation: a relation x satisfying the condition that $\forall y \, \forall z \, \forall w \, ((<y, z> \in x \land <y, w> \in x) \supset z = w))$.

Matter: the information conveyed by the use of a statement, independent of its form.

Metalanguage: the language in the use of which we stipulate systems of signs, and their associated inferential and semantical systems.

Middle Term: in a syllogism, the term appearing in each premise but not in the conclusion.

Minor Premise: in a syllogism, the premise containing the minor term.

Minor Term: the subject term of the conclusion of a syllogism.

Modal Logic: a study of formally valid inference involving necessity and possibility.

Modal Operator: an operator for necessity or possibility.

Model: an ordered pair consisting of a set and a function; the function assigns elements of the domain to the constants and sets of n-tuples of domain elements to the predicates.

Model Set: a set of sentences in hnf satisfying various conditions; in SL the conditions are (C ¬), (C ∧), (C ∨); in QL they are those of SL plus (C ∀), (C ∃); in T they are those of SL plus (C G), (C □), (C G⁺); in S4 they are those of T plus (C GG⁺); in B they are those of S4 plus (C G₊); in S5 they are those of S4 plus (C GG₊); in QS5 they are those of S5 and QT; in SDL they are those of SL plus (C O*), (C O)$_{rest}$, (C P*), (C o*).

Model System: a set of model sets together with a relation R (called the alternativeness relation).

Mood: in a syllogistic figure, the arrangement of categorical forms.

More Membered: a set x is more membered than a set y if, and only if, there is no 1-1 function correlating the members of x and y and there is a 1-1 function that maps a subset of x onto y.

Null Relation: the relation that has no members.

Null Set: the set having no members.

Object Language: a language, which, in the study of logic, we stipulate and of which we write.

Onto Function: x is a function from set y onto set z if, and only if, the domain of x = y and the range of x = z).

Operator: in SL, the expressions, ¬, ∨, ⊃, ≡; in SML the operators of SL plus G and □; in SDL, the operators of SL plus O and P.

Ordered Pair: set x is an ordered pair if, and only if, $\exists y \exists z$ (x = {{y}, {y, z}}).

Pairing Axiom: $\forall x \forall y \exists z$ (Sz $\forall w$ (w ∈ z ≡ (w = x ∨ w = y))).

Peano Axioms: $\forall x$ (0 ≠ sx), $\forall x \forall y$ (sx = sy ⊃ x = y), $\forall x$ (x + 0 = x),

$\forall x \, \forall y \, ((x + sy) = s \, (x = y)), \, \forall x \, (x \times 0 = 0), \, \forall x \, \forall y \, (x \times sy = (x \times y) + x),$ plus the induction axioms—all sentences of the following form: $(A \, (0) \wedge \forall x \, (A \, (x) \supset \forall x \, A \, (sx)) \supset \forall x \, A \, (x).$

Peano Proof: a sequence S terminating in a formula F is a *Peano Proof* of F if and only if S is a derivation of F from the Peano Axioms.

Peiorem: in traditional logic, the notion (sometimes rule) that the conclusion of a valid inference cannot exceed any of its premises in strength.

Perfect Syllogism: a syllogistic form that needs no proof because its validity is immediately evident. The four syllogistic forms in the first figure are perfect.

Polish Notation: a system of logical notation that uses place order, rather than punctuations such as parentheses, to disambiguate strings of symbols.

Possible World: circumstances that might have occurred.

Power Set: a set consisting of all subsets of a given set.

Power Set Axiom: $\forall x \, \exists y \, (Sy \wedge \forall z \, (z \in y \equiv z \subseteq x)).$

Predicate: in general, a declarative sentence less one or more occurrences of one or more of its singular terms.

Predicate Letter: in QL, uppercase letters with arabic numeral superscripts and with or without arabic numeral subscripts.

Predicate Term: in TFL, a term on which a qualifier is operating.

Premise: in an argument, a statement meant to help establish the truth of the conclusion.

Problematic: an expression in the range of a necessity modal operator.

Proof (Derivation): a finite sequence of lines, each of which satisfies a rule of inference.

Proposition: what is expressed by a sentence (often called a "thought").

Qualifier: in TFL, a formative indicating whether the information conveyed by the term to which it is attached is affirmed or denied.

Quantified Modal Logic (QS5): QT plus S5.

Quantifier: in QL, a sentential formative that binds the free variables in the formula to which it is prefixed; in TFL, a formative indicating whether the information conveyed by the term to which it is attached involves the entire set of things the term is true of or only a part of that set.

Quantifier Logic (QL): a formal language suitable for the study of quantification.

Quantifier Logic, with Identity (QLI): QL plus =.

Quantifier, Particular: in TFL, a quantifier indicating that the information conveyed by the term to which it is attached involves a part of the set of things the term is true of.

Quantifier, Universal: in TFL, a quantifier indicating that the information conveyed by the term to which it is attached involves the entire set of things the term is true of.

Reduction: a method of proving a syllogism by converting it to a perfect syllogism in the first figure, using rules of immediate inference.

Relation: a set of ordered pairs.

Relational Term: in TFL, a compound term, one member of which is relational.

Schema: the result of replacing expressions in one or more sentences by letters.

Semantic Consequence: a relation between a sentence and a set of sentences in which the set is included in a truth set only if the sentence is a member of that truth set.

Sentential Deontic Logic (SDL): a study of the consequence relation in a language that results from the language *SL* for sentential logic by adding the two unary connectives "O" and "P" (for obligations and permissibility), and the three binary operators "∨," "≡," and "⊃" (for disjunctions, biconditionals, and conditionals).

Sentential Logic (SL): a study of the consequence relation in a language consisting of simple sentences and their compounds resulting from using negation and conjunction as primitive operations.

Sentential Modal Logic (SML):

> **S5:** S4 plus G □
> **S4:** T plus GG
> **T:** SL plus D, ND, □I, GI, GE
> **B:** T plus $\phi \rightarrow G \square \phi$

Sentential Term: in TFL, an unanalyzed compound term used to express an entire statement.

Soundness: in SL (QL), the derivation system is *sound* if and only if for any SL (QL) sentence φ and set A of SL (QL) sentences, if φ is derivable from A, then φ is a semantical consequence of A, that is, if A / φ then A G φ.

Split (Unsplit) Copula: in TFL, a binary functor that is (not) analyzed into its two fragments: a quantifier and a qualifier.

Statement: any sentence used to make a truth claim.

Strength (of a Statement): in traditional logic, the notion that apodeictic statements are stronger (provide more information) than assertoric statements; assertoric statements are stronger than problematic statements; universal statements are stronger than particular statements; affirmative statements are stronger than negative statements.

Subject: in TFL, an expression consisting of a quantifier and a term.

Subject Term: in TFL, a term on which a quantifier is operating.

Subset: a set is a subset of a set if all of its member are members of that set. A set is a **proper subset** of a set if it is not equivalent to that set. Two sets are **equivalent** if they have all the same members.

Syllogism: An argument consisting of two premises and a conclusion, each of which has a categorical form.

Syllogistic: the system of formal logic initiated by Aristotle based on an understanding of arguments as consisting of categorical premises and conclusions.

Term: in a statement, an expression determining (in part) the matter of the statement.

Term Functor: a unary or binary functor that operates on a term or pair of terms to form a new term.

Term Functor Logic (TFL): a system of formal term logic that construes all statements as consisting of pairs of terms (each of which may be positive or negative) connected by a binary functor (which may be positive or negative).

Term Logic: a system of formal logic that construes all statements consisting of pairs of subjects and predicates.

Term Variable: in a formula, a symbol (usually an uppercase letter) used to indicate the occurrence of a term.

Theorem: in logic, a sentence derivable from the null class of premises; in set theory and arithmetic, a sentence derivable from the axioms of the theory.

Traditional Logic: Aristotelian syllogistic logic amended and emended by logicians from Aristotle's time to the late nineteenth century.

Truth Claim: an implicit claim accompanying the use of a statement and asserting that the proposition being expressed is true.

Truth-Functional: a sentential operation such that the truth-value of a compound sentence constructed by means of that operation is entirely fixed by the truth-values of the component sentences to which it is applied.

Truth Set: in SL, a set of SL sentences such that (1) a negation is a member of it if, and only if, the negated sentence is not a member of it, (2) a conjunction is a member of it if, and only if, both conjuncts are members of it; in QL, a set of SL sentences such that (1) a negation is a member of it if, and only if, the negated sentence is not a member of it, (2) a conjunction is a member of it if, and only if, both conjuncts are members of it, (3) an existentially quantified sentence is a member of it if, and only if, some substitution instance of that sentence is a member of it.

Union: the union of a pair of sets is a set each of whose members are members of one or both of those sets.

Union Axiom: $\forall x \, \exists y \, (Sy \, \forall z \, (z \in y \equiv \exists w \, (w \in x \wedge z \in w)))$.

Unit Set: a set having just one member.

Universal Quantifier: in QL, $\forall$.

Variable Domain: a domain of discourse whose number of constituents can change.

Variables: in QL, lowercase letters "s" through "z" with or without arabic numeral subscripts.

Valid Form: on the classical view, an inference is formally valid because it is truth-preserving; on the constructivist view, an inference is formally valid because it is defense-preserving.

Validity: a property that an argument has if its premises cannot all be true while its conclusion is false.

World: a variable domain of discourse.

Index

Made in the USA
Middletown, DE
22 February 2019